THE LAST DAYS OF APRIL, 1975

FOR ALL THOSE SOULS WHO LOST THEIR LIVES DURING
THE VIETNAM WAR

AND ALL THE OTHERS WHO DIED ON THEIR WAY TO
SEEK FREEDOM...

IN MEMORY OF MOM, MOTHER-IN-LAW,
AND MY SISTER/HER HUSBAND

TO MY TWO BROTHERS, MY TWO SISTERS-IN-LAW,
AND THEIR CHILDREN/GRANDCHILDREN

TO MY SISTER'S CHILDREN/GRANDCHILDREN

TO MY WIFE XUAN TUOI

FOR DAUGHTER SOPHIA

THE LAST DAYS OF APRIL, 1975

HOA NGOC HOANG

Library of Congress Control Number: 2024909904

English Translation:
Hoa Ngoc Hoang
Edited by: Byron Allen Black
Cover Art Design:
Khai Co Vu – Australia
Publisher: Nhan Anh
2024

ISBN: 9798330214341

HOA NGOC HOANG

THE LAST DAYS OF APRIL, 1975

NHÂN ẢNH
2024

TABLE OF CONTENTS

PREFACE

This book was composed as the result of perpetual encouragement of friends – Vietnamese as well as American – and of family members, particularly the "second generation", all of whom were eager to learn just *how it happened* that I had strayed, all the way from the Southeast Asian nation of Vietnam to the United States of America, living the life I have at present.

This is not really a memoir, since I am not a famous person narrating a life of fame. However, it is *my story*, a story that I hope others can relate to, perhaps find interesting, and even draw inspiration from, to motivate them to share their own stories.

My book is a *personal living document* that existed before and after 1975, in the form of diaries and manuscripts, some of which were published in newspapers, submitted to competitions, and printed up as books. However, because of the unique nature of each article, in summary, it is difficult to avoid certain incidents and overlap. For most of the people you will meet in this book, I was granted permission to use their real names; with others, however, due to delicate matters, I gave them pseudonyms or abbreviated their names, to respect their privacy.

It is difficult to imagine what life was like in Vietnam after the US military withdrew, if one was not present there, in person, like me and my family. We witnessed the *"Vietnamization program"* of the war, subsequent military aid to the Republic of Vietnam vetoed by the US Congress, and the violation of the 1973 Paris Peace Accords by the North, acts that led to the dissolution of the Republic of Vietnam polity. In Saigon, Vietnam's capital, during the last days of April 1975, chaos was rife, and there were more rumors flying about than accurate, useful information, rumors such as there would be a *"ceasefire"* or that there would be a division of land to the other side, so that Saigon might remain the capital of a Southern rump state, all spread because the South Vietnamese government at that time shifted, according to the demands of the enemy.

OMNIA VINCIT VERITAS, "Truth Triumphs Above All", and this is proven in the story I will narrate to you. My family and I went through the events and experiences with the Communists, including all that we saw in those last hours, and were in fact much more fortunate than the majority of those trapped without means of evacuation – or trust in the *"new government"* – to treat them kindly when assuming power.

Even the United States government, innocently believing what it had been promised by the other side, endured anarchy right in its own Embassy, including at its Defense Attaché Office (D.A.O.), when *"Operation Frequent Wind"* failed to evacuate all those vital people they had promised to bring safely out of Vietnam. The world-famous news photo of an Air America helicopter on the roof of the Embassy is a testament to what is beyond the expectations of both insiders and outsiders during war, or any conflict between humans.

Some of the articles that I composed during my *"first days of freedom"*, about my own hurried exodus from Vietnam, were simply sad diary pages, forgotten for nearly 50 years until after my retirement – when I came across them and took the opportunity to do something much more useful with them. To tell my life's story in a way for others to read and understand my experiences, in addition to including what I personally saw during the Vietnam War and lived through while escaping Vietnam, I wrote about my experience during my many years living in the United States. It took more than a year to complete the Vietnamese-language version of my life's story, an account at once typical of any Vietnamese who had to abandon his homeland during the last hours of the Vietnam War, by evacuating and taking refuge in the faraway United States – and unique, since it is about me, my journey and my destiny.

The purpose of my book is not to brag about myself or anyone else in my life. Instead, I wrote this book about my life in the faith to make certain that generations of Vietnamese people, whether living outside of Vietnam, in the US in particular, or still living in Vietnam, having returned or never left, can have an idea of what *life was like for me,* a person born and raised in Vietnam, one who lived and survived a major civil war, a war that I absolutely did not want, yet could not stop or change, and who, within that historical moment, made the decision to be a reluctant refugee, ending up penniless on American soil. Please understand how our *"first generation of Vietnamese in America"* had no way to predict how our future or the future of people in similar circumstances would proceed. Making a living in America was hard, and full of problems, and each person had a different outcome, some of success and others bitter failure.

Such was the challenging life of the first generation of Vietnamese to settle in the United States. By telling my story, I thus honor all Vietnamese people's stories.

In those last dark days of April 1975, many Vietnamese fled Vietnam, exploiting any means of evacuation whatsoever. Those who remained did so largely to exact revenge and trample on the dignity of the new regime. Those of us who managed to get out traveled by water alone, or by sea and land afterward, and because of this, we were awarded a special new name for the history books: *"The Boat People"*.

Whether *Boat People* is a properly respectful name matters not. What *does* matter though is that those Vietnamese who escaped were a people in search of ***FREEDOM***, a people that thinks that honor and dignity are worth more than economics, or even one's life, because honor and dignity are trampled down more than economics, accepting death more than life. There are no statistics on those who go unaccounted for because *many families have no survivors*. How many unfortunate souls rest in the cold depths of the Pacific? How many people fell into the hands of Thai pirates? And, how many had to eat like cannibals to survive, when lost on deserted islands?

Despite escaping to the US under such awful and challenging (instead of "special") circumstances, the first generation of Vietnamese people successfully integrated into a community of different cultures and languages, extremely smoothly and incredibly quickly. They were willing to work hard in *any* job that could earn them a living – no matter how dirty, a few had to live on welfare at first. The new immigrants were willing and motivated to go to school, in order to survive and even better to make a meaningful contribution to their new, second homeland.

"Thank you!" to the United States, in general, for welcoming us Vietnamese, and my family in particular. I am extremely grateful to our sponsors *(Mr. and Mrs. Ted and Patricia Srygley, Director of the University of Florida Health Science Center Library from 1966 to 1993)* for their sponsorship and support of my family's emigration, as well as their support of those refugees who, like us, escaped Vietnam because of the ongoing conflict, physically as well as mentally to get to where it is today.

In less than a year, it will be exactly half a century since Vietnamese people left their country in large numbers. Looking back in time, one might ask, what have the Vietnamese people gained? *Hatred* and *jealousy* still exist among those in the powerful Vietnamese government and, instead of joining forces to serve the country, those leaders continue to lead the country on a downhill slope. The imminent danger of losing their country is approaching ever closer once more, which should be a warning bell for those still slumbering on their victory, after nearly 50 years.

For *one thousand years* of Chinese domination and *one hundred years* of French colonial rule, the Vietnamese people stayed in their country. It wasn't until April of 1975 that great numbers of citizens in the South, and now even in the North, sought to leave Vietnam, desiring *Freedom* and a better life by escaping its Communist regime. And yet, the question remains: Why does such a cruel regime still exist in Vietnam today?

Although I have no pretensions of being a professional artist, I created this oil painting (24x42) and titled it "Hope" when I heard that in Da Lat, my cousin's four children, led by her eldest daughter, crossed the sea on a boat ... one that never arrived...

– Painted at Lee Gardens - Arlington, Virginia – 1980.

Five persons whose names must shine: Kieu Duyen, Quang Dinh, Quang Tuan, Quang Huy, and Quang Hoang (BiBo). Remembering these and all others who lost their lives on the road to freedom.

ABOUT THE AUTHOR

Hoa Ngoc Hoang graduated from An Cuu Primary School, before attending high school at the National Academy of Quoc Hoc, in Hue, where he studied from Grade 6 to Grade 12, during which time he participated in the Cub Scouts and Boy Scouts of the Bach Dang League; he was also a member in Hue. He continued his education in Saigon, at both the University of Saigon and the College of Law, until April 29, 1975, when he was evacuated to the US with his eldest brother, serving in a helicopter squadron of the Vietnamese Air Force. They found themselves in a crowded Pendleton, California refugee camp.

From the refugee camp, Hoa first settled in Gainesville, Florida, because his brother was studying there for a Master's Degree in Civil Engineering. Hoa then attended Santa Fe Community College in Gainesville, Florida, before transferring to the University of Florida (UF), from which he was awarded a Bachelor of Design Degree in Architecture, on March 22, 1980, as one of the first refugees to graduate from UF.

Hoa then left this small town and settled in Arlington, Virginia, where he lived for a while before moving to Montgomery Village in Gaithersburg, Maryland. After working in Gaithersburg until 1983, Hoa agreed to relocate to Tampa, Florida, to open a branch office for an Engineering/Architecture company whose main office was in Greenbelt, Maryland. Later he moved to Palm Beach, South Florida.

The final stage of Hoa's lengthy career occurred in South Florida, where he was part of the Community Redevelopment Agency/Projects for the Town of Lake Park, as well as being placed in charge of the establishment, design, and maintenance of the city's new Fiber Optic-based computer network system, which he had personally designed.

1973-1975 College of Law, at the University of Saigon, Vietnam.

March, 1980 University of Florida, Bachelor of Design in Architecture.

May 5, 1986 American Institute of Architects (AIA) - Associate Member, Florida

1998 International City and County Manager Association (ICMA), Full Member

2002 Florida Local Government Information System Association (FLGISA), Member

2003 Florida City and County Manager Association (FCCMA), Full Member

2011-2023 Certified Government Chief Information Officer (CGCIO)

October, 2021 Retired* from Town of Lake Park government in Florida

*Retired at the end of October 2021, after working there for over 23+ years, having held the positions of Assistant to the Town Manager, Interim Town Manager, and finally Information Technology Director and Chief Information Technology Officer.

CHAPTER I
THE VIETNAM WAR
AND THE NORTH-SOUTH CONFLICT

INTRODUCTION:

We now find ourselves in an age of ***information technology;*** *thus, people simply need to "Google" to get immediate access to many documents about the war in Vietnam, first with the French colonialists and then a civil war that lasted for more than 20 years. Among these many documents, there is truth and there is falsehood because it is convenient for some to load more or less distorted facts online. It is thus up to each person to divine the correct answer. Document storage centers in democratic countries such as France or the United States are relatively closer to the truth than many on the Web, in Wikipedia, or in books printed in countries subject to state censorship. There have been many accurate documents about Vietnam from the war against the French colonialists (1945) to the period of division of the country (1954) and then until 1975, so here we do not mention the details, just the facts. understanding and witnessing a part of the author through school, the mother's narration through events.*

FRENCH COLONIAL POLICY AND WORLD WAR II

COLONIAL INVASION WAR

Prior to the onset of World War II, the French sought control of a number of colonies, as did the Portuguese and the British. Napoleon III's July 1857 decision to colonize Vietnam led to a 100-year-long war with the French. Unlike the British, who established colonies to expand their territorial power, the French took over other people's countries to exploit resources. At first, their policies were ostensibly to assist poor countries in enjoying the same advanced lifestyle as they had. A closer look at the policies revealed their downside. Exploiting the religious opposition of the

Hue Court of that time, which was under a hereditary monarchy, they convinced many Vietnamese to become pro-French, following their instructions to avoid the opposition of those who did not serve them. The Nationalist or Communist factions of the Vietnamese people pursued the same goal of opposing French dominance, fighting against foreign invaders, and endeavoring to regain the country's independence. Nevertheless, they did not move in the same direction and were always quarreling with each other. Taking advantage of this division, the French increasingly weakened opposing factions. My mother recounted to me how when Japan and Germany were apparently winning the war, they went to Vietnam and formed a pro-Japanese, anti-French faction. When the Japanese military effort began to crumble and they withdrew, the pro-French numbers returned to settle other factions, meaning fewer and fewer people truly loved the country and were willing to sacrifice for the nation, instead seeking perks for individuals. The various empires eventually found it impossible to hang onto their colonies forever, without opposition; as foreign policy weakened them, they gradually ceded governance back to the people. Particularly for Vietnam: taking advantage of the *"sticky beans situation"* at that time, the Viet Minh worked under the guise of fighting against the colonialists, foreign invaders, and loving the country, and thus struggling to regain independence from the French.

But this proved not to be so easy. With the intervention of the United States, Vietnam was divided into two parts, like Korea or Germany through the Geneva agreement of July 1954, taking Ben Hai River, the 17th Parallel, as the border between the two regions.

AMERICA'S INVOLVEMENT

Assuming the matter had been resolved, whoever was there, the French withdrew, and the South, supported by the United States of America, was named the *"Republic of Vietnam"*, while the North, supported by the Communist bloc, including the Soviet Union (USSR) and the People's Republic of China (PRC), called itself the *"Democratic Republic of Vietnam"*. ("Democratic" was of course ***not*** how you and I understand the term).

The dream of annexing the South festered in the ruling

circles of the North, but with the signing of the Geneva Treaty, witnessed by the world, and the anti-Communist policy of Southern President Ngo Dinh Diem, especially *"The Strategic Hamlet Program"*, they did not get on with what had to be done and had to wait until the ruling faction in the South started quarreling for power (1963) before jumping in to *"get the fisherman's benefit"*. They created a puppet government, a.k.a. the *"National Front for the Liberation of South Vietnam"* in 1960 to attempt to delude people, thinking that the South would solve the matter on its own, but at that time the North did *not* intervene. After a major military campaign to capture the South, backed by the PRC, they dissolved this government in 1977. In fact, the 1968 Tet Offensive not only failed to capture the South, but also backfired, so they created more *"summer fire"* in 1972, and *still* failed to take the South until 1975.

The important factor behind this incident was that the United States' effort was impeded by antiwar groups, vociferously campaigning against American participation in the Vietnam War. As U.S. Vice President Spiro Agnew resigned for tax fraud, and President Nixon was forced out of office by revelations of Watergate wiretapping, Republican foreign policy weakened, adding to the left-wing media coverage of the scandals. Mounting numbers of American soldiers killed in action in Vietnam undercut popular support. The successor to the President, who had not been elected by the people, but acceded to the Presidency according to the law, was Gerald Ford, a Republican who led a majority of the House of Representatives, and only had to engineer a solution to withdraw from the South *"with honor"*. Secretary of State Henry Kissinger was a Jew who had been in bed with Communist China and abandoning the South was *"killing two birds with one bullet"*, as by no longer proffering military support to South Vietnam, the US could turn its attention to Israel, always in need of strong support. The fate of the Republic of Vietnam was predetermined, and the Vietnamese people themselves had no say in the matter. The North's propaganda policy against the invasion by the US as well as the French colonialists had been successful before, although the truth was heavily distorted and massive foreign intervention was supporting Northern military forces.

Currently, declassified documents reveal that, under President Nixon, the strategy of blockading and bombing Hai Phong Bay for

3 additional days would have forced the North to surrender, as it could not withstand such economic and political pressure; alas, the Americans discontinued their efforts earlier. Could they have been so naïve that they didn't know what was going on, even with their sophisticated intelligence? But only because they wanted the South, with their support, to take the North? Looking at history, the United States won World War II because Japan surrendered after two atomic bombs gave the USA the burden to take care of the country they won, so they *did not* want history to repeat itself.

The United States helps countries following the war; it no longer wins battles but continues to withdraw: Cambodia, Laos, Republic of Vietnam, Iraq, Afghanistan, and one where the battle is still equal at this time: Ukraine. Will the Americans help this nation to win and resist the Soviet invasion, or will they also throw up their hands and declare to the people of that country that they do not *"want"* to fight and *"lose the battle themselves"*, not because the US did not support or give up first.

Back at that time, the important milestones were the Geneva Cease-fire Agreement of July 1954, and the division of the country, which led to the civil war endured until April 1975, one that was fatefully arranged by compromise of a foreign country, eventually wiping out the name of a country known as the *Republic of Vietnam*. Although this erasure has led to the unification of the country, whether the people have Freedom, Independence, and Happiness is another matter. The Geneva Agreement allowed a number of wise Northerners to jump aboard the American army's open-mouthed ships headed to the South, to seek freedom in 1954 and the reunification of the two regions in 1975 made the people of the South find ways to cross the border for a "Second Freedom", something indisputable and erased in the history of Vietnam. Since then, a new word has been added to the dictionary: *"The Boat People"*. How many people reached the shores of freedom, how many people are lying still, deep in the ocean depths, or "unwanted guests" in Thailand, Malaysia, Cambodia, Africa, Indonesia... No statistic can pinpoint the exact number of disappeared, because for many families there were simply no survivors. This is the stain of history, so *"Winning Side"* has sought to justify and erase the truth, a question arises: *"If a country is unified, the people live peacefully without revenge, well trampling on honor, dignity or forcing those who 'lost', people evacuate, try their utmost to escape out of the country ... and for what?"* Someday history will answer, because it is too early now.

The war has ended for 49 years, since the so-called unification of the country, but the hatred still lingers here and there.

In the final days of the Republic, the US government was able to evacuate only a small number of its Vietnamese employees. The pilots of the Republic of Vietnam Air Force and Vietnamese Naval ships found their own way out through Thailand, the Philippines, and U-TAPAO airport or they landed on US 7th Fleet carriers waiting off the coast of Vung Tau. Their purpose is only to save as many as they can, to avoid the revenge of the *"winning side"*. Recover some weapons that had supported the South, so they might not fall into enemy hands. Funneling through Guam, before checking in to the mainland of the United States, just over one hundred thousand Vietnamese and about 900 previously-displaced Cambodians were brought to the first and second Camp Pendleton Marine Corps barracks. At this point, they were forced to open more refugee camps, in part to carry out immigration procedures.

The United States withdrew from Afghanistan in 2021, and only a small number of people escaped. Of course, the number that is left behind cannot avoid the revenge of *the winning side*. History repeats itself because people want it to. The civil war in this country began on October 7, 2001, because of 9/11 in the United States to find the perpetrators of terrorism and ended on August 30, 2021, also nearly 20 years.

Particularly in Vietnam, in addition to the survivors who were sent to brutal *"re-education"* camps, the dead also cannot avoid revenge. The cemeteries of the ARVN soldiers were wiped out, they only respected the soldiers who died because of the war of the side they called martyrs, but the other side, even if they died, was still the enemy. Looking at the American Civil War, after it ended, the northern victors respected the living or dead of the South. Revenge is no longer the answer in the post-war era. Vietnam is not like that: how many people died in concentration camps because of revenge? How many people enduring their stay in the country suffer trampled honor and dignity? How many people died on the way to freedom? How many graves of those who died before 1975 are revenged? Although no one wants to talk about it, they still have to return the truth to history. Half a century later, hatred still exists and history is distorted; it may be a long time before there is *real* ***peace***.

Making many mistakes after occupying the South, including the bureaucracy of the ruling elite, losing *"brainpower"* both at home and abroad, not knowing how to use talent, and discriminating against the losers, has resulted in corruption and dictatorship, party-rule leading to the risk of losing roots and losing the country.

Before being executed by the Communists on August 14, 1975, in Can Tho, the last heroic words of a former Junior Military Academy cadet, Colonel Ho Ngoc Can began as follows: *"If I win the war, I will not condemn you as you condemn me. Nor have I humiliated you as you humiliated me. I'm not asking you the question you're asking me. I fight for the freedom of the people..."*.

Do not focus on History and you can thus give up on this subject. Just a few decades from now, succeeding generations no longer know whether Vietnam has 18 Kings Hung Vuong or Vietnam belongs to a province of China. Whose evil plot is this? The late Professor Lam Tai and Chau Tang, while teaching Literature at Quoc Hoc, taught us that: *"If you wrong culture, you harm an entire generation"*. Today, that consequence may come, because many people intentionally choose a "wrong culture" and tomorrow there will be no more Vietnamese or the right Vietnamese country with the saying *"Vietnamese language alive, Vietnamese people are still there"*.

TCS's anti-war song (still banned in Vietnam because of its first line):

"One thousand years of domination by the Chinese invaders, one hundred years of domination of the French invaders, twenty years of civil war every day... The legacy that Mother left me is a sad Vietnam..."

CHAPTER II
CHILDHOOD (1953-1965)
HIGH SCHOOL IN HUE (1965-1973)

MY CHILDHOOD – 1953-1965

A midwife came to my home on Ton Nhon Street, Thai Trach Ward, Hue Citadel to assist my Mom in giving birth. She had indicated that she preferred birthing at home to going to a hospital. It was 1953, "The Year of the Snake" and was, Mom relayed to me much later, infamous for terrible flooding. Water from the Perfume River surged through the inner city, including my family home, and we were forced to get up on a table and chairs to keep away from it.

Before I was born, a fortune-teller in the village informed my mother that she would give birth to a son – definitely a boy – but he would be inflicted with a small defect. The mystic predicted *"Having talent, later fame, illustrious in foreign countries"*. When I was born, my mother inspected me closely but could not discover any defects – only that my *left* eye was slightly smaller than my *right* one. It is a peculiarity that you cannot see unless you inspect me closely; Mom was in fact a bit concerned, but she wasn't totally convinced the predictions would come true.

She also related to me how my Dad had noted that *"This boy has long fingers, very beautiful hands... he has a talent for Fine Arts, so later let him learn about Architecture and become an architect"*. The statement actually exerted a strong influence on my choice of a major field of study later on.

Precisely one year later, my Dad, Commander of Battalion 255[1], was ambushed and killed by the Viet Minh (VM) at around

1. *According to the Report of Battalion 255, KBC 4,070 dated March 2, 1954, there are many doubts about the unjust death of my father. The Dodge 4x4 vehicle had broken down and the driver became ill when the vehicle left Hue, arrived at An Lo to wait for a convoy of 11 vehicles, including*

Kilometer 17 of Highway 1, nicknamed *"the Boulevard of Horrors"* while leading a convoy from Hue to Quang Tri (where he was stationed), following celebrations of the New Year of the Horse (1954) at home.

February 24, 1954; he proceeded down a silent, empty road. Curiously, the driver of the 4x4 Dodge was suffering a cold and running a fever (possibly poisoned by the other side, in an inside, pre-planned job?) My dad sent the convoy ahead and ordered the driver of his Jeep to continue, while he followed behind in a Dodge sedan. A while later, Viet Minh ambushed the Jeep from both sides of the road, thinking that he was in it. Observing his Jeep on fire, with two drivers in front, he stepped on the gas, attempting to escape – but the Jeep had stopped and blocked the highway. Unfortunately, there were drainage ditches on both sides of the road, so his car got jammed on the verge and stalled. He got out of the car and attempted to flee on foot, but a VM shot him, severely wounding him.

It took more than three days for the Army to bring in troops to retrieve his remains. Although he had in fact been promoted to Major three days earlier, he was still carrying the Captain at the time of his death. Before that, his younger brother, Uncle Hoang

---

ambulances and armored vehicles, leaving An Lo at 3:30 pm. If the driver had become ill or the car had broken down, he should have stayed in Hue or An Lo, instead of following the convoy to get closer to the rendezvous point with the other side already prepared, ambushed, ready to attack with the aim. to kill my Master and take away the personal belongings that must have been arranged by an insider in advance. He was posthumously awarded the Vietnam National Order Medal, 5th Class, but no one has ever investigated the details of the death of the Battalion Commander of the 255th Battalion.

Vietnam Gallantry Cross Medal.

When occupying Hue in March 1975, the VC took revenge, by trampling and tearing the National Order Certificate 5th Class hanging on the wall, messed up his picture on the altar wearing the Master's military uniform and medals. His Vietnam Gallantry Cross Medal on the left was damaged. I have collected the 5th Class National Order Medal (the middle picture has four words "Fatherland of Gratitude").

Dai Hai, had gathered to the North.

What is even more unfortunate for Mom was that before leaving, he took with him all the savings for construction materials for the new house; he had hired an Architect to design a home in which each child would have their own room. This was in fact special – a rarity at the time.

Having lost most of her assets and her husband, Mom's life was impacted severely; nevertheless, with a strong will, and always thinking of her four young children, the youngest less than a year old, she rose in pain and continued onward, to provide for her family. Another year passed and my paternal grandfather, who was living with my family, also passed away. Afterward, my mother, suspecting that the house on Ton Nhon Street was bringing bad luck, decided to sell out. She moved the family from Thanh Noi to An Cuu, to build a house on land they purchased earlier, and hopefully make a fresh start.

A family picture, taken around the fall of 1953. Mom is sitting and holding me. My sister stands on the left; behind her, from the right, are my brothers. My Dad's military photo, in uniform.

ELEMENTARY SCHOOL 1958-1965

Once settled in the An Cuu house, I was able to enroll in Ngu Binh Primary School, located at the foot of the mountain. After only a year, I reported to my mother that classmates had been threatening and bullying me on the way to school. My mother thus determined to avoid trouble and had me transferred to An Cuu Primary School. From my house to the two schools the distance is approximately equal. The front of the school overlooking the An Cuu river *("...cloudy when sunny and clear when rainy...")* goes from the first to the fifth grade. Boys and girls studied together but had to sit on different sides of the room. I only studied there until the third grade, when I remember a dramatic moment when the teacher own daughter had a *seizure* and fainted while studying. The entire class came to a halt, as the teacher held his daughter and massaged her. After a few minutes, she regained consciousness, and the class resumed.

My handwriting was even and beautiful, so the teacher encouraged me to stand on the board and write for the whole class to copy, especially the spelling (meanwhile the teacher is dictating to the whole class). He/She then dramatically pulled a dark curtain to cover the board, only opening it after all had completed their writing chores. I was happy to see how my spelling was very good, with rare errors, so I always got 10/10 points. For those whose transcription had misspellings, they could look at the board to correct it, once the teacher completed reading and pulled back the curtain.

What was most memorable for me in the fourth-grade class in the 1963-1964 school year was the way the teacher clearly cherished me; there were even rare compliments in the notebook. I remembered that the year she became pregnant, she often wore a white coat outside – one that people jokingly referred to as *"the ceasefire coat"*. During the latter part of her pregnancy, she often got tired in class, sometimes resting her head on the desk for a moment. She allowed me to lead a lesson, writing on the blackboard, with the entire class silently copying after me. Since I was standing and writing on the board, I had to pass my notebook to the two girls sitting on the left row to copy for me – one with the long royal name Cong Tang Ton Nu Doan Trinh. She was a small girl who lived next to the teacher's house near the school. The second, smaller one, was named Vo Thi Kim Phung; these were the two people who were asked to copy articles into my notebook every day. On the bottom of the pages, I drew a landscape, coconut trees, apricot trees, or a row of houses, and often received a compliment from the teacher for my artistic talent. It is an honor and advantage to be able to write on a blackboard, and when you finish writing, you will always remember what you inscribed, much more vividly than sitting down and copying in a notebook.

My teacher was given a beautiful name: "My Ky". Her husband was Ton That Quynh (indicating that they descended from a royal family). By coincidence, he taught a Science class that my brother attended at Nguyen Tri Phuong High School.

Studying with her, every month, I earned an honor card *(the commendation board for the top 5 students in the class)*. She and her husband are now retired and settled in Fairfax, Virginia with their successful children and grandchildren, after both worked in banking with the US government for many years.

Up to the fifth grade, there were two classes, designated "A" and "B". Since I was studying with Ms. Chuong on 5A, she preferred to stand on the blackboard and compose text by hand, so I did not have another opportunity to write for my classmates. The upside was that I no longer had to ask Doan Trinh or Kim Phung to copy text into my notebook. I do remember Miss Chuong was known to be a notoriously difficult teacher; decades later, when I met my fourth grade teacher in Virginia, I asked why she (Miss Chuong) had been so ferocious at that time with such small students. Her response that she was single at that time, while all the other teachers in the school were already married with children.

HIGH SCHOOL - QUỐC HỌC (NATIONAL ACADEMY) 1965-1973

Upon completion of the fifth grade, some students applied for the sixth grade, taking a public school entrance exam. This was on the right bank (south of the city Hue, divided by the Perfume River at that time): people divided the city into two parts for easy reference. If looking from the west (Kim Long or White Tiger bridge), toward the East and Thuan An, the territory on the left-hand side of the Perfume River is known as the *left bank*, while the right-hand side is called the *right bank.*

Public schools (enrolling students who do not have to pay but must take the entrance exam, according to a quota program), National Academy (grades 6-12), each year allow 200 (male-only) students to take the exam, with the highest scores selecting the candidates. In 1965, the number of candidates who took the exam was 2000, with just 200 selected. Nguyen Tri Phuong School (grades 6-9): the institution was less popular because the school was smaller. Girls entered Dong Khanh High School, sixth grade, the only girl's school on the right bank. Later, there was another Co-Op High School, a prototype public school named "Kieu Mau". The remainder of the private high schools that imposed tuition fees were Ban Cong (Hung Dao), Binh Linh (Pellerin), and Thien Huu (Providence).

The family photo was taken around 1963, in front of the family home in An Cuu, Hue: from the left: brother Chau, Hoa, Mom, brother Lap, Sister Gai, and Mr. Bang (cousin). Many family photos were lost or destroyed during the war and post-1975.

On the left bank, there are public schools such as Ham Nghi, and Nu Thanh Noi (girls-only High School), and private schools such as Nguyen Du and Bo De. There are not many options for students in Hue; if they fail the exam to enter a public school, they either go home to farm, get a job as a manual worker, or if their family is wealthy, they study in private school and then have the opportunity to take an entrance exam for public school, once a place to admit more students was opened every year.

The number of students selected is limited; failing the entrance exam to enter the sixth grade, one's future is uncertain (also nicknamed in Vietnamese: *The Crab Legs exam*, perhaps using the French language *"Concourse"*). The tuition fees and study expenses are not that high, to the relief of many students and their families, but it is not easy to pass. That year, I passed, coming in at the 100th place out of 200 students selected. Exam questions included subjects such as Mathematics, Literature, and Science.

The title of the essay (Literature) that year was as follows: *"Please describe a dream you have had"*. I thought this must have been a proverb, similar to the previous year when the exam included an instruction to explain the sentence: "*Good woodwork is better than good paint; ugliness with a good personality is better than beautiful"*. Thanks to reading books, this topic also allows students the freedom to tell any story: *I describe in a dream that I passed the exam...* Perhaps the examiner wanted to challenge the imagination of 11-12-year-olds, but at that age, I slept like a baby. Even if I had had a dream, I would wake up only with wet pants, and not remembering anything! When I came home that day, Mr. Tin (a professor) asked how I felt about the exam. I told him; he said *"You will surely pass"* because according to him, to describe such a dream is to get what they had been asking for.

Glad to have passed the exam, now I had to worry about how to go to school. In elementary school, I simply walked across An Cuu Bridge every day, turned right, passed the market, had to cover my nose because of the fishy smell of fish and shrimp, and then went to school. Now I had to ride a bicycle, pass by the mill, cross An Cuu Bridge then to Mieu Dai Cang, turn left along Nguyen Hue Street until Ben Ngu, then turn right to go to school. The best-known school in Hue is only for boys, but most of them go on to successful careers after graduating because the number of students who pass the Baccalaureate One and Two is very high compared to students in private high schools. In 6th grade, I chose French as my second language, so I was put in class 6-1 and studied in the one-story row overlooking Dong Khanh Girls' School, (The School's management board allowed younger students to study on this side because they were considered too young to interfere with the girls' classes, like older students).

MẬU THÂN 1968 (THE 1968 TẾT OFFENSIVE)

In the 1967-1968 school year, I was in the Eighth grade at Quoc Hoc School (QH). Near the end of the "Year of the Goat", every class holds a small year-end party and everyone goes home to celebrate. Mom made all kinds of jam cakes, such as ginger jam, lotus seeds, coconut ... then lotus seed cakes made of special beans, rounded into small balls, wrapped in colorful glossy paper, sometimes clear paper, sometimes opaque, with both ends cut into tassels. She also made melons, flowers trimmed from papayas, carrots, or radishes, dried, and shriveled in small pots, but when put in a bottle, with cooked fish sauce and sugar together, they bloom beautifully. After the 23rd day of December in the Lunar year, which celebrates and lets the Kitchen God's family go back to present a yearly report to God, Mom prepared an even greater variety of cakes: green bean-printed cakes, moon cakes, glutinous rice cakes, and *banh chung (sweet rice squares)* and *banh tet (sweet rice balls)* which are usually simmered overnight in a large pot.

That year Mom made all kinds of delicious food, because her eldest son had just completed his pilot training in the US, and he chose the assignment at Da Nang Airport, to be close to home. My brother Lap was studying in Saigon; after going to Hue to celebrate Tet (New Year), he would return to Saigon and on the 7th day of Tet, was scheduled to travel and study abroad in the United States, through a US/AID scholarship. My sister had just completed her teacher's education in Quy Nhon and also returned before taking up a position in Quang Ngai. Thus it was that the entire family was at home: Mr. Tin, relatives, Mr. Luyen, and my cousin would also come to celebrate Tet. The whole family was busier than in previous years, because except for me, the children were far away from home celebrating Tet, so Mom looked happier than usual.

On the 28th of December, the lunar year calendar, the whole family took each other to the Tet flower market; this is a park in front of Tran Hung Dao Street, on the left bank of the Perfume River, a park on the left of the Truong Tien Bridge that people have cleared to display melons, jam cakes and especially flowers in bloom; this year's *"flower market"* was unusually crowded... Hue city is small, most people know each other quite well... but this year we saw a lot of strangers. My oldest brother Chau had just returned from the US, looked pale compared to others... still slurred voices, others a little dark-skinned, more tanned... and who would have thought that most of the VC commandos had infiltrated Hue, ready for what they called the *"General Offensive"* at the most important hour of the people to celebrate? All the families are happily reunited, thinking of the safely returned beloved, because the two sides had previously agreed to sign a ceasefire for three days of Tet.

On the evening of the 28th or 29th of the New Year, we noticed many people coming in and out of the next-door neighbor's; so we suspected that Nha Ca's father had just passed away. Our house was behind her house, and in other houses, children and grandchildren came home to celebrate Tet, so it was also unusually bustling. Honda motorbikes were zipping back and forth on Highway 1 in front of our house.

After offering Tet to invite grandparents to the altar as a tradition, the entire family enjoyed a meal. After Mom and my sister finished cleaning up and started playing cards, although I was in eighth grade, I was the youngest in the family, physically I was also small, so when the table was crowded, children could only sit and watch others play. And since it was not the beginning of the year, I had not yet received my gift of *"lucky money"* – folding new money to spend. New Year's Eve came, firecrackers exploded, but there was also strangely the sound of machine guns, from two military strongholds near our home: the Le Loi transport fort in the south and the Trang Bia fort in the north. The gunfire was punctuated by sounds of explosions. Loud rumbling echoes from afar, and then a power outage, confirming for people that the explosions are no longer the joyful sound of firecrackers… My cousin Luyen wanted to go home to An Lang, on a red Honda SS50, while the rest of our family stayed in place. There was no news. In the cellar of the house, Mom had made an improvised shelter: the lower half on the ground, covered with sandbags to avoid shelling. Everyone crowded in and tried to go to sleep.

Early in the morning, everyone went out into the front yard to try to tell what was what, but saw nothing. Highway 1 was deserted, with no traffic or people passing by, while on New Year's Day, it should have been bustling. Then Mom and my brothers decided to stroll north, to get closer to the city, because they thought that if the VC took over, they would have to come in from the outside, south from Da Le. My brother took Mom with me on a black Suzuki motorbike, with a Samsonite suitcase full of clothes he had brought back from the US, we ran after him. Going to An Cuu Bridge, we noted that while the bridge had not collapsed, it had been badly damaged: there were many holes in the middle of the bridge, so large vehicles could not cross it: only two-wheelers or pedestrians. Arriving at the shrine, everyone turned left to go towards the Redemptorist Church located on Nguyen Hue Street; this was the road I still cycled to school down every day, just a short distance from Mieu Dai Cang to the west. Two other directions: one goes across the crossroads; one goes to Bridge number 7 across from the stadium. Neither direction had any shelter; maybe that was why people headed to the church, not knowing that if they went straight, the Truong Tien Bridge ahead of them was damaged because of a broken span resulting from an explosion the night before: the VC intended to prevent support vehicles from crossing the river, making them unable to cross the left bank, while the Kieu Mau High School on the right bank was occupied by refugees from the previous night. Most people were streaming in from the Phu Vang direction (East).

At that time, most people assumed that the wisest way to seek shelter would be in solid buildings, both avoiding bullets and shelling. Places of worship should probably be safe from attacks from either side. The Redemptorist Order in Hue met these conditions, so people sought refuge, in a large number[2].

We did not enter the church from the main gate, but instead from the Disciple Institute's gate on Nguyen Hue Street, diagonally in front of Sao Mai printing house and Thien Huu School. This area is known to be a Christian area and my family is not very knowledgeable about it because we are practicing Buddhists. My experience had been limited to scouting and collecting stamps; I often visited the Sao Mai printing house or Xavier Center next to the church, or friends who study at Thien Huu but go to the Vietnamese-American Association in the evening at Quoc Hoc, for English classes taught by an American.

After my brother left the Suzuki on the back wall of the church, entering the side gate, we observed a lot of people sitting or lying in the corridor, an area wide enough for refugees to huddle together, with walls and windows on both sides, while leaving enough room for people to pass through in the middle. We were struggling to find a place with our belongings when a man in a black robe with a white collar showed up; he was scowling fiercely. I noticed that he had bright and serious eyes when I looked directly at him. He pointed to my brother's brand-new Samsonite suitcase, including a tag with his last name, and commanded: *"Let Father keep it for you in my room instead of leaving it here"*, and then carried the suitcase to the end of the hallway. Later when Mom returned in February to receive the suitcase, with all the belongings intact, I found out that he was in fact Archbishop Nguyen Kim Dien, whom the VC had killed after a 1975 incident. At that time, he was still Archbishop of Hue. I did not know when he stored the suitcase in his room whether he knew we were Buddhists or not, but this action left us with an unforgettable impression of him – because

---

2. "The Tet Offensive in Hue (1968)" was rewritten by famous writer Nha Ca, during the time she returned to mourn her father, Uncle Phu, who had died a few days earlier. In fact, her home sat right next to ours, and like my family, the people there fled for refuge to the Redemptorist Congregation after New Year's Day. They also witnessed the tragic scenes that took place here on these days. Her book was denounced and publicly burned by the Communist government after April 1975. Please read the English edition of Olga Dror, titled "Mourning Headband for Hue" to better understand the brutal policy and the cruel treatment by the Communists, in Hue in particular and in South Vietnam in general. True stories and real people – told by a famous writer, more complete and detailed for those who want to learn the truth.

he knew how easy it would be to reveal our identities to the VC.

There were many refugees along the corridor; we had not realized that the main church was already full. Our family only consisted of five people at that time: Mom and me, two brothers, and my sister. Around the 10th of the Lunar New Year, at 10 am, one person ran in from the outside, in a hurry, running and shouting: *"VC, they are coming, run, run... go...go..."*, he ran down the corridor and disappeared, and my two brothers ran too. A few minutes later, a young VC wielding an AK-47 forced everyone outside and made us follow in a row to the backyard of the building. I saw quite a few people herded out there Some of the men were tied together with long electrical wires. They were sitting on the floor on the other side of the fence; women and children were guided across to the opposite side. Mom held my hand tightly as if she was afraid they might separate me from her, my sister followed; all three followed the people in front, VC guys on either side, with guns and full of young faces. I thought I saw a familiar face resembling a guy who lived near the railway tracks; even in the Eighth Grade, thanks to my small body, or because someone covered my face from them, I escaped death. A few hours later, when they had driven all the people to the other side of the fence, they let the women and children back into the church, but the view was no longer the same as it had been in the morning: the corridor was now empty, the furniture scattered about. Although Mom didn't say anything, I knew that she was worried about her two other sons. I had no idea where they were; the family was separated. In the evening, my brother Lap returned, his face still full of terror; he said a small group ran to hide in the Sao Mai printing shop next door, when the VCs came in and shouted, a few people came out and were taken away, but he still hid until the evening, before sneaking back to the church.

Seeing such a chaotic situation, not knowing when they (the VC) might return, and observing how the place of worship was also not a sanctuary, Mom decided that the rest of the family should move along Highway 1, across the crossroads, past Thuan Hoa Hotel (MACV station), to the Kieu Mau School, next to the College of Sciences. Here, there were quite a few refugees, but the VC did not show up to arrest people, so it was relatively orderly. Two days later, my eldest brother appeared; he said that when they entered the church, he and a few others ran towards the An Cuu Bridge and bumped into a group of VCs who challenged them: *"Why are you running away?"* Thinking fast, he blurted out *"Americans – there were a lot of Americans GI back there"* so they let them continue on their way. It was the VCs who were detaining people; there were no Americans at that time. Had he opened his mouth to say "VC", the results would have been different. There must have been someone to speak on his behalf, and the group at that time, to save their lives. When he got home there was no one there. He stopped by Luyen's house but felt uneasy, so the next day, he went back to the church again. Finding that his family was no longer there, he continued to the North and eventually met up with us. We stayed there until about January 21st when my eldest brother went to the front of the park and met up with some of the pilots of his 213th squadron from Da Nang Airbase for an H-34 in front of Toa Kham. He and his brother Lap went back with them to Da Nang, then sent Lap to Saigon via military cargo plane, as he was concerned about being late to leave for the US. Fortunately, incidents abounded in Saigon and other cities, so the Vietnamese Study Abroad Education Department and US/AID rescheduled the date to go to the US later.

My Mom was at ease; no one had been lost or captured by the VC, so when the family returned to the house safely, she discovered that the American soldiers had entered the house. They weren't able to use a squat toilet, so in the boxes of green beans and rice she kept were *"American Pu's bombs",* we had to get rid of them all, unfortunately.

The neighbor in front of our house, a single woman named Aunt Diu, had an only son named "Hue", who had just graduated from the Field Police Academy. He was arrested by the VC and taken away; later, his family was unable to find his body. Another neighbor was Mr. Ton, also a Field policeman; when they came to arrest him, Mr. Ton hid on the roof. They said that if he didn't get down, they would take his two younger brothers and his friend instead. By the time they got to the railway, he ran after them and gave up, exchanging his life for those three people. He went missing; his family could not find the body either. As for

Mr. Dieu, my aunt's son, having just completed a course in the Education Teaching College of Quy Nhon, he hid in his sister's basement near the railroad tracks; when the American soldiers came in to clear them out, he presented himself, speaking English; when he showed his papers to them, the American soldiers let him accompany them. Approaching the Mieu Dai Cang, the Communists shot them from inside the Temple, because they suspected they were going to follow the American soldiers. He and another Vietnamese died in a hail of bullets from two sides. People covered the body temporarily, in front of the Temple gate.

After a month of eating old moldy bread, and canned foods, not taking a bath, and lacking sunlight, my whole body started to be covered in scabies. When I went back to school, there were still students in the classroom; two professors had been arrested and went missing, while one Scouter of the team was killed by a rocket shell.

The class returned but it was no longer the same as before. In the weeks following, mass graves were discovered, one by one: Bai Dau, Phu Thu…Khe Da Mai… mass funerals were held across Le Loi Street, the wail of weeping mixed with the scent of incense… every time a mass funeral passed by, the school let students line up in two rows in front of the main gate, to greet and say goodbye to the unfortunate victims; DK girls' school did the same. Along Le Loi Street, under the Royal Poinciana trees, were a group of students in blue and white clothes, and on the white Ao Dai side, standing solemnly to say goodbye to innocent victims for the last time.

Even the bravest could not help but shudder. I was only 14 years old at that time; the cruelty of innocent people being unjustly killed, and then repeated in the summer of 1972 and 1975 – no matter how I might try to describe it in print, a book cannot even capture the feeling. You had to be there to witness it.

Hue City is small; almost everyone knows everyone else, from left to right bank, down to Gia Hoi, Phu Thu. Hue, after Tet, should have had fun all the month of January, but now it turned gloomy and mournful, parents weeping for lost children, wives crying for husbands killed, children crying out for parents and siblings who had been massacred. Leader of the Scouts Tran Dien[3] even though he admitted that he was an active Vietnamese Senator, he was not treated any better than any other. At Ben Ngu, they arrested Vo Thanh Minh[4], another famous Scouter, who took him along with them when retreating and then killed him. Professors Le Van Thi (Sciences) and Chau Khac Tuy (Mathematics) of the National Academy were buried alive. There are people in every village who were buried alive, destroyed, or taken away, but whose remains were never found.

As a result of the naked Hue massacre, many left-leaning liberals suddenly opened their eyes to the reality of a massacre of innocent people. A small city, once the capital of an ancient land, Hue was fortunately recaptured by the army after nearly a month of combat. During this time, I called it *"The Hell City"*. There was a general mourning for the Vietnamese people and a private mourning for Hue City.

Now that the Mau Than Tet offensive is 56 years in the past, some of the victors are attempting to justify their crimes, or trying to suppress or erase the history of what happened – since by now most of the witnesses are gone. Young people in Hue rarely know

---

3. *After New Year's Day, Chief Scout Leader Tran Dien and his family also took refuge in the Catholic Church, because he was nearby and familiar with the church. Along with his two sons, Tran Tien San (served in the military and Tran Tien Ha) was arrested when the Communist guerrillas entered and drove all the people out of the church. Mr. San and Ha untied themselves and escaped when they weren't paying attention.) Mr. Dien claimed to be a Senator for the Congress Republic of Vietnam and they still took him away. His body, after his having been buried alive, was found at Lang Xa Con, Huong Thuy District, once the ARVN recaptured Hue.*

4. *Chief Scout Leader "Hong Son Da Ma" (Wood Badge named) Vo Thanh Minh was the one who set up a tent and played the flute outside the conference room of the 1954 Geneva Conference, hoping to receive an audience from the two negotiating delegations of the National Socialist Republic of Vietnam and the Viet Minh. But only a few old friends, members of the South VN delegation (Tran Van Tuyen, Cung Giu Nguyen) visited, to persuade him to stop going on a hunger strike, and Mr. Ta Quang Buu – his successor – held the position of General Member of the Council in the Central, representing the Viet Minh in signing the armistice agreement, not seeing him again at all (perhaps not having been allowed to contact him). A few years later, he returned to live in seclusion at Uncle Phan's temple in Hue. Arrested during the Tet Offensive and brought to a prison in the forest, we heard that since he could not escape his captors, he was beaten to death by the guards. (According to the document of Scout Leader Nghiem van Thach-Paris, France 2007).*

or hear about this. But for me, such a stain on history cannot be casually erased but should be learned to avoid happening again. I have seen this as similar to the 9/11 incident in the United States, but the difference is that the people responsible for 9/11 had to pay for their crimes. Those responsible for Mau Than atrocities in Hue continue to evade the law, simply because they were the winners of the war.

The political situation in the United States after the Tet Offensive became more and more confusing, and left-leaning media and press took the opportunity to report false information, benefiting the anti-war faction. President Lyndon B. Johnson announced his decision not to run for re-election on March 31, then just a few days later, on April 4, 1968, Dr. Martin Luther King, Jr. was assassinated, leading to days of riots in several cities. Yet again, on June 6, Democratic presidential candidate and former Attorney General and New York State Senator Robert F. Kennedy was shot dead. Riots between police and protesters erupted at the Democratic Party's national convention in Chicago in August 1968, leading to Democratic candidate Hubert Humphrey losing the election to Republican candidate Richard Nixon in the November election of the same year.

This is a mass murder: burying innocent people alive, including foreign professors at the College of Medicine of the University of Hue. It should have awakened the conscience of the world, but all political developments in the United States took over the media National News. Thus the Tet massacre in Hue and Vietnam were easily lost in the shuffle and forgotten.

Hoping that after nearly 60 years, hatred will be gone, and no one has to think about the common mourning for the Hue compatriots in any year of the perpetrators, because they themselves will die so that the unjustly-treated souls can rest in peace eternally. Hoping for a confession, guilt, and admission of responsibility from those in power who caused it in later days.

Following the incident, a few classmates suddenly disappeared; no one asked for details or the reason why, but later I found out: they had applied to go to a private school, in exchange for a younger birthdate in the school records, to avoid the mandatory

Military Draft, total mobilized to reduce the age of one year to compulsory enlistment in 1972; they then applied to rejoin the National Academy. The number 1 adds a dash to the number 4, 52, add the hook becomes 55… How did they predict this in advance? No one has wondered until now.

"The Diplome" or Thanh Chung's high school exam after the 9th grade, was canceled so students could continue to the 10th grade. Every year there are two exams in class, called First and Second Semester Exams. The students with the highest scores in the subjects assigned to them are assigned to a rank division called a *"shirt folder"*. Few students are at the top of all subjects, so it is an honor to make a folder for a school with all students, but you would be placed on top. An honor even though the subject might be of little importance. Whether the subject is important or not depends on its "coefficient", such as choosing B: Math, Math has a coefficient of 4 (multiplied by 4 times the number of points). This coefficient is important because if a student is good at a main subject (A=Sciences, B=Math, C=Language, D= Literature), then taking the exam is very beneficial.

Quoc Hoc's curriculum is not easy, because it is a famous boys-only school in Hue and the teachers and supervisors have a reputation for being strict with students. The uniform is dark blue trousers, a white collared shirt, and a blue embroidered name badge worn on the pocket; it must be neat at all times. Must wear sandals with straps or closed shoes, not allowed to wear thong sandals (nicknamed *"Japanese open sandals"*). Students will be disciplined. Students are also not allowed to smoke and must attend school on time, as a mandatory requirement.

Professors usually enter the school through the front gate, while students go in and out by two side gates, next to the Governor's office. There is no entrance to Nguyen Truong To Street because it is shared with Dong Khanh Girls' High School, to avoid clutter. In the past, students at the two schools entered and left at the same time; later, when they saw the boys and girls leaving the school, after school time, not shy about it, boys and girls were waiting, so they began to dismiss girls 15 minutes in advance, to avoid traffic on the same Le Loi road at the same time. After signals to enter the school (QH used a bronze gong to signal and DK used a large drum) because the two schools were close to each other, the school staff locked the gates. Those who are late to class will either have to leave, or be more rebellious, climbing the wall, but wanting to go to class if they are late is a different story, because the teachers call attendance when the students have entered class after lining up outside. Classroom attendance is also an aspect of school discipline, approved in the year-end report card.

Since entering the sixth grade, we started looking for new friends, because meeting the same elementary school friends is quite rare, as only 200 students are divided into several classes, I saw that there were 62 students in my class at that time who chose French as a second language.

After passing two yearly exams and not giving up because of family circumstances, students will move to higher grades together; each year a few new members are admitted for reasons of moving from public schools inside or outside the province, areas that are not secure because of war… or other legitimate reasons. Every year when old friends are lost, there are also new ones, so by the end of the 11th grade when we go to the Baccalaureate 1 exam, also known as the Semi-Baccalaureate, the remaining students will pass together, then go up to 12th grade. The secondary language, French, the number of students is becoming smaller and smaller, so the two classes are combined into one. From the 10th grade, we studied both foreign languages, French and English, or vice versa.

THE FIRST LOVE AND THE PURPLE AO DAI

At this time, in high school or from the 10th grade and upward, friends often met to study together or go to movies together, visit each other, ask questions... no house had a phone. If you want to meet anyone, just drop by and knock on the door or make arrangements before the weekend. Friends' sisters are often shy especially so with their brother's friends, so they hide behind or in the kitchen, but rarely dare to show their faces when their brother's friends come to visit. It is not easy to flirt with your friend's sister; when you go to their house, you can't easily meet her alone because your friend is there with you.

During a visit to a friend's house when he is not at home (actually this is just an excuse to get to know each other after you have spotted one another), since your goal is not to meet your friend but his sister, you come in, risking an excuse to get to know your friend's sister, especially girls attending the girl's high school next to yours. It is also a golden opportunity to ask questions and gossip. Thanks to that, I got accustomed to the practice, and a few times when I asked to go out, it became more intimate. In Hue, the city is small, so either just go to Ngu Binh, go down to Vy Da to eat rice cakes (banh beo), visit Linh Mu Pagoda or go down to Con Hen to eat sweet bowls, sometimes go to the cinema at Tan Tan or Chau Tinh theaters a few times. Everywhere there are people watching, people spotting and recognizing you. She often wears a purple long dress, and white pants when going out, the special purple color of Hue girls. White Ao Dais are only for when going to school. We call the girls in DK by the affectionate name *"Girl Love Banh Nam"*, abbreviated as CYBN[5].

The first love was so pure and innocent, the two were very compatible, although we did not dare to promise anything.

The name badge on my white shirt for school was challenged

5. ***"Banh nam"*** *is a special kind of cake of Hue people, made of rice flour and filled with shrimp, ground pork with a little minced or pounded skin, thinly-wrapped in banana or dong leaves, eaten with Chili fish sauce. When making it, put on the cooked rice flour first, then a pistil on top, fold, straighten, steam, open the cake to have a rectangular shape, eat it with a thin bamboo stick called a pointed paddle to divide the cake into pieces in the manner of how the King ate them. Many people who are not used to eating this way use a spoon or chopsticks to pick it up, or some people eat it boldly, rolling up the whole cake, dipping it in fish sauce, putting it in their mouth, but eating the cake slowly, square by small piece, is the right tune. I don't know since when, but the slang for female students is Con Yeu Banh Nam (CYBN), love is "goblin", aka "chimpanzee", we boys mischievously call our girlfriends or friends studying at a girls' school in Hue, during high school. This slang term was probably used by a group of students to call each other from the time before mine until 1975. In the song "One realm going back" by musician Trinh Cong Son, composed around 1974, there are the lines:*
"Clouds over my head and sunshine on my shoulders.
My feet go but the river stays.
The love elf accidentally called. ***(Con tinh*** *yêu thương vô tình chợt gọi).*
I see a human shadow on me again."
Many people who are not originally from Hue, or there are singers who do not know the origin of these two words have changed to word ***"heart" (con tim)****, which is not the right meaning for the song.*

by my sister; she embroidered it for me, but when she washed the shirt and discovered the badge was not hers, she questioned me about it. I had to confess, so she was the first to know my secret[6]. When my sister returned to Hue after April 1975, she was very close to her, often coming to her house because she was in the education teaching profession and thus learned that her brother also escaped with me in the last hours. At that time, no one dared to think about going any further without a complete education and career path. God has arranged it all, because if I had stayed in Hue to study like my friends after 12th grade or got stuck in the last days of April, and then returned to Hue to live, my life would have changed, with a three-generation background that I had to declare. I would only have to work as a freelancer to survive, but I couldn't continue to study or work, since no one would dare to hire me, only to get married, but the person I would choose is probably none other than her.

Once, when my friend and I drove out of the house on Honda motorcycles, there was a young man in the village who stopped us and demanded a fight; he must have noticed that I often drove my CYBN out for a date so he was jealous. Fortunately, that day with my friend, nothing untoward happened, because that village was not very secure, so my friend, a boy in the village, had to stay at his aunt's house in the city to go to school, but his sister still stayed

6. *My sister is good at cooking, baking, knitting and embroidery. She was very skilled at learning Home Economics from Dong Khanh girls' school. My school shirts' name tags are embroidered with navy blue thread on a piece of cloth and sewn up every year. Mom had a Singer sewing machine with a foot pedal at home; since we go to Scouts, even though we are boys, we all teach ourselves to sew, sew team flags, sew up pants, even know how to change the bobbin thread below, the hardest task. I automatically changed all the nametags on my shirt because she (my girlfriend) embroidered them for me herself. My sister was observant and caught on that that wasn't her work, so I had to confess to her. When I was about 10 years old, once when she was away, I saw an unfinished sweater on the table, I had seen her make it before, so I imitated the up and down rows, when she went back to knit, I heard she say to herself: "Oh, why did I knit these lines yesterday not so bad but so wrong!", she took off a few pieces and reversed what I had done on my own without asking, because she didn't think anyone in the family other than her knew how to knit. Later, when Sophia learned to knit from my sister at the age of 8, she was surprised to see that her father knew how to knit without learning from her or anyone else. I confessed "I just watched her knitting or embroidering when I was young and then it 'entered' my mind, and I still remember the basics of how to knit or hand embroider."*

there with her paternal grandparents. The CYBN that I used to jokingly call every time: *"Long sideburn hair ..."* is now happily settled with her children and grandchildren[7] . (Perhaps Thanh, my friend, did not know about this until he read it here, having missed being a brother-in-law – but the love story was hidden).

BACCALAUREAT I AND II.

At the end of Junior year (11th grade), we took the Baccalaureate I exam. There is only one given year, so if you fail, you have to wait until the following year. Baccalaureate II after Senior 12th grade is administered in two exams; if you fail the first one, you must apply for the second one, otherwise, you have to wait a year to take it again; that's why there is a saying: *"We don't eat chili when taking exams, but it is spicy"* or *"Learn good but not the exam"*, *"Fall out of the Baccalaureate, here you go to Sergeant"*. If you pass Baccalaureate I, if you join the army, you will be trained at Thu Duc, you will have the rank of an Officer; if you fail the exam, you will enter Dong De (the rank of non-commissioned from private to sergeant). In 1973, the Ministry of Education abolished the Baccalaureate I exam, and the Baccalaureate II exam became multiple-choice, IBM computer-graded, instead of a written test (students jokingly called it *"IBM Baccalaureate"*).

PEOPLE DEFEND THEMSELVES PROGRAM

Before the exam year, we studied together in groups; the

7. The song "Sideburns hair are short and long" by musician Pham Duy, composed in 1969 opens with two folk verses:
"Tóc mai sợi vắn sợi dài... *Lấy* nhau chẳng đặng, thương hoài ngàn năm".
" Sideburn hair is short and long... If we can't get married, love forever".
This song is famous for the female singer Thai Thanh, the timeless voice of Vietnam
**Previously, in 1956, musician Pham Manh Cuong composed the song "Love Forever" based on the above two verses. Two different songs composed by two famous musicians, one taking the last half of the verse, the other taking the first verse of the folk song as the title; both muse on romances of school days, whether successful or not, depending on each situation. For anyone who has confided about love and first love, listening to these songs is very meaningful.*

Baccalaureate is important if you have to choose a military career, whether you want to or if you have to, so the students have to at least try to become officers. Good students in the class like Liem or Chanh often help other students who are weaker in Math or Physics (two important subjects of group B have high coefficients). At this time, there was the People's Self-Defense program[8]. After that, physical education for the war was replaced for Junior and Senior years with a military subject to familiarize students. This subject has points added to the total score for the Baccalaureate Exam II, up to 10 points, for the purpose of dissuading students from dropping out of class.

Class 11B3 National Academy School year 1970-1971. Picture taken by Instructor Phan Khac Tuan (wearing glasses, standing with a tie, on the left). He was the Principal of the 11th National Academy from 1973-1975. He was also a professor of Physics, Chemistry, and Photography at the school.

8. *This is a military training program in each city, so that male members over 18 years old familiarize themselves with weapons, in case they have to defend their area if attacked by the enemy. Because of "The 1968 Tet Offensive" in Hue and Saigon, in June 1968, the government of the Republic of Vietnam launched this program to suppress local terrorism and avoid revenge. Every evening the young men in the neighborhood meet, take turns guarding, train in the use of light weapons (Carbine M-2 or Garand) by soldiers, to get acquainted in case of need to use and meet, also to identify familiar or unfamiliar people in the case of strangers appearing in their villages, as before Tet Mau Than. The Hue people were alert and learned from this experience to avoid a repeat tragedy.*

THE RED FIERY SUMMER (EASTER OFFENSIVE) 1972

Based on the famous book of Nam Nhat Phan: *"Mua He Do Lua"* (The Red Fiery Summer) the American military called it the Easter Offensive (American Easter Holiday, 1972).

The war escalates and draws closer to the city. This year, a 122mm Russian made rocket of the Communist forces shelled at night fell into the back corner of our family house, inflicting damage; my family was safe but neighbors were injured. The final year of high school, so the exam in the summer has just ended (July 5 for the first exam offered and August 30 for the second), the order to enlist in the army by the Ministry of National Defense, students born in 1953 are being drafted. The deadline to report is September 23, 1972, except for students who are deferred due to health, or family circumstances, or those who have *"declared a younger D.O.B."*. At this time, peace talks for the four-party Paris Agreement are taking place, so military pressure will have a lot of influence on the negotiations. Knowing that, the Communists massively ordered a total attack by their people throughout South Vietnam, decisively ending hostilities – but we had not yet failed.

My classmates who were born in 1953 went to the Thu Duc, respectively, and some of them took the entrance exam to the Da Lat National Military Academy School for military careers, such as Phuc Van Le (d) and Thieng Ngoc Nguyen. I went to Saigon University without knowing that Liem Nguyen was also attending Van Hanh University. The others continued to study at Hue University. The University of Hue only has Education and Sciences to choose from, or the School of Medicine, Law, or Literature… not as many majors as Saigon. Particularly, Military Academy school applicants must pass the first section of Baccalaureate 2, majoring in Mathematics B, apply and take the entrance exam, because the program four years later is equivalent to the College of Science, and this is a school specializing in military careers and leadership, similar to West Point in the US, students graduating with a Bachelor's Degree in Science.

My friends from Quoc Hoc school since 1965… More than

half a century… Now some have gone, others are doctors or professors, some are freelancers, a number are overseas, and some are staying in the country. The name *"Dong Khanh"* has been retired; the school has too many memories for us, but now boys and girls study together, Dong Khanh girls' school, next to us makes our hearts flutter every time we see color-coded nameplates in Ao Dai white dresses that we remember with verses: *Senior Purple, Junior Pink, Sophomore Blue, Freshmen Red.* Now it is no longer the same as before because the school has been renamed.

CHAPTER III
COLLEGE LIFE IN SAIGON
1973-1975

COLLEGE – CHALLENGING AND REAL-LIFE EXPERIENCES 1973-1975

When I attended high school at the National Academy in Hue, I intended to continue my studies at the University in Saigon. My strongest supporter in this objective was my oldest brother; alas, Mom seemed to be sad, as there would be no one to stay in Hue with her – even though before I finished primary school, she had intended to send me to Saigon to continue my studies at Quoc Gia Nghia Tu *(School for the Children of the Nation)*. Established in 1963 along strict French high school standards, this was the only educational institution in Saigon dedicated to the children of servicemen who had died on duty, sponsored by the Ministry of Defense and the Government. Later, branches opened across more provinces. Automatic admission for those who qualify and no tuition. Those whose results are promising are then given priority to apply for a US/AID scholarship to study in the USA. If there is a father in the army who died in battle, families often with many children only have a mother receiving a small pension; life is difficult, they have to send their children to government schools and only two schools are available: to become a cadet specializing in military science at *Junior Military Academy* or *School for the Children of the Nation.* Although students do not take an entrance exam, they must qualify and meet the conditions to enjoy the benefits. I was more than qualified for both of those two schools.

The first difficulty was to determine to go to Saigon to study at *which* university, and *where* to stay. My brother Lap had gone to Saigon (1966) and was fortunate to have been accepted by Dac Lo Residence; brother Chau (1963) lived with a friend at Minh Mang Residence. By the time I entered, it had become more difficult than before, so the first thing was to see if any relatives had houses to stay at temporarily. We could ask Mrs. Dung, daughter of my maternal uncle: she had a husband and child on Nguyen Huynh Duc Street, but it was not convenient there because you have to get prior consent for whenever you leave, you can't bring a pack; you have to knock on the door and ask to enter. There was Mr. Luyen, who was studying Architecture, but he had been assigned back to school by the Corps of Engineers to complete his education, so he lived in An Dong dormitory and as a civilian, I could not stay there. My oldest brother often went to Saigon on official duty; happened to meet a distant relative, Mrs. L., who lived with her family right at Phan Thanh Gian (PTG), he made a request and she eagerly accepted immediately.

Hitching a ride on a military cargo plane from Da Nang, I flew into Saigon in June 1973 [9], with only a suitcase of clothes and a few books. My brother agreed to ship my Honda motorcycle later on because he could only carry it on one of his squadron's helicopters; we were not allowed to transport bikes by C-130. So I had to take the bus or walk until I got my wheels.

---

9. *Why I was one year late in my education is explained here. I was supposed to arrive in Saigon in the summer of 1972. I took the first Baccalaureat exam in 1971, but for unknown reasons, my exam was altered by someone, and I consequently did not score high enough to pass. When a professor in Hue reported that there was a problem at the exam center in Hue, Chau, my oldest brother flew all the way to Saigon, went to the Exam Section of the Education Department to file a complaint, asking them to let me take my test again, so they might re-exam the scores and compare the handwriting. They said they couldn't do that because they couldn't even find my test and there was no way to retake it. At that time, all candidates had to take the test on the same white paper, scored with the same horizontal lines and distributed in the exam room. Each aspirant had to use blue ink to avoid intentionally making any marks for the examiner. Before marking the exam, they cut off the upper part of the profile, so the test was blinded, and judges did not know the names of contestants. After scoring, they reassembled the first part with the second part containing the scores. All this manual system, a large number of contestants, a small number of judges and staff meant they could have made a lot of mistakes or intentionally pasted "one man's beard on the other's chin". Later, the IBM test in 1974 was marked by machine, which didn't take as much time; it got results sooner, because it didn't have to remove a candidate's name before scoring. I passed the Baccalaureat I the next year and the Baccalaureat II, first section in 1973. My closest friend, Chanh, the class leader, was the best in his class, took the Baccalaureat II exam in 1972 but failed the 1st section. Because of the war, people evacuated to Hue from the northern provinces, occupying schools for temporary accommodation. Students thus had to reside in their own homes, and did not complete the curriculum that the exam questions had been given by professors from Saigon, an area not affected much by the war, the last part of the learning book. Fortunately, both Chanh and I passed the next course, it just didn't mean that we did not study hard, took the exam, and failed the test even we did well. No one in school expected us to fail the exam; nor did we. This was the first and last time in our life that he and I both failed an exam, without knowing that it was our fault.*

UM BA LA...MY CHILDREN, YOUR CHILDREN AND OUR CHILDREN.

When I entered the house of Mr. and Mrs. L. *(Here, I would like to abbreviate the names of their family for sensitive and delicate reasons)*, at 650/20 PTG, I realized that this was a house in an alley, two floors of a concrete-reinforced structure, a flat roof and on the top floor there is an arbor with bougainvillea in front and a covered terrace. Under the roof was a *divan*, large enough to sleep two people, for Tu (who is a fourth-year student at the College of Architecture, who entered from Quang Nam to tutor Bu, the youngest son, who was studying in 10th grade at Cao Thang Technical School. Entering through the front door was a living room with a wine cabinet and a few bottles of French liquor and wine, then a place to store some motorbikes, the stairs, and under the stairs a small dining room; then there was a kitchen and a toilet, with no bedroom on the first floor. The second floor, behind the stairs, was the owner's room, with a window air conditioner installed. Separating the room with a wall is a small altar hanging above, below is a *divan (bed)*[10] and stairs next to it, then there are two large beds for 4 girls to sleep, with a small common area and a door to the terrace.

There wasn't much room left for me to get onto the terrace, so they told PH (her stepdaughter) to let me have her bed under the Buddhist altar above, and she would have to share two large beds with three sisters: PN, PA, and PL. At this point, it must be mentioned that this narrow two-story house, is very separate because there are three generations in the same house: mine, yours, and our children. The husband has two children of his own, the son was a troublemaker, so he enlisted in the army, and the younger sister PH, because of the addition of me, had to give up her bed for the distinguished guest whom she called "Uncle". The stepson belonging to his wife was sent to France beforehand. Only three daughters and the youngest son, who is a common child, live in the house. The youngest boy is naughty all day long; although his parents have a tutor for him, he refuses to study at all, so he gets

10. *A divan is a wooden bed with solid hardwood on top and without a mattress; a twin size sleeps one person. Because of the warm/hot and humid weather in Vietnam and a paucity of air conditioning, we don't use mattresses.*

yelled at and scolded many times. Mr. L., in my opinion, is a very kind, if hot-tempered and strict person with his youngest son, but even with soft or hard styles, he still cannot train or change his son, like a *"wild horse"*, completely out of control at home and unsuitable for a school education. His son, who was a paratrooper, would come back every once in a while, and sometimes be forced by the military police to ask my brother to take him out of military jail, but he was still a troublemaker. She is too kind but does not like her husband's children, for good reason. As for PH and their three daughters, they are very polite, and well-educated and also know my shyness, that of a distant relative, when entering this house, one full of *"trouble"* that I knew absolutely nothing about before.

Every time S. (Mr. L.'s son) comes home, the house is rife with screams, things like money, jewelry, or a bottle of wine are lost or taken away... Perhaps the family is used to this, but privately Tu and I feel uncomfortable because we are outsiders.

Their eldest daughter, PN, is only one year younger than me, and is studying at the College of Education, majoring in English, and is very observant, so she also feels uncomfortable for Tu and me[11].

Observing the situation of a house so crowded and complicated, it was difficult for me to have time to meditate or study, for a long term. I tried to contact Mr. Luyen, asking if I could rent a house or have a temporary way to help me solve the housing problem. After going to see some places with rooms for rent, both cramped and not affordable, he took me down to the corner of 6 Tran Quy Cap Street, near Turtle Lake National Park (also known as International

---

11. *When I met Tu while he traveling to the US for a meeting of Saigon architects in Clearwater, Florida, he recalled the old story. Tu said that after I left, "You are luckier than me. I still had to stay, because I had no other choice, to continue studying and graduate, to become an architect working in Saigon." Tu recounted how, in the last days of April, the whole family of Mr./Mrs. L. and siblings tried to get to Bach Dang Pier to evacuate but failed. Tu was very angry because they attempted to escape without telling Tu, even though they were in the same house. His son, named S., who was naughty, also died in '75. He died in SG. PN and her husband escaped by boat and settled abroad with Bu, her sisters and Ms. L. in France with a guarantee of her son Mic. I heard that PH, his daughter, who gave me the divan under the altar when I first came to Saigon, escaped by boat from Phu Quoc Island, settled in Washington State and completely cut off contact with everyone in the family.*

Square).

Right around the corner is Saigon University Institute, behind the College of Law and College of Architecture (on Phan Dinh Phung Street) is Tran Quy Cap Elementary School (TQC), a school that teaches 1st grade to 5th grade, with a gate, car entrance and a small side gate for motorbikes or pedestrians. He introduced me to the school's staff, Uncle Thich, and then I found out that he had previously let several students from Hue… stay temporarily in the school to be able to study. He has 3 girls and 2 boys who are still young, so when he accepted, I also promised to help tutor them while I studied in the evening. He let me stay in room number 5, right in the middle near the flagpole.

Every morning, I had to take off my pajamas and put them in a closet behind his house, go to school all day, and when school was over, I came back and was free to bathe near the restroom. There was a garden hose mounted on the wall, cold water only and with Saigon weather, you never need hot water – which is very expensive to have anyway. After studying, I slept on the desk at night, then got up early in the morning, before the teachers and students came, brushed my teeth, washed my face with a garden hose, then took a motorbike to the nearby National Library if there was no class on that day, or if there was a class, leave the bike at home, walking through Duy Tan Street, where there are long lines of shady trees, special lunch and dinner can be eaten for University students only, or a popular rice plate with fish or meat sold on the street for $1.00 to $1.50 per plate, with free iced tea.

After dinner, I would come back to school, just take a shower, change clothes, and go to *bed* after studying. Sometimes, early in the morning, I would oversleep; the teacher of the class would come by, knock on the door, and get me up; I'd wrap a blanket around my body and run into the house after her, just keep running and saying *"Sorry"* plus *"Thank you"*. Perhaps the teachers and principals here knew that there were poor students who stayed temporarily to study; they did not cause difficulties for the school staff because they let us live for free and did not take any money. Later I found out that the school principal was Mr. Bao Van Bui(d), who had written many books for elementary school children. I don't know how old he was at that time, but I see they often call him Uncle.

Despite this difficult accommodation situation, I was very comfortable, especially on weekends, there were no students, the whole school was empty, and I did not have to go to the library to study. This was an area with only a few crowded residential houses, very quiet, just walking to Turtle Lake National Park or up to Notre Dame Cathedral of Saigon or the main post office is enough, straight up is Le Loi Avenue, Nguyen Hue or Tu Do Street, Bach Dang Pier. Although I was poor in material wealth, I had the good fortune to walk on the most beautiful streets and parks in Saigon at that time.

From the time I arrived in Saigon, Mom had sent me a *mandat postal* (money order) for 5,000VND [12] every month. The amount was too small to be called enough for a month there, but it was her total pension, so only two months later I urged her to stop sending it to me, because I had money from my brother Lap, transferred to me from the US. Every month he gave me USD$50 (exchanged for 30,000 VND), and he sent me these transfers every 3 months via Chase Manhattan Bank [13] (in Vietnam it was called *"Ma Nhat*

---

12. *Not sure how I could survive in Saigon on such a small amount of money. My mother did not tell me, but when I came to Saigon, she personally sent Chau two pieces of 24k Kim Thanh gold leaf, telling him that when I needed it, he would give it to me. Perhaps she trusted him because she was afraid that if she gave it directly to me to keep, I would have spent it when it was not yet an emergency. These two pieces of gold were brought to the US in 1975 and my brother sold them at Camp Pendleton; the price at that time yielded $300 a piece. When the Vietnamese escaped here, many rich people brought suitcases of gold and diamonds from Saigon as they were evacuated. Because of security issues and to avoid robbers in the camp – they would even kill each other to get their hands on such a fortune – they would store their valuables in a bank armored truck, recommending this to anyone who had gold or US dollars to exchange and depositing it in the bank for more security.*

13. *Chase Manhattan Bank, headquartered in New York. When I arrived in the US, I sent my savings book and asked them to respond and confirm the amount of money left in the Saigon branch. They replied that the US government had closed the facility because of the evacuation, so it was not their responsibility to return the money to their clients in Saigon. They actually blame the Vietnamese government on the legal side, but I know they closed their branch on April 24, 1975 and evacuated their staff to Bangkok-Guam. Deposits not withdrawn before the 24th are considered lost; many clients have sued the bank in court in New York but the bank/US Department of Treasury has responded to them as well as me: both the bank and the US government bear no responsibility in this case. The "responsible agency" would be the new government (Central Bank) National Bank of Vietnam, when it took over the Saigon branch on May 1, 1975. The amount I lost is too small, not enough for a lawyer to go to lunch in New York, so I don't dare to make a big deal out of it.*
Case #1 in 1984: 616 F. Supp. 10 (1984) TAT BA, Plaintiff, v. The CHASE MANHATTAN

Tan Bank", with a branch in Saigon). This money was used to buy books, meals, and monthly expenses, so I didn't need to find a job or tutor anyone for profit. There was no fee paid to tutor the two sons, but after a few sessions, they also gave up because it seemed that it was not interesting to go to evening classes or study with me, and the family did not force them. (He often called them in a Southern accent "Dinh anh, Dinh em" because of the pronunciation of the South for the V and D).

My brother's scholarship was only 200 USD per month, but he gave me 50 USD; at that time the exchange rate was about 30,000 VND, so I understood and respected him, never asking for more or wasting anything. At that time, the cost of living was not very expensive: a plate of popular rice at a student price was 100 VND, and a burger cost only 50 VND. Thus it was that sometimes I didn't have much money left, so I had to eat bread without anything inside and drink cold water to survive.

The small motorbike I bought from Duoc, my elementary school friend in Saigon, was enough to move to Ms. Dung's house, eat, go to the post office to send letters, or go to the University Library. The school right behind me was the Law School, and when I had free time, I would go to the College of Architecture (KT) to help as a *"Ne"* for Mr. Luyen (*"Ne"*, French *"Nègre"* is a proper noun, the slang word of the people in French Architecture school use to call other students to help them with projects during their 7 years of study). The person doing the project is called *Patron*, in the tradition of the École des Beaux-Arts School of Architecture in Paris. These projects can take weeks, months, or even years and are usually large-format drawings on *croky* paper, using various colors or Pelican ink, which I call Architecture ink. *Ne* may be lower-class students who need experience, and know about drawing or painting, and the reward is usually cups of soot plum bought from

---

BANK, N.A. and Citibank, N.A., Defendants.No. 83 Civ. 9421 (EW). United States District Court, S.D. New York. (The judge dismissed the case because it was 6 years overdue, although they had previously contacted the bank and the US Treasury Department to ask for a refund of the money sent).

Case #2 in 1981: Vishipco Line v. Chase Manhattan Bank, N.A., 660 F.2d 854 (2d Cir. 1981) *This case belongs to Mr. Tran Dinh Truong and was lodged in the Court of Appeals, related to to the 200 million VND (Certificate of Deposit CD) deposited at the Chase branch in Saigon. The upper court overturned the lower court's decision and Chase lost the case.*

the small corner store at the Architecture School. The iced soot glasses here are delicious, especially after focusing on the large analog drawing. Most of the Architecture students were also poor, so this small gift also melted away the fatigue after focusing on the drawing *(at that time my friend Chanh's salary, as a Second Lieutenant in the Air Force, was about 26,000 VND a month. Even though it was very low it was enough to live because accommodation was free at the government house in a bachelor's dormitory. the government vehicles were provided but if you had to worry about housing costs, motorbikes, and gasoline, it probably wouldn't be enough to spend).*

Mr. Luyen studied in 4th year of Architecture and was assigned back to College by the Army Corps of Engineers because he had completed his lower degree in Architecture beforehand. He was paid a monthly salary and lived in An Dong dormitory, owned by the government, so every day he took a Vespa down to park at TQC and then walked through Architecture school. Seeing how I was living comfortably, he asked Uncle Thich to move back after being chased away by girls from TMG.

Since Mr. Luyen moved in, he let us into the Medical Room, which seemed more private, because only the school nurse used it during the day and the students rarely needed it. Here was Uncle Tu, a mysterious person who was only exposed after April '75 that he was embedded from the other side as a spy. He was a driver for an unknown rich man, so at the end of the day, he drove the car (Toyota) back to school and slept in the Medical Room. The new car had private curtains, so I guess its owner must have had money. However, why he gave it to the driver to keep it and not leave it at their house, no one knows and we didn't ask. Woke up early in the morning and found him gone. We lived like that, no one knew anything about the other's life, free to go and come back and Uncle Thich does not care. The principal, staff, or teachers of the school never disturbed us, because we abided by the silence agreement, leaving early in the morning when the school was not in session, and returning at night when the school was empty. Students, probably don't know if it weren't for a few times when we slept late or had to return in the middle of the day to exchange books to go to school or take a motorbike for an urgent matter. It was best to leave the motorbike there and walk on foot. I often go to the Post Office to send letters to Hue to my Mom or my brother Lap in the US and buy newly-issued stamps for collection, so it was not too far to walk there. In Saigon, there was a fee for someone to watch your motorbike, so it does not get stolen while you are inside the building.

The kindness of many people at that time must be acknowledged: they helped each other to the limit of their ability, sometimes even beyond their limited capacity, but still did it to help others, even though they were in the same situation, not better than the people they helped. Uncle Thich had his first son-in-law, a paratrooper, taken to protect the Presidential Palace nearby; he thought it was a happy thing, he drank every day, came home, and beat his wife and children, sometimes waving his handgun, the second son-in-law also in the military but gentle, knowing how to do business – every school break, his wife and her sister displayed sweets and cakes to sell to the students.

It seemed that everyone lived within their framework, with difficulties they endeavored to solve themselves, no one bothered anyone else and rarely went beyond the established framework for each situation. Life was limited, but freedom was not lost and that is important for everyone to be comfortable, because while the material life was limited, the spiritual life was full, to see that they were more fortunate than many others and could afford to be willing to help those less fortunate than themselves whenever possible.

With my family, school, and Scouting education as a *"luggage tag"* along for my life trip. I have found myself more confident to adapt to real life in any situation. I am not capable of helping anyone, so it is good to receive help from others.

When my Mom and my sister got to Saigon at the end of March, 1975 after losing Hue and Da Nang to the VC, we stayed temporarily at Mrs. Dung's house on Thieu Tri Street. After the bombing of the President's Palace on April 8 caused an uproar in Saigon, the Law school was still open but not many students were attending classes before the end of the year exam, even though cars and motorbikes were still running on the street. Everyone was staring at each other and only saw worrying faces; no one knew whether Saigon's fate would be like that of other provinces or even worse. The TV only showed scenes of people evacuating, running, or at the Presidential Palace, policies had changed every day to please the other side. Since the day the President's Palace was bombed, I didn't return to my temporary residence at TQC anymore, so I wasn't aware of the situation there, but after April, when the new government took over, they kicked Uncle Thich's family off campus. Now being *"equal"* to Communist policy, everyone was the same, so you shouldn't use your kindness to help those less fortunate. They lived a peaceful life and had no ties to the military or politics, so the new government only forced them and their families to move out of the school.

THE LAW SCHOOL AND DUY TAN STREET, ARE ALL SHADED WITH TREES

In the song *"Give it Back to my Love"* composed in 1972 by musician Pham Duy the scenery of romantic Saigon is described, as "*high shady trees on both sides of the street"* and "*the university life"* that I was fortunate enough to enjoy… I had both. Right behind the Law School and College of Architecture, just walking from the corner of University Offices, a short distance from Duy Tan (now Pham Ngoc Thach), to Phan Dinh Phung (now Nguyen Dinh Chieu), then turning left is the Law School. Only the second-year students could study there because the first-year group was too crowded: so many students had to attend classes at Thong Nhat Theater, located on Thong Nhat Street, where the National Lottery was held every Tuesday.

Studying Law at that time, you were not required to attend class daily, but when going to school, the professor's lectures were often included in the year-end exam. I lived closest to the school, so I had the duty to hold a good seat in the class for my friends. I would go to school early, sit at the first two tables, remove the books, and get a few seats for my friends who are far away. B. Lien, Nga, Nghia, Elizabeth... Perhaps because of that merit, they organized my first birthday, *(many Vietnamese families at that time did not have a tradition of celebrating birthdays)*. At the beginning of March 1975, in Saigon, the school was still teaching as usual. My friends gave me gifts and shared a picnic in Thu Duc, the first birthday party of my life and then I never saw them again [14].

---

14. *University of Saigon, College of Law before 1975, the first two years of study were*

If it hadn't been for the big change in April '75, I would have continued to study at the Law School and would have continued with a Master's Degree and graduated from law school around 1980. My time in Saigon was only two years, away from home just to continue my education and hoping to have a stable job after graduation, at least to be able to take care of my family. After two years of busy studying the atmosphere of war is getting closer and closer to the capital, so in terms of *love*, I had no chance to have any girlfriends in Saigon; my first love was left in Hue with L. already.

Such a life, continuing until the end of April; if I was stuck and did not know what the future would hold, only the poem "*I Dreamed*" could express my feelings at that time[15].

---

the same. In the third year, you had to choose one of three majors: Justice, Public Law or Economics. The Judiciary Committee offered Civil Law, Criminal Law, Procedural Law, Ethnic Minority Law... The Law Department had Social Studies, politics, International Public Law, Public Freedom... The Economics Department specialized in Economics, Commercial law, International Economics. All three departments studied the subjects of Civil Law, Economics and Public Law together. Thus, when students completed 4 years of a Bachelor's Degree, they could continue to study at Master's level 1 and 2 or higher, even for a PhD.

If you want to become a lawyer, after you have obtained a Bachelor's Degree, you must enroll in a solicitor group at a real lawyer's office (each lawyer can only accept two interns. If any Law's office wants to accept more than 2, they had to receive permission from an Associate Attorney, up to 4). After 3 years as an apprentice, you had to pass an exam. If you pass, you are considered qualified to practice law and are only allowed to take the exam three times within three years. If you do not pass, your hope to become a lawyer is lost.

15. *Composer/Musician Pham Duy, composed Thich Nhat Hanh's poem "Peace" in 1964 with the first "Song of the Heart" titled "I Dream":*
"I'm still alive, I'm still eating and I'm still breathing... But will I ever, ever, be able to say what I dream straight...".
This dream is the true aspiration for Peace in the country, knowing when it will really come, but dare not say it, because they would condemn that as "anti-war".

CHAPTER IV
SAIGON, THE LAST DAYS OF APRIL, 1975

SAD...EVACUATION – THE LAST DAYS OF MY MOTHERLAND

Multiple witnesses have documented in writing the last days of the Republic of Vietnam, important historical milestones, and as well the North Vietnamese Communists (NVA) breaking the agreements signed in 1973 *(Paris Peace Accords),* crossing the border of the two regions, advancing to occupy the South from the Ben Hai River (the border from the 1954 Geneva Agreement - 17th Parallel) into the city of Saigon, the capital of the South, on April 30, 1975. Here, I just relate the story of important days affecting my family and friends during this period, according to personal documents and a daily journal.

January 27, 1973: The Paris Agreement for Peace is signed in Vietnam [16]

On March 20, 1975: The Communists occupy An Loc.

Quang Tin is lost on March 24, including at Chu Lai airport.

Quang Ngai falls on March 25.

March 25, 1975: Hue is lost; Mom and my sister escape from Hue to Da Nang by helicopter, with Colonel Phuoc, 51st Tactical Wing Commander, then following along with Mr. Thanh and Major Hieu (233rd Squadron Deputy Commander) to Saigon by helicopter on March 26. Without any home to go to in Saigon, they were forced to temporarily move into Ms. Dung's house at 8/1 Thieu Tri Street. Mr. Thanh, a family friend, before saying

---

16. *The Paris Peace Accords, also known as the "Agreement on Ending the War and Restoring Peace in Vietnam", was signed on January 27, 1973 in Paris by four factions but after signing, the North intentionally and continued to violate the peace treaty. The political situation in the United States through the Watergate case forced President Nixon to resign, but Vice President Spiro Agnew had previously resigned because of tax fraud and President Gerald R. Ford take over was having to put all his efforts into the internal affairs of the United States, no one thought about sanctions for violators as President Nixon promised to the South at the signing.*

goodbye and going to his wife's hometown, told us the story of my Uncle Gio's family, traveling from Hue to Da Nang as refugees: the boat they were in was overcrowded and sank, about as far as Lang Co; everyone else in the family, including his wife and children, died. He was the only one to survive, clinging to a nylon bag. He went to my aunt's house in Da Nang and when Mr. Thanh came to leave the motorbike, he told him to suppress the news when entering the airport, because she was at the Da Nang military airport at that time. If she came to know about it, my uncle was afraid that she would change her mind about staying, so when he arrived in Saigon, before returning to My Tho, he told Ms. Dung. my uncle's biological daughter, with my Mom and my sister present. Everyone was shocked to hear about this, but at that time no one dared to follow Major Hieu back to Da Nang. Major Hieu said goodbye and proceeded to fly back to Da Nang alone, even though everyone advised him to report to TSN airbase [17].

Da Nang AFB on March 29, 1975:

Da Nang Airport, on the evening of March 28, helicopter squadrons, part of the flight to the South, via Monkey Mountain airport to avoid shelling. It should also be noted here, an important factor, according to the lunar calendar, this night (February 16, lunar year of the Cat) the 16th and full moon, thick fog creates virtual light, and helicopter pilots, if not used to flying at night, succumb to *"vertigo"* dizziness. Some crash along the way before reaching their destination, further south.

Some fly directly south, along the coast, before having to stop

---

17. *Major Hieu Nguyen, Deputy Squadron Commander of Sky Hawk 233, even though he had previously entered Saigon by a flight to take his family, my Mom and my sister for a ride in his chopper, he was still afraid that he would be reprimanded to leave the office early, he once was demoted, so he decided to fly back to Da Nang airport, he said, when he arrived, he was too tired because he had flown all day, so he went to the crew's office and fell asleep. He woke up on the morning of March 29, the VC shelled the airfield heavily since the evening of March 28, preventing the tactical evacuation of the RVNAF. He ran to the runway, which was empty because the pilots had left the night before. The helicopter he brought home yesterday was no longer there, he was lucky to find one intact, full of fuel and some crew members wanted to go to the South. Knowing that Chu Lai airport was no longer safe, he flew towards the mainland, was shot several times but no one was injured, the plane stopped at Phu Cat to refuel and then went to Nha Trang and TSN. "A trip to remember," he said. He stayed and was jailed for 13 years in "Re-education camp", escaped by boat and resided in the US.*

at Chu Lai airport to replenish fuel. There, they already fell into the hands of Communist soldiers, the rest were shot down from the ground; some ran out of fuel, had to land, and were arrested as prisoners of war. Some brought extra drums of JP-4, then had to land to refuel sufficiently to fly to Phu Cat Air Force Base or Nha Trang Airport. The helicopter of Lieutenant Colonel Le Ngoc Binh (currently living in Louisiana), the Commander of the 257th Salvation Squadron, was shot, crashed close to the coast, and flipped upside down, across Quang Ngai province. He was the only survivor, wading ashore. Brigadier General Diem Colonel Toan and their followers on the helicopter all died. When he was on shore, another helicopter following behind luckily landed to refill, from the barrels they had brought; he followed them into Nha Trang Airport and then Saigon. Captain An's plane, the 257th Salvation Squadron, ran out of fuel and had to land in a schoolyard. Lieutenant Hung, short of fuel also landed, but all were surrounded there by the VC. The story of Captain An's sacrifice will be told in another article with the witness, Lieutenant Dang: his copilot was a living witness at that time. (Vietnamese Nguoi Viet Daily, California published this tragic story, in a November 7, 2011 issue, entitled: "The Tragedy of War").

Quy Nhon lost on April 1.

Nha Trang on April 3.

Da Lat on April 4.

April 8, 1975: The President's Palace was damaged by two bombs because Air Force Lieutenant Trung Thanh Nguyen turned out to have been a VC operative. His F5 took off from Bien Hoa Airport; his mission was to drop bombs behind enemy lines, but he made excuses, claiming a radio malfunction; he left the crew behind and dropped his bombs on the Palace. It was about 8:30 a.m.; I was sitting in Professor Vu Van Mau's class, teaching Civil Law at Law School, on the corner of Duy Tan and Phan Dinh Phung streets. The whole class huddled under the table after the loud report of the explosion, because this place was very close to the Presidential Palace where the bombs hit. The teacher let the students disperse. I took the *cady* and went straight to Ms. Dung's house because Mom and my sister were staying there temporarily at that time. Cong Ly Street was crowded with people; at the intersections, there were still public police with red and green lights on. The city of Saigon was still orderly.

Phan Rang lost on April 16.

Phan Thiet lost on April 19.

South Vietnam President Nguyen Van Thieu resigned on April 21, 1975.

My brother Chau returned from Bien Hoa Military Airport. He had worked 2 days in a row, then 1 day off, when he returned to Saigon to spend time with me. This time he returned, observed the tense situation, and after talking with Mr. P. (at that time the attaché officer to the Chief of Staff of General Vien, Ms. Dung's husband), Mr. P. advised us to bring the family to TSN airport. He took Mom and my sister on his Honda motorcycle. I drove a motorbike, following to Phi Long Airport Gate, He showed appropriate documents to the sergeant at the gate. The airport security guard told the whole family that if we wanted to enter then we needed a guarantee paper from the Airport Security Office, because Captain Chau did not work at this airport but rather belonged to Bien Hoa Airport, so only he could enter but he could not bring his family in. Feeling stuck because if you do the paperwork through security, you may have to wait a week or more so I told the guy, can you lend me your Motorola walkie-talkie to call Officer Chanh in the Security Office, not that far from the gate? He asked: *Do you know him?* I said: *We were high school best friends, go out drinking all the time.* Fortunately, at that time, this person knew Second Lieutenant Chanh [18] and he was in his office, not out on the field.

18. *Chanh studied with me since the 6th grade at Quoc Hoc (National Academy), went to grade 12 in 1972, the government dropped one year younger to stay at school because the mandatory military draft, my class went to the military more than half, National Military Academy in Da Lat, officer training in Thu Duc, Chanh was supposed to apply for entrance exam at National Military Academy, but because he failed the first offered for the Baccalaureate II, the requested letter from the Department of Defense came back, he had to report to Thu Duc, in here Chanh passed as the valedictorian, he could choose any military branches, he dreamed of going to the air force, flying a jet fighter pilot. However, as an only boy in the family, Chanh lived with his grandparents from a young age, when they heard that he wanted to choose a career in fighter aviation, his grandparents cried and begged only his grandson to continue the line, so Chanh chose Air Force, working on land, not to fly, was sent to train at Cay Mai School, graduated as the valedictorian of the Air Force Security, so he chose to serve at TSN but did not choose Da Nang for being close to his family, the military rank system at that time was to choose a job or branch depending on how high you passed the exam, most of the people who passed the high scores chose the combat services such as Paratrooper or Marines,*

In less than five minutes, when I saw Chanh driving a black C-90 Motorcycle running out, I asked to take my Mom, sister, and myself inside the airport. Captain Chau was authorized to go in and out whenever he wanted, but he couldn't bring his family, including me. I saw Chanh whispering something to the sergeant, and he opened the gate for us to come in, showing that the power of the security officer (now promoted to Second Lieutenant but not yet *"celebrating"*) is higher in security than the captain of the flying branch while on the ground. The problem is that Mr. Chau did not serve at this Airport; now where to go because he did not have a dorm there, I said to Chanh, can I visit your dorm? This is a single officer's dormitory – two people in one room, Chanh's room upstairs, right next to the stairs and balcony. My family stayed downstairs temporarily with Major Hieu's family at that time; his whole family had gone to TSN. Chanh lived with Cuong before I met him. Chanh gave the room to me while Chanh and Cuong stayed in their office. The next day, I saw many families gathered downstairs, they began to bring their families in, mostly crew members of C-130s of two transport squadrons 435 and 437 to Con Son/Phu Quoc Islands, the purpose being to avoid the shelling, because the airfield would be a prime target.

With my Mom's Sony radio, I started listening to BBC radio: the Vietnamese-language program on 31m shortwave, and only heard bad news, from the central region that fell, Quang Tri went to Phan Rang, then rumors that President Thieu would only go to Ninh Thuan, his hometown; other rumors said there was an agreement to divide the land with the other side. Curious about BBC radio (7:30 pm every night) I found the post office shortwave station, an open channel where people with relatives abroad talk to each other about the price of gold, transferring money and comfortably evacuating abroad by civilian plane, because at that time there was no private telephone system.

Having nothing to do, I invited Chanh to go out for a drink; in the evening Chanh rode a black motorbike to the dormitory to pick me up and the two of us went off down the street. I only remember visiting a restaurant; we ordered fried frog leg with butter, and a few cans of beer, sitting and talking about his girlfriend, I asked Chanh why didn't he bring her to the airport, as he had the

---

but with his family background, I understand why Chanh must have that choice.

opportunity to evacuate. Chanh told me "*I will stay here and die with my M-16*", but then said, *"How could we lose Saigon?"*. I told him I thought the same, but only a month had passed and we lost territory from Quang Tri to Phan Rang. I also hoped there would be a ceasefire or peace talks, but with this situation and the Americans evacuating their planes from Saigon, it is impossible unless the NVA voluntarily stopped, only accepting Phan Rang, because the ARVN troops withdrew to the South. We would have run out of domestic routes, like in 1954. I advised Chanh to think again, then suggested: *"You take me to evacuate with the American C-141 plane, if possible, bring your friend in and continue the next night to fly out."* Hearing the suggestion made sense; on the way back to the airport, Chanh told me *"...to prepare to depart tomorrow"*.

April 23, 1975: Near dark, Chanh stopped at the dormitory, just giving me enough time to say goodbye to my Mom, brother, and sister, I took with me some plastic-wrapped diplomas stuffed against my stomach. Chanh told me to put on Cuong's uniform to make it easier to go out and give me the passcode. It was dark, sitting in the back, so the guards also thought I was a security officer like Chanh. On the way to the airstrip, Chanh told me to wait behind an abandoned bunker, there was a boy who was younger than me, shivering in fear, and he was Quang's brother, working in the same office as Chanh and Cuong. Waiting at the end of the runway, I listened to each US Air Force C-141 aircraft take off, the announcement in English of the American staff behind the plane calling out the passengers' names in a manifest to board the C-141 aircraft to evacuate under the Defense Attaché Office (D.A.O.) That clued me into the fact I was not to evacuate on an American aircraft. So that night, suddenly the US Marines took over guarding the airport security and boarding their aircraft, not allowing anyone else to board unless their name was in the *manifest* of the US. Quang drove his brother, Chanh drove me back to Chanh's barracks before dawn to avoid being exposed.

April 25, 1975: Chanh returned to the dormitory and said that the next night, the US would again turn over Airport Security to the Vietnamese[19], but neither Chanh nor I mentioned anything

19. *I think the US DAO staff took back the consideration screening of the people boarding their evacuation plane instead of the South Vietnamese Airport Security as in the previous days because when the evacuees boarded the plane, the remaining*

about leaving, because if it had been revealed, not only mine but also his career would have been destroyed, because Quang took his brother back to the city, no longer intending to evacuate with the DAO. Chanh also revealed to me that the US had given us a few gas bombs (CBU-55 Cluster Bomb Units) that had been installed by the Air Force on an AC-130 [20], ready to drop when the Communists reached Long Thanh, at least to slow down their progress, but later I learned that those were bombs that could not detonate because the Americans had not given us the detonators. These bombs each weighed 750 lbs., equivalent to 340 kg.

Airborne Captain Pharmacist Trinh Mau Nguyen, who was in the Capital Area, stopped by to visit my brother Chau, visit Mr. Vinh Ho, a helicopter pilot flying for General Ky, and evaluate the situation. Saigon was still orderly, still not thinking about evacuating or having to land a helicopter on the roof of his house on Tu Do Street to pick up the evacuated family as my brother planned with him.

My brother Chau privately told me that in case we needed to evacuate by helicopter (he knew that I was very familiar with helicopters, even though I was a civilian), it would carry only enough fuel to get from the coast of Vung Tau for about 30 minutes. If you are heading to sea, if you don't see any ship to land

---

Vietnamese money was left in their pocket, knowing they wouldn't need it anymore, they gave it all to the South Vietnamese Security staff behind the plane. Seeing it, the Americans thought it was the Vietnamese employees who took as the bribe. Later that day, knowing this misunderstanding, they gave the South Vietnamese Air Force Security back to allow people boarding the plane to evacuate. It's also because I was mean to fly on an evacuation plane flown by the South Vietnamese Air Force and if I went that day, I don't know what the evacuation status of my brother and my family would be.

20. *USAF's C-130 is dubbed Hercules (Greek God of Health), built by Lockheed, has 4 Allison T56-A-7 propeller engines mounted on two wings as transport aircraft. The US Air Force provided aid to Vietnam and the pilots were sent to train in the United States, returning home to serve at the 53rd Tactical Wing, 5th Air Division, RVNAF based at Tan Son Nhut Airport had two C-130 435th and 437th Transport Squadrons. Four propellers are mounted on both sides of the low wing, so when the four propellers rotate, it is very dangerous. These aircraft were used by the RVNAF as the last day of evacuation from TSNAFB to U-TAPAO AFB, Thailand, including military personnel and their families. The Americans knew and calculated in the past how to withdraw some of the military aid to the Republic of Vietnam from falling into enemy hands. Some C-130s that arrived at U-Tapao on April 29 had tail numbers: HCC, HCL, GZA, GZM ... The aircraft is classified by the United States as* ***STOL*** *(**S**hort **T**ake-**O**ff and **L**anding), only needing the short runway. That why it was be able to take off by taxiway on the last day.*

on but fly for more than 15 minutes, even if you return to shore, there will not be enough fuel, and he said in case a small boat does not have enough space for a helicopter to land on, he will put one landing gear and touch down for everyone to get off, then he will be the last to fly out to do *"ditching"*. As a volunteer of the 257th Helicopter Squadron, he brought a helicopter to the Vietnam Naval ship in 1974, to protect the Paracel-Spratly Islands when China invaded; so he had experience in landing at sea because he had previously landed on a moving ship that was very difficult. Rather than landing at a fixed place like an airport, it depends on whether the weather is good or bad, whether the sea is rough or not because the target is moving.

On the afternoon of April 28, 1975:

Around 5:20 pm on April 28, 1975, while the handover ceremony between President Tran Van Huong and General Duong Van Minh was taking place in the Presidential Palace, outside sky it suddenly dark and started to rain. The overcast sky seemed to herald a great sad event for the country.

6:20 pm: Five A-37s Dragonfly aircraft, led by Trung Thanh Nguyen, a former RVNAF F-5 officer taking off from Phan Rang, dropped six Mk81-250 lb. bombs on TSN airport, damaging several aircraft. The airport was still usable but closed, airport security and military police had ordered no one in and out, except for soldiers who were outside: they had to go to their base to report, 100% "NO EXIT" orders. These A-37s landed in Phan Rang. *(NTT alone, after bombing the President's Palace on April 8, had to land his F-5 at the VC airport temporarily in Phuoc Long, because Phan Rang AFB had not yet fallen to the Communists).*

April 29, 1975 – Tan Son Nhut (TSN) Airport

From 4 a.m. to about 6 a.m. on the 29th, TSN airport was heavily shelled; the women soldier's barracks were on fire, and the main airstrip was damaged by shelling, all but the Davis military base [21]. Peace talks were underway among the four sides, because

21. *The four-sided meeting located at one side of military base is Camp Davis, named after Thomas Davis, killed by the communists in 1961, southwest of TSN airbase, under the control of the USAF, the meeting place after the Paris Agreement. 1973 to implement the treaty signed by 4 factions: the Republic of Vietnam (South), the Democratic Republic of Vietnam (North), the Front for the Liberation of South Vietnam*

the communists knew there were high-ranking North Vietnamese officers (General Tra Van Tran) present, so their artillery avoided this place.

Around 6 a.m., I saw Major Thanh Nguyen, the 233rd Squadron Commander, walking from Phi Long gate to our barracks to investigate the situation and inform my Mom that his wife had just given birth to a daughter the day before. He knew my family was staying there temporarily because Major Hieu, his Deputy Squadron Commander, and his family were also there.

Around 7:30 am, standing in the yard, in front of the barracks, everyone saw an AC-119K continuously firing bullets down at the airport perimeter; the plane was flying at a really slow speed, every time the mini-gun howled. The pilot knew the risk of flying at such a slow speed and low level, but that was the only way to be accurate and avoid hitting people's houses around the Airport. Then suddenly a white smoke *(SA-7- Surface to Air Missile)* rose from the ground and touched the plane, cutting it into two pieces. The tail fell first, the fuselage spinning around. I heard people around me shouting: *Jump out, jump out*... but half of the plane fell onto the airport perimeter without a parachute unfurling. Everyone around fell silent. It was the last armed aircraft to be sacrificed for the military service at TSN by Lieutenant Thanh Van Trang, from the 821 *Tinh Long* "Quiet Dragon Squadron" stationed at TSN airport. Also, thanks to the firepower of this aircraft before it was shot down, perhaps slowing the advance of the Communists into the Airport.

Seeing that the situation was not good, hearing that the family of his deputy, Major Hieu, decided not to go anywhere, Major Thanh asked my brother Chau to drive him to Phi Long Airport gate to go home, to get out of the airport. My brother drove his Honda motorcycle, I sat in the middle, and Mr. Thanh sat in the back. I just overheard Mom say: *"Find any way to escape"* Even though she didn't know where to go, she was person who had experience in war with the Viet Minh, so she told me before: *"If you can't find the way to get out, hide somewhere, don't go home, it will be easy to reveal your identity and get revenge"*.

(NLF) and the United States. The North violated the Paris agreement of 1973, occupied the South, which they blamed on the NLF, which everyone knew, was killed after clearing the South in 1975 because it was a puppet agency of the North, was born to cover the eyes of people who do not understand the Vietnam war.

8:30 am: Go directly to Phi Long gate, with a distance of about 100 meters, a Vietnamese Military Policeman (MP) holding an M-16, stopped the motorcycle and asked my brother: *"Captain, where are you going?* He responded: *"I have to take Major Thanh to the gate"*, he shouted: *"Captain, you can't get out the gate. We are not allowing anyone to leave; please get back!"*, I pointed to the front of the Security Office Building, not that far, and told him we needed to go and see Second Lieutenant Chanh. No answer, he raised his gun to the sky, and the MP (QC) shot a volley of bullets warning my brother not to go in the direction of the gate. Not convinced, my brother turned the Honda around. This soldier's action saved Major Thanh from more than ten years in a *"re-education camp"* prison. His Squadron Deputy Commander, Major Hieu Trung Nguyen got 13 years in prison.

We went straight to the helicopter section and saw that there was no one in charge, everything was in disarray, and the airport was a scene of destruction after the shelling at night, a Chinook CH-47 had quite a lot of people around it but there was not enough fuel left. When crossing the DAO (Defense Attaché Office) airstrip, the American Air America helicopters were parked full and orderly because it seemed that the shelling did not fall on this area the night before due to the *pre-agreed staging* between the US and the Communists, the 4-party military group was still here, an American Air Force Lieutenant Colonel came out in his full uniform and greeted us when my brother asked: *"May we have your Huey?"* (My English at that time only remembered him saying *Help yourself!*), but after sitting up, and turning on, the gas was full and the battery was still good (when starting the helicopter, you have to use the battery before the engine starts up), Mr. Chau and Thanh suddenly changed their minds because they took this "CIA" plane, either side could have shot it down, the US side might think we stole it, the VC side thought it was the CIA's Air America, I sat in the back and threw the headset down to the seat, jumped out the chair when the two brothers turned off the engine, signaling not to go this way.

Getting out of the new blue and white helicopter full of gasoline, we drove the Honda motorcycles through the Chinook CH-47 area, the Chinook with two pilots and many people sitting inside and behind, went inside, heard the pilot say: Not enough fuel to fly and if we get out with the chinook, no one thought that at that time, this heavy helicopter could land on the ship, if you fly to the west, there was not enough gas to get to Thailand, Cambodia already fallen, so my brother continued to drive through the airstrip of the C-130s of the 435th Transport Squadron. Ruined by shelling in the night, vehicles were scattered because of those who had left, then suddenly a C-130 emerged from a hangar, the rear ramp slowly lowered, and viewed from the rear, I saw it was empty inside. About 200 yards away, the three of us dropped the motorcycles still running on the ground, and ran together to the end of the airplane, the airplane stopped, and I saw the two pilots waving their hands. Turning my head and looking back, I saw about 200 military men and civilians from the back of the hangar running to the back of the airplane, the rear port of the C-130 didn't come down to the ground but was about chest height; I was trying to climb up and suddenly someone behind pushed me up and so that the latter lifted the first person into the fuselage, the engine noise drowned out all other noises, later I found out that the C-130 had to start the engine number 3 first (standing from the rear looking forward, in order from left 1, 2, 3, 4) because this motor gives power A/C and D/C, then 4 then 2 and 1. Artillery shells were still scattered on the airstrip, because of the panicked situation, the pilot started his engines without following the orders in manuals 3, 4, 2, and 1.

The C-130 closed the tailgate and side door after everyone had boarded, over two hundred I guess, everyone was sitting on the floor because this was a military cargo airplane. Slowly using the force of the propeller to go back and forth and then suddenly stop, the pilot on the speaker announced and asked who had let the Jeep block the plane's way back because the propeller might collide. He turned the two engines on the left to increase the rotation speed thinking he could push the car back, but it still stood there, probably someone had put the handbrakes before leaving there. The front left side door opened, and a person wearing a flight suit jumped down; he moved the car; when he grabbed the door to jump back up he fell and a propeller hit him. He fell dead right on the taxiway, the side door could not be closed any longer, (checking later: he was Lieutenant Colonel Chau, nicknamed *Chau flickering* because he blinked his eyes when he talked) and when we landed at U-Tapao, I saw bloodstains on the left landing gear.

Listening to the pilot say on the speaker, everyone piled

forward to make the tail light for take-off, the main runway was damaged, so it would take off from the taxiway… the plane pulled forward, picking up speed, surging into the air for a short distance at an angle and speed not allowed in the manual or flight safety – but kept on climbing and then flew around to say goodbye to Saigon, the door on the left side couldn't close completely, so the oxygen system couldn't be turned on. That is why it only flew below 10,000 feet, flying along the Cambodian coast (see attached map) lost to the VC a month before, fortunately, their air defense did not mind at that time; otherwise, I would no longer be telling my stories here… maybe the VC was afraid anti-aircraft fire would hit an American plane by mistake, because the two sides had come to a prior agreement.

Directed to Thailand, but could not use the plane's radio to communicate with U-Tapao Airport. The captain of the C-130 plane (later I learned that it was Captain Minh Duc Nguyen nicknamed *Crazy Minh*) set off an emergency signal and flew above the runway dipping its wings, then turned around and landed, out to the taxiway, stopped. The back door opened to the ground this time, the engines were shut down, and everyone scrambled to get out; many US airmen standing around, and they collected all the weapons of evacuees. Walking into a nearby hangar, I looked back and saw two bucket trucks with two American soldiers painting over all the signs of the Air Force and the South Vietnamese flag on the back of the plane with new paint. They were doing it very quickly. The hangar accommodated more than a few hundred people, some standing or sitting, some running out to find acquaintances or relatives when they observed new airplanes landing. I went around but couldn't find Chanh; I only saw Quang, asked and he didn't know where Chanh was. About half an hour later, looking at the airstrip, an ACK-47 just arrived. As the group streamed in, I saw Chanh and Cuong; I ran out to welcome them, Cuong looked at me and told me to remember to return my uniform. (When I left TSN, I was wearing Cuong's Second Lieutenant uniform). Chanh said: *"How did you get here before me?"* Looking at him, I replied, *"Because you were still defending our land with your M-16, it's okay to be late".*

The military plane flown by South Vietnamese pilots that brought me and a large number of soldiers and their families to freedom was probably the last big cargo plane to leave TSN Airport because I saw no more C-130s landing at U-Tapao after that.

The next day, my brother ran into his friend in the helicopter squadron, Major Du Van Huynh (d) (brother-in-law of Airborne General Luong Quang Le), and asked how he got there. He told him that when he was looking for a helicopter late in TSN Airport, the good planes were already gone; the remaining helicopters were either damaged or out of gas. He luckily found an acceptable one, only missing the battery and gasoline; he went to find a good battery to replace it[22], and for gasoline, he took the metal helmet, removed the fuel tank of the A-37, and filled the helicopter's fuel tank. The A-37 and helicopters use the same JP-4 [23] fuel. He also did not know whether it would be closer to go to the sea on the East side, because as my brother had planned, if he went to the sea without a ship to land on, he would not have enough fuel to return to shore, whereas if he went west, he could land on the shore, if he ran out of gas. It took a long time for this but it was done. he also brought along two spare barrels, because he knew he did not have enough to get to the Thai border. He picked up his wife's family and children and flew to Thailand, but had to fill up with more fuel along the Cambodian coast. Fortunately, the Khmer Rouge did not appear, and he also had his brother (the paratrooper) sit in the back with a mini-gun ready if it was necessary to use it. He is the pilot who brought the only helicopter to Thailand.

THE LAST EVACUATION SIGNALS FOR AMERICANS

It should also be noted about the South Vietnam broadcast system that all daily news was bad, because of the tense situation after refugees near the DMZ (*DeMilitarized Zones*) poured in

22. *To start the Huey UH-1 helicopter, you must first use a 24VDC battery, open the fuel pump, and then turn the propeller (counterclockwise), the battery must and still have at least 12V, the engine may started.*

23. *Jet Propellan 4 (abbreviated JP-4) is a 50/50 mixture of kerosene and gasoline so it smells like kerosene, used for jet aircraft. Vietnamese Air Force soldiers, because they are poor, do not have money for fuel, can use this type to use Honda motorbikes, but the muffler is louder than using 100% 90 octane gasoline. The smoke has a foul smell of oil/ kerosene. A UH-1 filled with 4000lbs of gasoline theoretically flies about 450km at 110 knots (127mph), 1 knot = 1.15mph.*

since the central provinces from the 17th parallel had fallen into the hands of the Communists. Local Southern radio stations were all broadcasting on the inexpensive AM (Amplitude Modulation) system; only American radio stations used FM (Frequency Modulation) because music programs can be broadcast in "stereo". Particularly, Vietnamese-speaking program stations, such as BBC (British Broadcasting Corporation) only broadcast 30 minutes in the morning and 60 minutes in the evening, VOA (Voice of America) had more Vietnamese programs, including the Voice of Freedom *Guom Thieng Ai Quoc* (targeted at Northern listeners) transmitting by Shortwave (SW) on 13, 16, 19, 25, 31, 41 and 49m bandwidths, as well as the main Saigon radio station.

The South did not prohibit its citizens from listening to broadcasts like they did in the North. In addition to the public listening, soldiers, either local or at the front, could also hear broadcasts if they had a radio. My Mom was a fan of these radio programs; she had a Sony radio that used batteries and could pick up programs on all bands, with an antenna that extended up to a meter long when she needed to tune into distant stations. When to broadcasting time arrived, especially in the evening of the BBC, she would turn on the 7:30 Vietnamese program a few minutes beforehand, usually on the 31m wavelength until the music signaled the program starting. The neighbors also listened in at the same time and with the quiet outside (because at that time few people were out on the street), sometimes the whole neighborhood was tuned in. Listening to the radio was the only one-way communication medium at that time, until around 1966 when black-and-white TV stations had been set up by the US military; then local Vietnamese stations started broadcasting: people preferred TV because they could see -pictures instead of listening only.

At this time, listening to the news on the radio every day, the *more* you hear, *more* nervous you get. Vietnamese programs for Vietnamese people hear the news that they can't keep up with the military withdrawals outside of tactics more than accurate news. If you understand and listen to American radio, only a few mentioned any means of evacuation. Foreign news agencies, although not censored by the South Vietnamese government, but left-leaning and focusing on anti-war demonstrations in the United States, knew the Vietnam war would end one day, not decided on the battlefield but at the conference table.

In the last days, the Americans prepared for an evacuation program out of Saigon, but few people knew about it. The program was originally called *"Talon Vise"*, then because it was leaked, it was changed to *"Operation Frequent Wind"*. Few people paid attention, because listening to American radio on FM you had to know and understand English. I often listened because of popular music at that time and also to practice English, so I sometimes tuned in to FM radio stations. We did not know that in preparation for the evacuation, the American Embassy in Saigon had distributed a 15-page booklet called **SAFE**[24], short for *"Standard Instruction and Advice to Civilians in an Emergency."* The booklet included a map of Saigon pinpointing *"assembly areas where a helicopter will pick you up."*. There was an insert page that read: *"Note evacuation signal. Do not disclose to other personnel."* When the evacuation is ordered, the code will be read out on Armed Forces Radio. The code is: ***The temperature in Saigon is 105 degrees and rising***. This will be followed by the playing of ***"I'm Dreaming of a White Christmas."*** Frank Snepp later recalled the arrival of helicopters at the Embassy, while the song was playing over the radio as a *"bizarre Kafkaesque time"*. Japanese journalists, concerned that they would not recognize the tune, had to get someone to sing it to them. Few foreigners, especially Vietnamese, imagined that being summer, they would play Christmas songs repeatedly over their radio station.

Once the evacuation signal was given, buses began to pick up passengers and head to the DAO Compound. The system worked so efficiently, that the buses were able to make three return journeys rather than the expected one. The biggest problem occurred when the ARVN unit guarding the main gate at Tan Son Nhut Air Base refused to allow the last convoy of buses into the DAO Compound (Defense Attaché Office) inside the airport at about 17:45. As this was happening, a firefight broke out between two ARVN units, and caught the rearmost buses in the crossfire, disabling two of the vehicles. Eventually, the ARVN commander controlling the gates agreed to permit the remaining buses to enter the compound. General Carey's threat to use the AH-1J SeaCobra helicopter gunships flying overhead may have played a role in the ARVN commander's decision.

---

24. *President Gerald R. Ford Library Museum Archive:* https://www.fordlibrarymuseum.gov/library/document/0373/1555975.pdf

This famous photo taken by Dutch photographer/journalist Hubert van Es on April 29, 1975.

22 Gia Long Street, Saigon.

Air America Helicopter picked up Vietnamese Staff on top of the building at 22 Gia Long Street on April 29, 1975. This is the Pittman Apartment Building, not a "CIA building" as many have termed it. Photo Courtesy of Getty/AFP Forum.

Photo courtesy of Paul Blizard (left) and others (right) taken in 2018, 2019, then the same building at 22 Gia Long Street, 44 years later.

PREPARING THE LAST FLIGHTS OUT FROM SAIGON FOR THE AMERICANS

Documents from the Department of Defense and Defense Attaché Office: "THE LAST FLIGHT FROM SAIGON" written *by Thomas G. Tobin, Lt Colonel, USAF Arthur E. Laehr, Lt Colonel, USAF John F. Hilgenberg, Lt Colonel, USAF* and edited by Lt. Colonel David R. Mets and Lt. Colonel A.J.C Lavalle, were printed in 1978 and described in detail the planning and execution of "Talon Vise" and "Operation Frequent Wind" for American and Vietnamese evacuation during the last days of Saigon.

https://media.defense.gov/2010/Sep/28/2001330140/-1/-1/0/last_flight_from_saigon2.pdf

(Photo and caption courtesy of Little Rock Air Force Base, Arkansas)

https://www.littlerock.af.mil/News/Photos/igphoto/2001741050/

On April 29, 1975, Herc C-130A 56-0518, which sits on display at the base's front gate, flew the last mission out of Vietnam during the fall of Saigon. With more than 100 aircraft destroyed on the flight line at Tan Son Nhut Air Base, it was the last flyable C-130. In a panicked state, hundreds of people rushed to get aboard, as the aircraft represented a final ticket to freedom. The number of individuals aboard the plane and standing on the rear ramp required the pilot to taxi forward before hitting the brakes; this allowed the loadmaster to successfully close the doors. In all, 452 people were on board, including 32 in the cockpit. It was estimated the aircraft was overloaded by at least 10,000 pounds. Consequently, the Herk used every bit of the runway and overran it before it was able to get airborne. After getting lost, the pilots (Major Khiem and Captain Minh Nguyen) eventually landed the C-130A at U-Tapao, Thailand. The aircraft has been on display at Little Rock Air Force Base's front gate since June 1989 [25].

U-TAPAO: The Royal Thai Navy Air Force (RTNAF) airport, southeast of Bangkok, was approved for use by the US Air Force as a departure point for KC-135A aircraft supporting aerial refueling for B-52 flying fortresses and other fighters during the

25. *The US Air Force chose this aircraft for display, perhaps because it was the last C-130A to leave Vietnam. When the Republic of Vietnam Air Force received C-130A, the engine originally had 3 propellers. But when it was brought back to the US, it was still in good condition and used by the US Air Force for a while, they replaced it with a new type of 4 propellers, because 4 propellers are more difficult to damage than 3 propellers. The 3-blade motor is electrically controlled, so it is easy to damage, the 4-blade engine later uses a hydro-regulating system (Hydraulic) to adjust the angle of the 4 propellers, so it is more difficult to damage than the electrical system.*

Vietnam War.

<u>*The caption attached image was taken on the web, photographer unknown:*</u> *Some C-130s of the South Vietnamese Air Force, one GZA tail number has been removed with the South Vietnam flag when it arrived at U-TAPAO airport because this was Thai territory, a delicate political issue between Thailand and the US, when in fact the government of the Republic of Vietnam did not end that day. The other one GZM still has the flag of the Republic of Vietnam. The Thai government demanded the return of all South Vietnamese Air Force planes that landed here so that they could be returned to the "new government". The US Air Force and the US government cleverly refused by removing the RVNAF markings on the aircraft. All refugees were gathered in this hangar before the US Air Force C-141 brought them to Guam for settlement processing, starting the next day.*

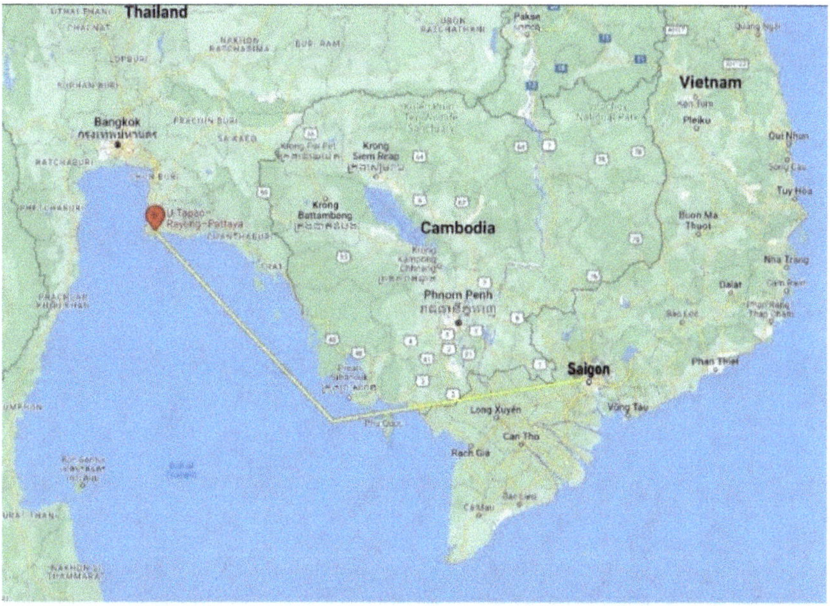

Google Map: *Saigon and U-Tapao Airport, Thailand.*

Military abbreviations in English:

RVNAF or VNAF: *Republic of Vietnam Air Force or South Vietnam Air Force*

USAF: *United States Air Force*

D.A.O.: *Defense Attaché Office – Office of the Department of Defense and the US Department of State for civilian affairs.*

ARVN: *Army of the Republic of Vietnam.*

D.M.Z.: *Demilitarized Zones, 17th parallel.*

VC: *Viet Cong.*

NVA: *North Vietnamese Army.*

TSN AFB: *Tan Son Nhut Air Force Base.*

This is a map of South Vietnam (Republic of Vietnam) from the 17th parallel (DMZ), with the military airfields of the Republic of Vietnam Air Force (RVNAF) mentioned in this book. (Central Intelligent Agency Map number 500874-5-72) Base Map Courtesy of the CIA and The United States of America Vietnam War Commemoration.

LOSING THE MOTHERLAND – STARTING A NEW LIFE AS A REFUGEE

April 29, 1975

11:00 am U-Tapao Airport (US Airbase in Thailand).

Theoretically, TSN and Binh Thuy/Can Tho airports were not yet in the hands of the VC, but the number of airworthy F-5, and A-37 jets or transports had already taken off, and no one else thought about flying to Thailand. Waiting from morning until evening, there was only one A-37 Dragonfly with a plainclothes pilot from Binh Thuy and Can Tho airfields; then there were no more RVNAF military planes landing at U-Tapao. Although the US Air Force (U.S.A.F.) knew that there would be RVNAF aircraft coming in, they did not prepare for the reluctant refugees, so they waited until the afternoon, when they queued up, thinking of delivering food. When I saw them bring out cigarettes to distribute, I saw all kinds of brands, from Salem to Winston, Camel, Pall Mall, Marlboro, Lucky Strike… beautifully displayed for non-smokers – like me! When Chanh and I were going back into the hangar, Mr. Thanh and Mr. Chau both said, *"If you don't smoke, just line up to get cigarettes for me"*. They gave out two *"cartons"* for each person (20 packs). In a dark mood, Chanh and I opened them up, and started smoking, both of us coughing, our mouths were bitter – so that was the first and last cigarette for us both: we never touched a second cigarette in our lives. (He saved the wrapping paper, as the back is a white paper where he could compose a short temporary diary). Later in the afternoon, they put fresh milk in a small box and cereal and distribute to us, so thirsty and hungry that no one noticed that when these two things got mixed on an empty stomach, none of us could help but stand in line at the restrooms because the lactase gave us diarrhea.

In the afternoon, there was a Thai person selling sandwiches. I had 10 dollars in my pocket from my brother who was studying abroad and sent to me; I bought 2 to share with a few people. Now that I think back to that time, I realize how the Thais in the airport sold food at exorbitant prices to the refugees in dollars, while a McDonald's burger costs less than 79 cents.

In the evening, the USAF sent a truck to bring in fried rice and water, and after eating, some people went to sleep right on the floor because they were too tired. Some sat in the hangar, talking. Saigon hadn't yet fallen; it was ***the longest*** night of waiting in my life.

April 30, 1975, 10:00 am: Today, Wednesday, President Duong Van Minh surrendered on Saigon radio at **10:24 am**. I heard the news at U-Tapao over small 31m short-wave radio carried by a soldier. Some people cried out loud; although people looked at each other, no one said anything. You could see blank faces and sad eyes – but the same thought that it was over. I was lucky to have escaped, but what about the rest, a life-changing era begins here for both those who got out and those who were trapped. None of us had any idea of what the future holds.

Since there were 13 Vietnamese soldiers in the group who had decided they wanted to go back home, the US Air Force in the U-Tapao base let us board two C-141s to fly to Guam right away. Later, I heard that they injected sleeping pills or tied up a few people in the back of the cargo airplane *(intelligence news of Chanh)*.

ARRIVAL ON GUAM

I don't know how long it took to fly, because I was too tired, but when I arrived in Guam it was the morning of May 1. This was the Andersen Air Force Base military airport, a post-war remnant of the Japanese occupation. They drove us to Orote Point by military buses, which already had pre-made tents on red soil that my brother later said the Army Corps of Engineers had been working on since early January 1975 to prepare and welcome refugees. They knew what was what for a long time; only I naïvely was unaware. They call this place *"Tent City"*. This was the first American island I had set foot on; later, I learned that there is another on Wake Island nearby also welcoming refugees, not belonging to any of the 50 states but under the control of the US military.

In May, the weather in Guam is hotter than in Saigon, the ground is brownish and dusty, they set up outdoor baths with water pipes connected to water trailers, one hot water pipe, one cold pipe, a men's bathroom, separate from women, but one room under a canvas tent could bathe dozens of people with a shower overhead. Temporary toilets were also set up in wooden stilt houses, squatting, and food included a few fruit crates with large cans. The box had peaches, pears, or apples (a fruit cocktail), a concoction that most Vietnamese were not familiar with. When they brought the refugees here, they changed it back to a program called *"Operation New Life"* because the evacuation program in Saigon to the Aircraft Carrier, called *"Operation Frequent Wind"* had ended [26].

The Americans set up temporary offices in the trailer to do paperwork. the first thing was to fill in our background. Then, they gave each person a social security number and an I-94 card. Those who had no papers would write down what they remembered. Any Vietnamese who passed through Guam at that time was given 586 as the first 3 numbers – the social security number of Guam.

The next day, while waiting in line to eat, I met Bich Lien, who had been in the same Law School class, because BL's mother worked in an American Bank in Saigon, and asked if anyone she knew in the class like Nga or Nghia got out like us. She shook her head.

BEAT PEOPLE WHO RUN AWAY, DON'T BEAT PEOPLE WHO RUN BACK TO YOU

Since there were in fact a number of displaced people demanding to return, the Americans brought together those who did not want to go to the mainland to settle. Mr. Thanh also wanted to return, but my brothers and I advised him not to do so: he would face at least 13 years in prison. 1,652 of these citizens chose to return, and found passage on the Viet Nam Thuong Tin cargo ship, departing from Guam in October 1975. Everyone was aware of the consequences of such a return so many had to find a way to escape a second time after being released from prison, having innocently believed the new government would forgive them [27].

26. *The Americans called the last evacuation of South Vietnamese out of Vietnam "Operation Frequent Wind", which took place only in the last few days of April, in the Vietnamese sense of "Cold wind coming from the North". Are these words both literal and figurative? The persons who named it have a very profound name.*

27. *Some people at the time of evacuation, military or civilian, could not bring their*

SETTLING IN THE UNITED STATES - LIFE IN A REFUGEE CAMP

American Staff began to organize us; family lines were separate from solitary refugees. Mr. Thanh and Chau: all were in the same family, so we only stayed here for 7 days, and then we were taken to Andersen Airport again, but had no idea where they intended to take us.

When we deplaned at the new airport, they took us on an air-conditioned military bus passing through orange groves full of fruit and the aroma of citrus flowers; the beach was on one side, and then the car drove up into the mountains, only to find out that it was Marine Corps Camp Pendleton in Southern California, north of San Diego and south of Los Angeles. This place is like a valley, surrounded by mountains. At the beginning of May, when we got off the bus, everyone was cold. The camp they took us to was number 5. The large tents were made of military fabric (Quonset huts), and inside were 2 rows of military folding cots with felt blankets. They gave us Military trillion battle coats filled with goose feathers – very warm to wear.

Camp Pendleton, California May 1975: Every day the Marines here cooked us food; they let us eat freely, the galley hall was open 24 hours, so we could eat whenever we wanted, then because many people would bring food into the tent, in the middle of the forest, all kinds of animals found their way in because of the smell of food. For this reason, they limited us to three meals a day, and announced a call for people who know how to cook to volunteer to cook Vietnamese dishes, because the dish they

---

families or wives and children at the last minute, or were operating in the area for the VC ordered to follow the refugees wherever they go, or women and children, to Guam and the mainland US demanded to return, but because the US government and the Vietnamese Communists did not have diplomatic relations, they could not be allowed to return because the US government was afraid of responsibility because the new government in Vietnam did not accept them. Those wishing to return were gathered at Camp Asan, Guam, and after repairs costing millions of dollars, were provided with a ship to return to VN on October 15, 1975. Everyone on board was isolated. and go to jail. Volunteer Navy Captain Lieutenant Colonel Tran Dinh Tru was sentenced to 13 years in prison and came to the US to reunite with his family in 1991 under the HO category. For details on this trip and how the Communist government treated the returnees as well as the US government's generous reception of refugees for the second time, please read the memoir "Vietnam Thuong Tin, His Ship of Destiny". He died July 2019 in Dallas, Texas.

usually cooked for us is Chop Suey, a Chinese dish that almost no one liked. The rice was three layers: raw on top, the middle mushy, and the bottom was overcooked.

In addition to lining up for three meals a day, we could get on the bus going from Camp 1 to Camp 9, then go look through the piles of old things they gave us and get whatever fits. All looked baggy on us because we were small compared to those donating clothes. Everyone harbored their feelings about losing their homeland, so no one was eager to talk or do anything. 900 Cambodians were off in their camp.

Every day, after meals, I also took the bus around the camp to look for acquaintances, only to run into Airborne Captain Pharmacist Trinh Mau Nguyen.

(He was a close friend of Quoc Hoc with my eldest brother; after finishing high school in Hue, he went to Saigon to study Pharmacy, but because he was the only man in the family, they sent him to work as an office in Can Tho. Later, he opened a pharmacy in Hang Xanh. He did not have to join the military like my brother, but the Mobilization Department, the Ministry of National Defense called him up, so he volunteered to go to the 10th class, but not to join the active military medicine like others. At that time, especially at the School of Medicine and Pharmacy, if you had to join the army, when you finished training, you would wear a Lieutenant's insignia, instead of that of a Second Lieutenant like other majors. He graduated at the end of 1967 and was licensed to return to school. He had visited his family in Hue right on the occasion of the 1968 Tet Offensive) after New Year's Eve, he decided to spend time with his cousin and instead went back to his family house and thus escaped death when the VC attacked and captured Hue on the first day of Tet).

He left Bach Dang Pier at the last minute with his wife, children, and niece, he said, despite the curfew, because of artillery shelling on the evening of the 28th at TSN airport, people were still moving into the city, but it was very messy. Soldiers and civilians carrying guns on the street; he followed a group of paratroopers and drove a Jeep to Khanh Hoi to see the situation for himself. An uncle of his specializing in shipbuilding said at that time that his ship had been stolen, and when chaos began to occur, the chances of evacuation became more difficult. Two weeks earlier, he had submitted an evacuation document to the US Embassy and also paid to register at the hotel on Bui Thi Xuan Street, because the US promised to send a helicopter to pick them up on the roof of the building. At noon on the 29th, he went to Bach Dang Pier to observe the situation.

Fortunately, he met his paratrooper friend, Dentist Tung *(who settled in Texas and was one of the first to regain his license and practice as a dentist in Southern California)* who informed him that his aunt had a boat named *Long Ho* (Dragon Lake), so maybe he could take the family up there to go. When he got there, he saw the ship with a large sign saying: **ENGINE BROKEN, SHIP DISABLED**. His friend Tung said *"It's okay, they just do it so too many people don't gather"*. Seeing hope, he went home, and drove the whole family to the pier in a VW, although it was not far from his house: Tu Do Street was not far away. Once aboard the ship, everyone lay down to avoid being spotted by people on the shore. Fortunately, when the whole family got on, the ship owner also cut the anchor and motored to the middle of the river, avoiding robbers attacking the ship or threatening the captain because, at that time, many people had weapons in their hands. Some people on the shore jumped off and waded to the ship. Whoever could climb up, clambered aboard. On the evening of the 29th, when the South Vietnamese Navy ships departed for the Philippines, civilian ships followed them. Since the Navy ships were guarding them, there was relatively little confusion. Many ships were not full (these ships on the last day brought more than 30,000 Vietnamese, escaping by sea).

They were in international waters when they heard the news of the fall of Saigon, on the morning of April 30, 1975. *(After he got out of Pendleton refugee camp, he returned to Texas and regained his Pharmacist license to practice in the US, the civil profession he and Dentist Tung had pursued from Vietnam to the US).* He is retired and currently resides in Maryland with his wife.

Every day I made a collect call to my brother who was studying Civil Engineer in Florida. Calling this way was the easiest: just dial 0 and that's done. The recipient pays; I didn't know how much those phone calls cost.

Activities in the camp, besides three meals a day provided by the US Marines: everybody went to study the bulletin board to find relatives, announced in Vietnamese on loudspeakers, or read the daily Vietnamese newspaper *New Horizons* and just waited for news before finding a sponsor to get out of the camp. Some families had to stay for up to 6 months, a year, or until the refugee camp closed.

Camp spokesman at the time, Lieutenant Colonel Arthur Brill said that within 24 hours they had to prepare the camp to accommodate 4,500 refugees. They had to open more camps [28]. They isolated the refugees at first in the barracks and tents for a variety of reasons, including political and security issues, also fearing that infectious diseases would spread outside.

Chanh's dream of flight has at least come true because he borrows Major Thanh's flight suit every day to wear. It fits him well, even though he took off the symbols of rank on the shoulders attached to Velcro, but everyone knows the difference between a Second Lieutenant and a Major. The girls in the camp fell in love with the handsome young *"Major"*, so he enjoyed and accepted the attention.

One afternoon, Chanh told me that the Camp's Chief announced that he wanted to reduce the number of people in Pendleton, so for anyone who wanted to go would be sent to the newly-opened Eglin Air Force Base camp in Florida, because he was an Air Force officer of Vietnam, and the TSN Air Force Security/Intelligence Team [29] volunteered to go, because he knew I would reside to Florida later. There would be many opportunities to reunite again. Chanh later said that this camp gave better, more luxurious, and fancier food than was available at Camp Pendleton.

---

28. *Refugee camps for Vietnamese in 1975 in the US in the order of opening: Orote Point, Guam; Camp Pendleton, California (open April 29, 1975); Fort Chaffee, Arkansas (open May 2, 1975); Eglin Air Force Base, Florida (open May 4, 1975); Fort Indiantown Gap, Pennsylvania (open May 28, 1975).*

29. *A group of Air Force Security/Intelligent officers working at Tan Son Nhut airport with Chanh, arrived at U-Tapao with the last EC-47, volunteered from Camp Pendleton, California to the newly opened Eglin Air Force Base, Florida in May 1975, perhaps because of their background served in Air Force, settled in Ft. Walton Beach was sponsored by an American family but eventually returned to California to settle down, except Chanh, listened and follow my advised, relocated to Gainesville, Florida and continued his education at the University of Florida in 1975, graduating with a BS in Computer Science Engineering in May. 8, 1980 then worked for IBM Raleigh, N.C. until retired in 2019.*

Once Chanh was gone, there was no one left to act as an intelligence agent for daily news. I got on the bus to go around the camp to find acquaintances, the number of people in the camp increased but then stopped, because the government opened new camps to accept more refugees: their goal is to avoid crowding the refugees into one state.

Quonset huts for refugees at Camp Pendleton. Credit: Photo by Don Bartletti-LATimes.

Life in the Pendleton camp is also boring; someone cooks three meals a day for you, the mountain climate is quite cold for people from the tropics, we are bored because of no homeland to return to, not knowing where our future will take us. I took 52 white styrofoam cups and cut out the round bottom to make chess pieces, and a thick piece of cardboard to draw a chess board to make it less boring. In our tent, in addition to our *"family"* of three, there was a husband and wife. The wife had worked for the US Embassy, the husband was a doctor named Con. Their families could not get out. She had a box of watercolors and lent them to me to draw two red and blue chess pieces. At the end of the tent, there was a couple with three daughters; the youngest was about ten years old, and the husband worked for a US agency, so the whole family was evacuated. Everyone had a sad face and heart, so few told anyone anything. In just over a week, the couple secured a sponsor to go to the prosperous capital of the United States; I heard that it was a congressman, so they left. After a month in the camp, the USCC agency gave us 5 dollars for travel, only to find out that the military items they gave the refugees were really good, but our brothers were afraid of soldiers' clothes, so we left all at the camp, not knowing that those things are very good, durable and expensive in Army-Navy surplus stores.

From the refugee camp, when we found a sponsor, they took us to the Los Angeles airport by bus. The flight from California to Florida was a civilian flight. So far, I had been on a military flight; now I saw stewardesses with blonde hair and beautiful clothes; every time they moved on the plane corridor, the scent of perfume was mixed in the air to create a really attractive scent. When I set foot in a civilized country, I found everything strange. The plane arrived at Gainesville Airport, Florida, where my brother and our sponsor's family picked us up, arriving at the Glen Springs Manor apartment he had rented with 3 rooms. In the room, there were a few mattresses placed in the middle of the floor to make a bed. There was a small dining table with some old wooden chairs.

This was a rental apartment, with many rows of two-story buildings and flat roofs. They opened most residences to students because it hosts the largest university in the state. My brother told me to relax for a few days, and then go find a job. The sponsor gave us an old blue American-made station wagon; we went to the school volleyball court in the afternoon to play with Vietnamese students who were stuck studying abroad. Then, we went to report to the City Employment Office. We had an I-94 and that allowed us to work in the US legally. The city has two main roads: University Ave. perpendicular to 13th street, and the SW area of the intersection is the University of Florida. The city is very neat, as long as the name Avenue is perpendicular to the Street, finding a way into this small city is not difficult for us. Because of their background in the Air Force and military training, and their good English, getting a helicopter pilot's license was not difficult for Mr. Thanh and Mr. Chau. Those two were the people who first obtained their driver's licenses and helicopter licenses in the United States. Mr. Lap gave me his 250cc Yamaha motorcycle, so it was easier for me to get a license than for a car. Later, when Chanh followed my advice to move here to study, I took the car driving test, thanks to Chanh's small yellow Opel.

An Opel, the first car of my friend Chanh-Gainesville – Florida in 1975

CHAPTER V
A NEW LIFE

GAINESVILLE, FLORIDA: FIRST JOB, WORKING AS A MAID

Both Mr. Chau, Mr. Thanh, and I went to look for jobs after settling in Gainesville, Florida in May 1975 and after visiting the City Employment Office to fill out an application [30], we discovered they only had jobs for construction firms specializing in roofing – since we were all terrified of heights, they suggested we apply for a job at a hotel, if we knew how to cook ("Cooks"), wash dishes ("Dishwashers") or clean up and prepare rooms ("Maids"). Holiday Inn Hotel, located right on 13th Street, consists of two sections: one side is the hotel and meeting rooms, connected to the restaurant. When we entered, we immediately met the owner; his son-in-law was the Manager of the restaurant. After filling out an application, he told us that we have a choice of job for either side: anyone who wants to work in a restaurant or hotel can accept it immediately. Cooking is not my job, I only know how to cook according to the style of Scouting, and this is a big restaurant, so I chose to work for the hotel. Mr. Thanh cooks very well; we call him *"Hong Kong chef"*, Chau also knows how to cook and two friends want to work at the same place, so they choose to work in the restaurant.

On the first day, the hotel manager gave me a 4-wheel trolley with many compartments on it with enough items such as

30. *The job search office in Gainesville located at NW 2nd Street, come here, fill out an application and submit an I-94 card, say you want to look for a job, at that time there was no computer system on every desk. There is a stack of paper printed by a computer dot matrix printer with holes punched on both sides, white and light blue striped paper, writing jobs that need people, only the address of the place to be recruited and the phone number is also rare. Go straight to the places that need people, fill out forms and documents wherever you go. At that time, the job was easy to find, so when you completed the application, you would interview onsite and accept the job. If you don't have work or no income to go to school, they give you the application to fill in to the office to apply for government benefits. It was a time of economic glory. Minimum wage is $2/hour and gasoline is only $0.20/gallon.*

shampoo, soap, vacuum cleaner, toilet paper ... on the side of the trolley, there was a big word MAIDS. He led me into a room and then showed me what to do, with my current English, although I only partially understood what he said, I also knew what to do, when I saw him give a list of rooms to do, I saw 15 rooms; each room has a bedroom, a room with 2 beds, a bathroom, just doing the mental calculation that I'm sure I couldn't finish working all day and night, but I would only work until 5 pm for the sake of 3 brothers, go to work in the same car.

Thinking about that makes me feel tired, a Saigon Law student, who has never worked as a laborer, now has to deal with 15 rooms a day, but I can't give up, and if I'm scared, want to change jobs to work in a restaurant, maybe it's worse over there as the proverb warns: "*Avoid melon shells, meet coconut shells*".

Looking at the other housekeepers, my observation tells me that as soon as they finish one room, they pull the car to the next room. I think there is no way I would finish up in 8 hours; thinking so, I left the car at the top of the hallway, looked at the list of the rooms I had to work on, and then opened the door to each room on the list, took out all the dirty stuff and left it in the hallway, then I replaced clean items in each room and started working. There was no training at all, so I had to create and work out my own solution, the bottom sheet has an elastic band that is easy to pull out or put, up to the top sheet which must be straightened and placed under the mattress, then blankets, pillows and bed sheets lying on the top. By the 3rd room, I had started to get used to it and work faster. After I finished making the bed, I used the mop, cleaned all the bathrooms, and finally vacuumed. At noon, only 7 rooms were completed, the afternoon was very hard, I saw the Manager, and asked him how long the lunch break was, he said one hour but you can go to the restaurant to order food, whatever you want to eat in the menu, that would be fine.

Hearing that, I excitedly went to the restaurant because I hadn't brought anything when I went to work in the morning; the two brothers thought that working at a restaurant would have food, and since I worked at a hotel, I did not know there were free eats for employees. Sitting at a table for two, I ordered a plate of food, the price was not expensive, it was not cheap either because I thought it was the first time I would be criticized as taking advantage if I had ordered the most expensive item on the menu. After a while, I had almost finished a glass of iced tea, and I saw my brother bring up a plate of food, surprised that he had to serve his younger brother as a maid, sitting like a luxury customer. I ate fast and one hour was a bit long, I finished eating in only half an hour, I had no money in my pocket, I remembered I hadn't left any tips, rushed back to the hotel, I continued, this time I turned on the TV while listening and working, the speed was faster because there were 8 rooms left.

Around 4:30 p.m., I looked for the Manager, and told him I was done, just remember him looking at me and saying: *What?* My first English lesson was to learn the letter W, including the questions When, Where, and Who... now listening to him say only one word with wide eyes, I answered briefly with the verb to be: *"I am done, Sir"*. That's all, he took the paper I gave him in front of the number of each room marked with the letter V(Vacant), told me to follow him, from the beginning to the end of the corridor, he opened each room, viewed from the bathroom, towels, then flipped the sheet on the bed I made it up to see if it was a new sheet, going from room 1 to 10 he said *"good"* continuously, going to room 11 to 15, his word was *excellent!* Looking at me, he said a simple sentence: *OK, you can go home now.*

Walking to the restaurant kitchen, I saw two brothers still working because they were preparing for the evening, both of them were looking tired. He saw me and asked, *"Are you coming over for dinner?"* I said I was finished and was waiting to go home...In the car, they told me they worked so hard and got tired; it looked like I was in better shape, compared to the Major and the Captain, first time working in a restaurant, have to stand up all day, cut vegetables, cook, wash dishes, so "tired" is the right word.

The second day, when I looked at the list, I saw the Manager gave me 22 rooms; he saw that I had finished 15 before and played a prank on me, maybe tomorrow it would be 30. I would be miserable, but also I realized that working in the restaurant is too hard. The owner's son-in-law, the boss, has no respect for two RVNAF officers: once they had dozens of troops under their command every day, now they are at a loss, being used to the maximum, and can't sit down in a restaurant and order food like me.

This time I was more systematic, brought the dirty cart in front of each room and threw all the dirty things directly, not on the ground and then picking them up, because such an extra step would have been more time-consuming standing, with up and down movements, I just pulled the bed sheet and pulled it down immediately, clean things are left on the sofa because the bed is empty – easy to do. I ate lunch in the style of the scout, only 15 minutes to finish, and went back to work, taking an hour to eat is also a waste. I later learned that doing so was against the Labor Law, but because of my responsibility, I wanted to complete the work I had been assigned. At 5:10 pm, I met the Manager and said I was done. This time he just took the list of rooms I gave him and softly said *Thank you, go home*. Passing the restaurant, I saw two brothers still working; I went into the front room to watch TV and wait for them.

The third day, I expected I was going to be tired today, it wouldn't be fewer than 22 rooms, but the Manager told me to come in and see him, I think my job is over…maybe I'll be transferred to a restaurant…He told me to go check every room when the maids are done. This new job, because the hotel has several hundred rooms, and more than a dozen people working as maids, I get the list, see the names of people who have been assigned to work, so what room is left over to do? No one had over 12 rooms. It turned out that he had tricked and tested me, maybe because of the job application: I was studying Law, and applied for a maid's job!!! No wonder I did it all by applying the Taylor chain method, so he also knew how to look at people.

Now he assigned me to be a *Quality Control Inspector*, which means to sit and eat, and work leisurely but have to wait for the maids to finish before going to check and evaluate; with nothing to do, I ran over to the restaurant, saw the two brothers who had just finished picking up a bunch of lettuce that had just been smashed and split, took some old toasted bread that people did not eat, cut them into squares, fried them, since then I stopped wanting to eat these croutons, the two brothers asked the set of grooves. Why do you go to eat lunch early, I say now I just go to check the rooms, not working as a maid. Afternoon, I went around to meet each maid and saw that they seemed to be finished, so I only checked the rooms that were finished and then went to the clean room and turned on the TV to watch cartoons.

Mr. Thanh and Chau could not stand the restaurant manager's attitude, so they quit. I had no choice because we only had a single car to go to work together. Although I'm sure no one has worked for three days and been promoted as quickly as I was, I think no one would last long working there either. Incompetent management at the restaurant would make it hard to keep employees.

What happened with the restaurant management made me decide to go back to school to continue my education.

1975 – HELP RAISING THE BEACH HOUSE – THE HOUSE COLLAPSED

Our sponsors, Pat and Ted S. owned a small beach house for family vacations on weekends; it was located in the small fishing village of Cedar Key, Florida, about 60 miles southwest of Gainesville. The house is quite near the coast, overlooking the Gulf of Mexico, and built of wood. It has a small boat docking space and is so near the water that the floor of the house is built up to avoid any possibility of flooding the interior of the house. the posts supporting the wood floor with wood beams traversing them are made of concrete blocks. A special remark when entering the house is that the bathrooms and toilet doors are labeled with the word *"Library"* because he is the Director of the medical school library. The four of us were asked by our sponsors to come back for the weekend, to help raise the house because after some time the house had begun to sag and sink. It would thus require a stalwart group to jack it up. The plan was to take it up a notch, using portable hydraulic jacks at key structural points of the house, around corners as well as below wood beams when the whole house is lifted. One person would man each shaft; the hydraulic shaft has a 360-degree rotating movement. According to Mr. Ted's shout, each time should be a full rotation and then stop, so the house will rise slowly and evenly. I'm the smallest, so I chose the one in the middle, under the house because with my body size, it would be easier lying horizontally, and then rolling in. After all, the distance between the ground and the house was not so wide.

After a few hours, the floor was indeed higher. We took a break for lunch and then continued working afterward. Ted's neighbor brought ready-made wood planks to fill in the raised places. The floor was already much higher now, so I didn't have much trouble crawling down to the middle. After a few more shouts, I was about to continue when I heard a sharp crack, crack ... from above. Lying below, I only saw the house tilt to one side and collapse, the gap between the floor and the ground where I lay had closed up, but fortunately, the house had stopped moving and was not declining any longer. There was a shout outside: *"Is everyone okay?"* I quickly rolled outside; my two older brothers pulled me up, asking if I was all right. I answered in the affirmative, although my arm was a little sore because when my hand was on the handle, the wooden beam dropped and grazed my arm. Luckily, no one was hurt. At this point, everyone could tell that it would not be possible to continue with this method. The owner must hire a company specializing in house-lifting services to do it properly.

Later, when I gained experience and learned about Construction, Structures and Architecture, I realized that the correct method to have done it would have been to use wooden crossbars on the same level, raising them together at the same time, not just several points as we attempted. Luckily, the house only slid a short distance and didn't tip over or snap the horizontal beams – which could have entailed a lot of damage. Unfortunately, the house improvement failed and cost the owner a good deal to hire a company specializing in the restoration of wooden houses. But it was also a memory of our brothers and friends: we went to the coastal city, thinking we would have the opportunity to return. Since then I haven't ever had the opportunity to revisit the small town, famous for its smoked mullet.

1975: DECIDING TO GO BACK TO SCHOOL.

Right from the first time I settled in the United States, I could appreciate how my education path had been interrupted because of the war. Returning to school would not be easy, because at that time no one knew for sure when it would be possible to get a job, or whether they'd be able to return to their beloved homeland without retaliation or trampling on their dignity because of their background. If I stayed in Vietnam, there was no way the new government would let me continue my education at University or get a job, because of my *"wrong"* family background.

Staying in the US, the first problem was to overcome language and cultural barriers, to be able to integrate into a new society. International students awarded scholarships – like my brother – have overcome these difficult challenges, so I was confident that I would also be able to succeed, even though the proverb warns *"Thousands of difficult things start at a beginning"*. If you want to go to school or do anything else, you must first have money, but I overcame this difficulty when I went to Saigon to continue my studies: student life doesn't require a lot of money, only a few jeans, some shirts, and cheap foods. If you lack the money to buy books, you can go to the library – as we did in Saigon. That allowed me to become one of the earliest refugees to return to college; the other advantage is being right in a city with the largest university in the State of Florida. Continuing education is also a way to improve my English, in a way that will surely be a vital tool for the rest of my life.

I quit working at the Holiday Inn when my brother and his friend couldn't put up with their boss any longer and left. I took a 250cc Yamaha motorbike and ran to two colleges in town to apply for school enrollment: the city had only two institutions of higher learning: The University of Florida (UF) and Santa Fe Community College (SFCC). UF is the largest school in the state, offering a broad selection of fields of study; as a matter of fact, the famed School of Agriculture has many Vietnamese students who were studying at the graduate level before 1975; there are many types of plants and agricultural products here. It is suitable for the climate of Vietnam when they go home to serve or teach. Santa Fe is a small school, offering only 2-year AA (Associates of Arts) and AS (Associates of Sciences) degrees, the latter due to increased demand for 4-year BA and BS degrees. Santa Fe is farther from the city than UF, and the number of students is smaller; students only study for two years, and then go to work or transfer to UF to further their studies. Requirements for admission to UF are more difficult, including requirements for English: applicants must take the Test of English as a Foreign Language (TOEFL) and the minimum score to be admitted to the school is 500. For UF, you must first take a test, secure a passing TOEFL score, and then apply.

Santa Fe let me in right away to learn English: I decided I needed to upgrade my English, so I filled out an application. When it comes to submitting additional documents, including a high school diploma (or as I mentioned having completed a second year of study at the University in Saigon), there had to be documentation. You have to take the GED (General Educational Development), which is the equivalent of a high school diploma if you haven't completed the 12th grade. after the age of 19) or have no diploma.

The next day I brought three diplomas I had smuggled along with me when I escaped out of the country to show her. The American counselor said *"This is in Vietnamese! There must be an English translation."* There was no certified translator office in the US at the time, so I wondered just how long it would take me. Just *"going to school"?* Hearing me keep repeating the story of *"...going to school..."*, she responded that she rarely met a student who wanted to go to school so badly *("Really! Are you willing to go to school that much? Most people aren't!)*, I replied: *"Yes, I want to continue my education because I need to learn English first and to work later as I have lost my homeland; I do not know whether I can return or must stay here forever!"*

It sounded pitiful, so she asked: *"Can you translate these diplomas for me, then?"* Thinking I had heard wrong, I asked again, and she said *"Yes"*, so I asked: *"Do you trust my English"* She answered back: *"As long as you don't lie"*. I started with Baccalaureate I, passed Baccalaureate II, and was awarded my first-year certificate in Law. The basic English words for the degree were not difficult. *"You said 'Law School'?"* and I replied: *"Yes, Law School. I completed my second year"*. At that, she rolled her eyes and said: *"Then go to UF and continue to study Law!"* I explained to her that I would go to UF sooner or later, but I had to study here first, because the Law School program in Vietnam follows straight from high school, unlike in the US, where you must have been awarded a Bachelor's Degree (BS or BA) first, and must have LSAT for admission. Astonished, she said: *"But I thought the law school in your country was like here!"*

After struggling to translate my degrees, she allowed me to

enroll. My diploma would be sent to be translated into English and submitted later on. The next thing is to decide what to study for my first course. First, she advised me to enroll in English courses, which include English Lab, English Composition, English Literature, and Understand English… for 12 credits to qualify for a scholarship, she said (at that time there was no English as a Second Language, or "ESL" program). When I brought it home, my brother asked me which courses I registered for; I said I would start school next week. He asked me *"What subject will you study?"* I showed the paper to him; he skimmed it and said nonchalantly: *"You study like this, if you don't fail the first quarter, you'll lose your mind..."* He advised me, from experience, that if those subjects are taken together, while your English is not up to par, it will not only be difficult, but your test scores will be low because those courses are for Americans who have mastered English from childhood – not for foreigners who have just come to the US (and are enrolled in specialized ESL programs).

The next day, I went to see the counselor again, explaining to her that if it was possible I'd like to divide the English classes into several quarters; she said *"What subjects do you want to study, besides English?"* I explained how my brother had advised me to proceed, and asked her to let me take Math (Mathematics) and Science (Physics and Chemistry) because these subjects don't need much English. At this, she rolled her eyes at me like the day before and said: *"Study those subjects? Are you willing to die? Do you know that students here are afraid of those subjects like they are afraid of tigers?"* I said: *"Please let me try; if I can't master this course, I won't beg you anymore."* She did not dare to believe I possessed such talent, as I was the first Vietnamese to ask to re-enroll, so instead of giving me the Calculus Course I as I requested, she gave me Algebra.

Only later did I find out that for a student like me such a subject was not difficult, because I had studied it at the high school level in Hue. The next quarter she gave me the freedom to choose, after I won a 4.0 (President's List) for the first quarter. Later, when my friends like Chanh came in, she made it easier for students to register for math and science subjects without a degree, because many people weren't able to show them – they hadn't brought any documentation with them when they fled. They knew the details of the story, but it was not as difficult as before, and they saw that the Vietnamese students worked hard on their studies. Although they were weak in English when they first arrived, they made up for other subjects and diligently did not skip classes; some even asked their teachers whether they could record cassettes to listen to lectures again: the audio recorders were big and bulky, not as small as they are now.

My observation was that Vietnamese students like me could learn easily. Two teachers who specialized in teaching English to foreign students, Ms. Carnell (English Lab) and Ms. Lee Abbott (English Composition), loved Vietnamese students very much. The School had quite a few students from South America, but these two ladies were sympathetic with Vietnamese students, because of their politeness and hard work, beautiful and neat handwriting. Remember that around 1975, many Vietnamese students who had come here as exchange students or refugees had also finished high school in their home country, or were in the middle of university, or finished university in Vietnam, so most of them had passed the basic level of minimum discipline of a Master's, not to mention respecting teachers at home in middle schools and universities.

I don't know if I have a talent for essays, but the two ladies appreciated my fine, neat handwriting and the articles I described real-life stories. Even though my grammar at that time was full of errors, they corrected the entire page, in red. English teachers like students to write about their real-life stories and those around them, because most of the topics of articles are for students to choose from instead of being assigned, so it is difficult for the examiner but easier for new students like me: *Why come to the United States... the joys and sorrows of going back to school... an article on the virtues of Vietnamese women... and the difference between Eastern and Western cultures:* Cong (Work) Dung (Beauty/Appearance) Ngon (Speech) Hanh (Good behavior)". Other articles I wrote were about her: two years younger than me, going to school together in the dormitory, the charms and secrets of an Asian woman, not like a Western woman. She had very beautiful eyes but contained a sad melancholy that I jokingly called *"eternally sad eyes",* just afraid of suffering in a future love life. Not predestined, so just friends for life. A love story as beautiful as a poem: *"Love is only beautiful...when it is unfinished"*[31]. What a

31. *The poem "Hesitantly" by poet Ho Dzenh composed and printed in the poem collection "Grandparent Hometown", published in 1943, has 18 sentences but has two*

romantic… My diary is so rich and profuse in experience that it could be printed up as a book (!).

When it came to applying for grants, at first, I had to go to the school's financial office, when I filled out the application, the income my parents did, I filled it all with big ZEROS; ditto with my income statement: *no income*. They sent it back to make sure I had a suit to wear, but why was I so poor? They did not ask again later, because they had found out that everything I wrote was true, so the Government gave me the maximum amount of a Pell Grant and S.E.O.G. at that time. I helped several of my friends to complete their applications to get the maximum amount of scholarship. At that time, if you didn't use it all, you would stand in line at the Financial Aids office at the end of the quarter to get the remaining money, now they get it back. At that time, the Federal Student Loan program incurred 3% interest, but after graduation, it had to be paid back in a small amount per month.

Santa Fe is a small college, so everything is quick and convenient. After two years, you are done. After reaching UF, the school is large, the parking lot is far from the classroom, and you have to walk a lot from class to class, until the beginning of the Junior year, specializing in only one building. As for my architecture school, each student has a corner, with a large drawing table that can be adjusted up and down, under which is a piece of plywood with pillows and blankets to sleep on overnight. Because the projects including drawings and models must continue to be worked on and modified during the course, the students work day and night, especially near the end of the course. When we were hungry, we ran across University Avenue to buy ice cream, coffee, or snacks at Supreme Donut.

The city population was mostly college students, so in the

---

verbatim lines as follows:
"...Love loses its joy when it fulfills its oath,
Life is only beautiful when it is unfinished..."
Most popular when revised:
"...Love is beautiful when only unfinished,
Life is not fun when the oath is fulfilled..."
Taking the idea of the above poem, searching on youtube, there are five famous songs, namely "Story of Dating" by musician Tran Thien Thanh and "You can made appointment" by musician Anh Bang, "Love is just beautiful" by musician Thuy. Tien, "I keep making an appointment" by Hoang Thanh Tam, "Never stop" by Minh Duy.

summer the streets were empty because at that time, studying in a four-quarter system (Spring-Summer-Fall-Winter) did not require students to take a summer course as is the case at present.

The College of Architecture is located on NW 13th Street, near Tigert Hall (Administration), so few Vietnamese students came here: only 2 VN students chose this major, so we rarely met. As for engineering, I had a large number of friends; we would not only meet frequently but also get together at the main library (Library West-University Ave) on the 6th floor, or the Reitz Union. There were a few times when I had to walk over there; they were so happy as a group, but there was no one at my school. My school has its library, so I don't have to go to the main library; it was too far and I was tired of walking. At that time, almost every student focused on their studies; the scholarship was only limited to 4 years: if you didn't secure good enough grades, you lost, and if your grades were too low, you were *"kicked out"* of school. So everyone was serious and tried hard; apart from the students who go to school and the staff or professors, there were no one else around. What's more, there were no entertainment areas as in a big city; the scholarship money was just enough to live on. Thanks to that, the number of Vietnamese students graduating from school here in all fields is now quite large.

Everyone studied hard, so in the first few years, no love stories blossomed at my school; besides, at that time, they did not return to Vietnam to get a young and beautiful wife to bring over as they do now, so singles were valuable: *"one-way love"* stories are too many to tell. After graduating from school, most students find it difficult to get a job here because the city is small; they can only work for the school at a salary that is not as high as private firms, so everyone is forced to settle in other states or regions.

My luck, like that of many other refugees, was to come to a small city where there were not many options, and so the majority continued their education as a basis for later jobs when they completed their studies.

When we first arrived in Gainesville, we stayed at Glen Springs Manor 2130 NW 31st Ave. Many Vietnamese refugees live in this area, but at first, not everyone had a car, so we often traveled to school together, because the distance to Santa Fe or UF is nearly equal. Then I moved to Forest Green Village 3101 NE

15th St. B-1. At that time, 4 guys were sharing two rooms, Kha *(died April 6, 2017)* and Quynh, who shared a room; Chanh had one room and I occupied the living room because I often slept in the studio at school so I didn't need a room at home. Among the four guys, the only ones whose *"Love stars"* blossomed were Kha and Chanh. Quynh and I kept singing: *"Two years of unrequited love..."* (Poetry by Nguyen Tat Nhien, Pham Duy composed it).

If you go to school, you are allowed to work part-time. Work Study pays at least $2 an hour, a scholarship, and later with additional allowances for refugees and food stamps through the *Vietnamese Refugee Resettlement Program* was enough to live on. The house is under Section 8, so you didn't have to pay much. Remember Ms. Judie Gold, our social worker, when she came to the house to check for benefits, she told us that food should not be shared, and she put each person's name on the refrigerator for the sake of a government requirement. When we graduated from school, we invited her to attend the ceremony; she said that the following month the allowance would be over, and we told her that we would only ask for help temporarily, now that we could go to work, pay taxes and return money to our government to help others.

Looking back, the memories of our school days, after every final exam – we would get together to play ping pong, go bowling, or pinball... Although we were poor, our school life was quite interesting. After graduation, we naturally went to work, and had plenty of money but always remembered our student days: a poor, simple life but the time with the most vivid memories and the most romantic beauty in life.

WORK ON AN OIL PLATFORM IN THE GULF.

Since I had a full scholarship, I had a little left over for each course: the rule of the Pell Grant or Supplemental Educational Opportunity Grant (S.E.O.G.) scholarships for poor students like me is to keep their average scores higher than 3.0 (B average) and an annual income of no more than a thousand dollars. In 1978, I decided not to go to school in the summer and instead find a job. I bought an old Mazda RX2 that was sold by Mr. Hieu, my friend; he bought a used car and repaired it. The car was still running, so sometimes friends in the apartment would drive it to school together. I took a trip alone to New Orleans, then continued down to Houma. With a recommendation from an acquaintance, I stopped at Mr. Nhan's small house, where there are single beds, arranged in rows, I was offered a bed for $150 per week. I just slept overnight, and the next day went out to find a job. They told me to go to a shoe store to buy a pair of steel-toed shoes, and a hard hat, bring along any personal items that I need to use for a week, and then go to work the next day. I returned to Mr. Nhan's house, I paid the money and said that I would go to work tomorrow so I didn't need the bed.

Early in the morning, I saw a group of mostly white Americans waiting; I teamed up with two big fellows. A yellow helicopter with the 3 letters PHI (Petroléum Helicopter Incorporated) picked us up, this was a Bell model, with a capacity of 4 passengers. Lots of pilots working for this company are Vietnamese refugees, having served in the South Vietnamese Air Force (RVNAF) like my brother and his squadron, so they had plenty of experience. The salary was also good and they did not have to undergo any basic training. An oil drilling platform has 3 floors: the upper floor has a helipad, 4 trailers for eating and sleeping, one for an office, the second floor for oil pipes, pumping systems, and pressure gauges, while the lower floor is covered with mechanical equipment, the same iron beams as above, exposed, not sealed, so you can see sea water and waves slamming against the 4 main big round pillars of the rig. There is a boat anchored in a corner, as well as a small place for those who want to fish.

When we arrived, they immediately told us that if we heard an explosion or saw a fire, if we were still alive (not dead), for safety, just wear our life vest and jump into the sea; a rescue boat would pick us up. Just hearing that, I felt *"my manhood weakening "* right away, but after all, I had been in a country at war. I didn't die from bombs – would my fate be tied up with oil? Fortunately, during my time there, I never had to jump into the ocean, as instructed for an emergency.

In the staff trailer, there are double bunk beds and a bathroom; because of my small size, I took the top bunk. The next morning, a galley hand (kitchen assistant) went around to all the beds to wake us up on time; for personal hygiene, we brushed our teeth and washed our faces, then went to the next trailer to have breakfast, already hot and ready on the table, whatever you like including pancakes, waffles, omelets, cereal or the cook can customize for you if you like. After eating, the whole team had an outdoor meeting to assign work duties for the day.

My team consisted of 3 men, including the team leader, and an assistant and I became the assistant responsible for bringing the long oil pipes into place. The oil pipes are about 20 feet long, with some shorter and bigger. I guess they are made of metal or special plastic or stainless steel for a corrosive saltwater environment. The assistant is an American over 6 feet tall, and his arms and legs are full of tattoos and muscles; I just stand up to his stomach, and he points me to the end of the oil pipe, two hands already wearing thick gloves, he stands in position and motions for me to raise the oil pipe to my stomach, I crouched down, thinking it would be light; anyone who even tried their best could not lift it off the floor, holding my breath or no matter what, the oil pipe on my side still did not move, while over there he was swearing, using countless obscene words, should also know nouns and verbs all 4 or 5 letters like Dirty M. F---er.

He put down the tube, and looked at the team leader of the group as if complaining; without a word, he dropped the notebook, took my place, and lifted the pipe with another guy. I was standing there doing nothing; I ran over to pick up the notebook, my mouth shouting *"Sorry, sorry..."* Looking at the book – it is the notebook – I see the top line carries information about today's day and time starting work and a blank sheet, I find myself useless at work; maybe tomorrow I will lose my job, so I asked the team leader to let me write down what we are doing, such as a work report? He nodded his head; there was no other choice because usually, two assistants work: the team leader watches and records the work in the book. Each oil pipe has a different number, the size and length must be correct so that when drilling, each is used for a special purpose. When it was lifted by the crane from the carrier, they just left it there and the staff on the rig had to organize and handle it.

That day, working until noon, everyone taking a lunch break, I saw that the leader and assistant used many working nouns, but did not have any reaction about my *weakness*. After lunch, we continued to work, I kept the book, and the two men carried the oil pipes, working until the afternoon around 4 pm, then took a bath, changed into fresh clothes then went to the dining trailer. Dinner was handled by the chef and the galley hand, including almost everything. Meat, expensive shrimp, and desserts, I asked if I had to pay, and everyone laughed and said it was all *free*. There were no women on the rig, so after returning to the trailer, everyone jumped into bed and started reading books. I saw them all telling dirty stories; each of them had a Playboy or Penthouse magazine; all of them were looking at pictures, not reading, except that my book was full of words, grammar, sentences, and proverbs. They asked me what I was reading; I told them I had learned and studied more English because that was my second language. They all laughed very loudly and said: "*Did you see the words we used in your dictionary?*" I told them that for dialects, it was verbal only so I would learn from them, not from the dictionary. I learned *"obscene"* English here because every time they talked, they always started with a term that I called a *"special Danish word"* in Vietnamese (ĐM).

Still worried about my position and my job with the team; they were all quiet and no one mentioned my physical issues, but my sixth sense told me the whole platform had already discussed it behind my back. It seems that the team leader allowed me to keep the books, never looking or checking on them, and they handled the heavy labor work because they had no other choice unless they asked the Manager of the rig to change workers; that meant having to wait 7 days for a flight to bring in a new team. Having had the opportunity to talk a lot with these people, I found them to be very kind, most of them had only completed the 4th grade and then had to go to work to earn money. At home, their wives are lonely so they talk long-distance or have an affair, so when they return with their salaries, most of it has to be spent on these expenses. Each team worked 7 days on and 7 off; my team worked 14 days because the weather was bad; no flights, so there was no one to replace them on the platform.

The Manager of the rig was a tall, slender man whom I did not meet until the 10th day. Before the day of departure, the team leader told me to bring the books to the boss; I mentioned to him that we still had to work tomorrow. He said to write in cleaning and miscellaneous because on the last day, we wouldn't be doing much. I brought it to the office trailer and handed it to the boss – my first time in the office trailer. There were several desks with paperwork, a communications system, probably to talk with the helicopter, a ship or emergency broadcast, a large speaker and round red bell mounted on top near the outside, a small bed in the back, and a restroom. Someone probably stays there 24 / 7 to monitor the rig.

On the morning of the last day, after breakfast, the boss summoned everyone into the yard, divided the final work for cleanup before getting back on land, and then he looked straight at my team leader: *"Who wrote your report?"* I saw the face of my team leader turn red, his trembling hand pointed at me without saying anything. In the two weeks since handing the notebook to me, he had never asked or looked at anything; he let me do it, but later, during the conversation, I knew he only finished primary school: the workbook and report were the toughest for him and he didn't like to handle them because he didn't have enough writing words; he usually misspelled words. He's not afraid of heavy work, but not office paperwork. Then when I took the notebook over and he did my heavy work, he was happy with the exchange; now, if there were any problems, that would be his responsibility.

The boss gently told the group that he had never seen a report as complete as this, with *diagrams* and like a *spreadsheet*, no misspellings (at that time there was no software like Lotus 123 or Microsoft Excel) but I drew each cell division in vertical and horizontal, the name of each person, their duties and what had been accomplished, diagrams drawn and S/N tubes placed. He showed the notebook to everyone and then declared, *"He is a 'college kid', and won't be able to do heavy work so I don't want to see him next time, and don't expect anyone to make a report like this because I know your guys can't do it systematically like him"*.

The team leader and helper guy were happy to be praised, telling me: *"Next time you can team up with us?"* But I said that's enough, if I make too much, I will lose my scholarship, and I will have to work for the rest of my life like you guys, making a good salary but that's what I don't want. They cleaned up, let me go downstairs to fish, and waited for the helicopter to pick us up.

The next day, we were supposed to return by helicopter after receiving our salary, but the weather was bad. The two groups decided to return because they didn't want to stay on the rig without pay; they invited me to go with them by boat. Taking their invitation seriously, I followed the group back on a small boat, the waves high and strong; I saw that everyone had salt biscuits in their hands which they ate to fight seasickness. I slept the whole trip.

Returning to Houma, I gave the two leaders and assistants a ride home in my Mazda. After saying goodbye, I stopped by Mr. Nhan's house to tell him that I didn't need to rent a bed anymore because I thought if I had to go to work, I would go straight to the rig. Why do I have to sleep for two nights and pay up to $150 USD, a bit of a rip-off for a poor student like me?

On my way Eastbound on I-10… I returned to my student life, forgetting about all the hard work I had just witnessed in the past two weeks, and the expressions that were not in the dictionary that I would not dare to use even if I had to; thanks to that I know the language of the dusty people.

The amount of work I did was below the set amount of the scholarship, and I remembered the rig manager's words. So I never returned because I knew my body was not suitable for these jobs. Luck might not strike twice, to meet the same working team to keep the books and do the report. A job with many memorable memories for the first days in the country: *a university student working as a manual laborer in the United States.*

CHAPTER VI
WRITING ON AMERICA
VIET BAO NEWSPAPER AWARD

This is a chapter dedicated to an exposition of the author's articles, as submitted to ***Viet Bao California****, the Vietnamese newspaper headed by famous writer Nha Ca/Tran Da Tu, through a writing contest. "Writing on America" since 2000 includes an award-winning article from Viet Bao 2002. The original text is kept "as is". The author and Viet Bao hold the copyrights of these articles, which have been published into books by Viet Bao and are available online.*

MOURNING HEADBAND FOR AMERICA [32]- 2001

https://vvnm.vietbao.com/a162382/giai-khan-so-cho-nuoc-my

Participant number: 02-368-vb81007

I have things that I rarely use, so I put them in a small chest, when I have free time, I bring them out to see, as collectibles, sometimes old stamps, envelopes, maybe some Scout badges...But last week I remember one thing that needed to be used immediately, the little American flag with a wooden, gilded handle that the Chief Justice of Maryland gave to me when I took the oath of American citizenship in 1983. The small flag, I thought I would never have the chance to use, just kept as a souvenir of my second homeland, but today it is so noble and splendid proudly fluttering in the wind on the mailbox in front of my house. Neighboring Americans asked me where I could buy the flag because the flag stores were empty the week after the terrorist attacks in New York, the Pentagon, and Pennsylvania. I answered proudly about its origin. That flag is an unforgettable memory in my life. It came to me like a coincidence, like a pre-arranged fate, a crossroads between two roads, where I accepted myself as my second homeland, no longer having a choice because my first homeland was lost. Although the loss is only temporary because there is no permanent regime in history, looking back at ,the glorious times of our ancestors, Ly Le Tran, many heroic heroes, many kings just for the people, took care of the people. I can't escape change, let alone over here... The stream of thought suddenly stopped there, there was a little choking in my throat... Although only accepted as a second homeland, the United States has treated me in particular and the Vietnamese people. refugee in general in a broad way, unforgettable sentiments.

Just imagine a stranger, torn clothes, wild panic because of

32. *This article was published in Viet Bao Newspaper, section Writing On America and the title is based on the book by the famous writer Nha Ca when she wrote the book "Mourning Headband for Hue" in 1969 after the massacre of Tet Offensive 1968, English version by Olga Dror. This was also published in the special journal of the University of Florida student association (UFVSA) New Year Nham Ngo Edition 2002.*

war, no coin in the pocket, and no second set of clothes, like Mr. Chu in the history book. Coming to America because of the loss of its homeland...just less than a few years later, he had decent clothes, neat shoes, houses, cars, jobs, and hundreds of workers under his command. Success does not come as easily as many people think, but it can reach anyone if they work hard and believe in their talent, a Vietnamese businessman Truong Dinh Tran in New York gave the Red Cross two million dollars for victims of terrorist attacks, Vietnamese people who have settled all over the US also send relief money to their second homeland. In general, there are people who succeed in different ways, but in the end, it is also thanks to the country of freedom, full means, and no discrimination.

After the 911 attack, whether they like it or not, Americans will probably look at foreigners living in their country with a different view, good or bad depending on the person, there are also extremist Americans but the law strictly does not allow them to do outside the framework. My ex-Japanese boss who was born and raised in America always remembers what happened to his family after Pearl Harbor in 1941 and had to live in concentration camps in California. September 11 of this year will probably change America, and of course, the Vietnamese refugees will not escape this influence.

Although we have experienced the events caused by the war in the country such as 1945, then divided the country in 1954, then the Tet Offensive in 1968, the red fiery summer of 1972, and the event of 1975... we can't help but feel sorry for the victims of this 911 incident, regardless of anyone, children, innocent women, there are also people who come to settle or work in the US because they think this is the safest place in the world, part of the Pentagon was instantly turned to ashes, and thanks to the heroic passengers on Flight 93, although they died, they saved a number of innocent people. Mau Than (The 1968 Tet Offensive by the VC) was in Hue just a few days after Tet because of that took away 8,000 innocent people buried alive. In a peaceful country, this is a difficult thing to think about, so I borrowed the title of the book by the famous writer Nha Ca for this article, and she allowed it.

Tragic stories are being told in the radio and television press, a group of firemen number 6, only nearly died from slowing down while having to save a woman who couldn't get down the stairs. Love has saved them, *"cause and effect"* can be seen immediately without waiting. No matter what religion believes in there is protection, there are people who live by saving people, but there are people who lose their lives because of saving people. We Vietnamese people have come from a war country and witnessed many pitiful scenes, wives lost husbands, children lost fathers, and families separated, but before this scene, we couldn't help but feel sorry for the fate of innocent people, just because of this situation, villains can do anything, by any means, to achieve their inhuman ends. They believe they will go to heaven with many beautiful girls to serve them, but is there any heaven that accepts these people?

The number of Vietnamese in the US is not much compared to the local population, I rummaged through the newspapers and the internet hoping to not find any Vietnamese names on the list of victims, and then I received an email from a friend in the capital. Friends in the District of Columbia report that his friend who worked for the Pentagon has been killed. Khang Ngoc Nguyen is a relatively young employee for a US Navy contractor, enthusiastic about social activities since he was a university student.

Khang is also a successful immigrant in the United States, wanting to work at the Pentagon, he had to undergo background investigations, his past, and his family, but now he is gone forever, to his young wife and 4-year-old son, he probably didn't feel any pain when the airplane fly by terrorists crashed into his office, but painful for those who stayed, his wife cried, parents cry for their children, his child are too young to feel the grief of those who have lost their fathers. I have witnessed painful stories where I am also a victim that the war took away my father when I was just one year old. It wasn't until I had a child that I fully understood this loss and understood the pain boundless sacrifice of a mother who was there to raise their children. In tears, I can only pray for Khang's family to overcome this great loss.

My second homeland America has woken up from a nightmare. There will be many changes from domestic and foreign affairs, the economy to immigration programs, ideological warfare has faded into the 21st century, giving way to war on terror that can happen anywhere, any place, when there is no longer a place or country to fight a battle with only two sides. To win, there must be all three factors: the will of God, terrain advantages and human harmony, and countries where they no longer value human life or are so fanatical that they have destroyed priceless statues for two thousand years just for their own sake of another religion.

My brother used to say that after his travels to Arab countries, the most pitiful thing was to be born and become a woman in those countries. Women in Muslim countries sometimes do not have the right to go to school drive or go out on the street must be accompanied by a man in the family, with a **niqab** (hijab/burqa), no one will dare to flirt, no different than living in prison. Looking back at people and thinking about us, Vietnamese women in the past, although not as free as other European and American countries, we are proud to have heroines like Ba Trieu, and Hai Ba Trung. I wonder when will my first homeland have Freedom and the second homeland and common homeland of mankind live in peace. when hatred no longer falls on the heads of the innocent, when in our hearts there is no longer fear. Towards peace and freedom, may the less fortunate Muslim women one day enjoy what we are enjoying, the noble word FREEDOM.

October 2001

HISTORICAL PRESERVATION

Participant number: 2-615-vb70810

https://vvnm.vietbao.com/p222a162612/5/bao-ton-di-tich-lich-su

Viet Bao: The author currently holds the position of Assistant to City Manager, and serves in the Community Redevelopment Agency in a city in the southern state of Florida. His article recounts his work and thoughts on the process of preserving and restoring the Town Hall, an ancient structure of the city. I hope that intellectuals who are concerned about the fate of historical relics in Vietnam have the opportunity to "share the anxiety" of the author of this special article.

(This is the article that won the Honor Award of Viet Bao California in 2002).

Remember on April 29, 1975, he was *"stuck"* in Tan Son Nhut airport with his family, shells fell in the female soldier's barracks not far from the *"bunker"* area where he was avoiding bullets. Then early in the morning, he and his brother also crawled out of the airstrip, jumped on the last C-130 plane to leave the airport, headed to U-Tapao Airport, a USAF base in Thailand, took off on a *"taxiway"*, the main runway was badly damaged because shells from Nha Be all night before. He knows his life has changed since then...

Settling in a city with not many Vietnamese people, but having the second largest university in the state, he applied for school with less than a few hundred dollars that his brother gave to him, with a meager amount of English obtained from the Vietnamese American Association in Saigon when he was a second-year law student, it was enough to speak and listen with his hands, but then God bless the fool, the school's *"counselor"* helped him translate diplomas, helped fill out applications for scholarships for poor students, so he could afford to pay for his tuition, study, and spare time to work in a *"work study"* program with money to play billiards or bowling in the amusement, activities building.

After graduating from school, with a Bachelor's diploma in

hand, he took off with an old Mazda RX2 to make a trip around the United States, departing from the Southeast, he stopped at New Orleans, then Houston, then moved to the North, about a hundred miles from the famous musical city of Nashville, he felt the car shook, looking ahead, a wheel was rolling parallel to his car in front, that was his left rear wheel had left. Going for a ride is what he's afraid of, but he has no choice but to go to the nearest gas station to find a way to get his old car repaired, after a day of waiting, he finds old car parts in the junkyard, he got in the car, continued west, stopped in Kansas City, Central America.

In a week, seeing that it was not a good land to stay, he moved to the East, directly pointing to the US Capital, not continuing to the West, because he knew that California would be difficult to come back... again, he had to cross the desert with the iron horse had long hooves...so fate pushed him towards the capital, thinking that any country, the capital is more and always beautiful than other cities.

As he predicted, the capital of the United States was very prosperous, and only once on the highway along the Potomac River, he was inspired to write many *"frog"* poems. Well, he had to choose this place as the beginning of his temporary life, but for several years, he had not had the opportunity to go here and there.

After working for a few years, and having a house and a car, he saw the hustle and bustle of big city life, it took him more than three hours to drive to work and home, and then he understood the verse: *I was foolish, I found a place that no one here...*

In America, the more you worked, the more you spent, wanting to be able to quietly buy a home for his family, he volunteered to move to the branch of the company that had just opened in Florida, which was no stranger to him, secretly thinking about moving back because the work is the same everywhere in the US, life here is more leisurely, close to brothers and sisters, the climate is relatively similar to Vietnam, making him feel less nostalgic for being away from home. His ambition is to still have a peaceful day, with the experience he has learned, about contributing to rebuilding a part of his ruined homeland, the homeland is still the most beautiful thing in his heart since the day he left, so when he saw that there was a city that needed people to take care of Architecture and urban design, he applied immediately, thinking that learning this profession one day in peace would be enough to help the war country. So he changed his *"job"*, into a program to decorate and rebuild the city. Three years later, with the amount of experience, he was promoted to assistant to the city manager in charge of renovation.

It should also be known that this is just a small city of less than 20,000 inhabitants, including the snowbirds, half of whom are minorities from other countries, including Vietnamese, located along the East Coast. The whole city is no more than 3 square miles, the city he lives in has a pier, 2 parks, an elementary school, and the street that people call *"downtown"*, a town hall that has been built since 1920, so-called the ancient historical building designated through the state and federal. Government money subsidizes the city to preserve and improve these historic sites a lot. Looking at his homeland, he is sad for his thousand-year-old ancient city of Hue, which is getting worse and worse, with international (United Nations) funds subsidized, there is no government agency to spend time researching historical works to maintain and preserve for future generations.

This project, building the new town hall cost less, but they are willing to spend more than double that amount to preserve. To repair these historic sites, they spend years researching, and applying for construction permits through the city board, led by the mayor, and then the state historic maintenance agency, the federal government must complete the project under the supervision of a historic preservation council, there must be an entrance and a restroom for the disabled to use because the new ADA laws (Americans Disabilities Act), because ancient architectures often do not have many facilities such as today, electricity, water, drainage, toilets, windproof windows and especially air conditioning systems.

Lots of challenges in the project completion phase. According to the plan that removed, who knows the old people, building houses without reinforced. In the past, using only wood and bricks, when we unloaded it, were afraid of its structures. Construction and Civil engineers have to take care of the building not to collapse, and not to damage the old bricks, so the restoration work takes a lot of time.

Twenty years ago, they remodeled the town hall many times, but could only add a ceiling fan system to keep it cool, but did not dare to add an air conditioning system. With today's advanced technology, refrigeration engineers have been able to run small heat and cold pipes in the ceiling. However because the existing ceiling did not have much opening, so they had to create a false ceiling system to be able to bring the heating and cooling system to the whole area.

With a project on historic preservation, there will be many questions, the answers of which can only be seen, not predicted on paper like new projects. Only more than two hundred years since the founding of the country, Americans do not have long-standing historical sites like Asia and Europe, but preserving culture through historical sites shows us that they appreciate these heritages left behind by their ancestors, a part of a culture that is increasingly overshadowed by advanced technology and gradually lost. Meanwhile, there is a wild man in Afghanistan who destroys historical monuments that have existed for more than two thousand years, monuments that can be considered as historical monuments and wonders of the world, which the country is lucky to have.

From surprise to surprise, he did not expect to be confronted with the events before him. After 80 years of construction, the previous generation could not maintain the "maple" wooden floor because of the climate, so they used asphalt to spread a layer of vinyl. Then around the 70's, they spread out a thick layer of carpet, chiseled through the outer walls to install small air conditioners. Today, he, representing the new generation, has to strip the carpet, and then remove the vinyl and asbestos glue which is not acceptable with modern technology because of the contamination caused by chemicals that are banned.

The maple wooden floor is carefully polished, and 3 layers of colorless paint are applied for maintenance so that with today's advanced technology, women wearing high heels can not scratch this glossy layer. Now that the whole building has been operated by air conditioners day and night, the maintenance of the wooden floor is no longer as difficult as before. His predecessors had to roll out carpets to address the state's humid climate, also acting as sound insulation.

Because it is the city hall, with the 21st century and the state of democracy in the US, children and grandchildren in the village can also watch live broadcasts of the monthly meetings of the

Commission, unlike the old way have to go to a meeting in person. The City Council usually consists of the mayor, the deputy mayor, and three elected members of the council, odd numbers to avoid even votes when deciding any matter. A City Manager is hired to act as a shuttle between the people and five elected officials, and an attorney to advise the council in legal matters. It was because of this live broadcast system that made him sweat. Not only is there no room for cables to run, but the cables must be separate from the electrical and telephone wiring as required. All must run into a small air-conditioned room, where all the mechanical systems are transferred to the television station. This room is kept secure to prevent vandalism. He thinks far away that the young generation in the future will have to curse at the old men who run around. Now there's no need to use *"wires"* anymore, but in the era of *"wireless"*, even the wireless technology is still not good yet. However, thanks to advanced technology, restoration, and preservation are somewhat easier.

The restoration of ironwood doors also causes a lot of headaches. With time, the value has increased much, not to mention the old carpenters, meticulous in detail because of their time and cheap labor, did it in a very elaborate way. He came up with a way to cast the entire door out of metal, remove the insulation inside, look exactly like a wooden door, and take a long time to break, but the State Office of Monument Conservation did not accept the idea. That idea is because the paint will not be the same as in the old days. Paint they use a computer to *"scan"* the old paint, calculated by the machine to be almost the same as the paint when the new building was built.

The roof tile after 80 years was damaged, his predecessors wanted to be healthy and had little money, so they replaced it with a cheaper roof called *"shingles"*. Now restored to look like the old days, he had to let the workers turn it over, only to discover that trusses could not bear the weight of the new tile. Now more calculation by the civil engineers, adding iron here, connecting wood there, and done, the red tile roof replaced the old roof, making the town hall become more majestic, the poinciana tree shadow in front of the yard reminded him of the once heroic high school where he was born, now decaying over time. Will there be a day when they restore those historical buildings like he is doing, thinking about it makes him sadder.

The city he lives in, wants more money to restore outside the city hall, the government does not subsidize this money as grants. Why not think of ways to mobilize residents to contribute? Finally, the city organized a sale of bricks, each brick worth depending on the donor, individual, corporate, or family name, which will be engraved and lined on both sides of the main gate entrance, this is beneficial for both sides, the rich, the famous, the American-style gold plaque, he gathered this idea while visiting the Tay Lai temple in California, and the famous Disney World tourist attraction of the United States in Orlando, Some people do not hesitate to order dozens of bricks, engraved with the names of their parents and grandparents... So they have money to complete the project without having to ask or ask for help. However, this idea was put back on the shelves for the future but proceeded at the Marina instead.

His hair has been salted and peppered, and the retirement date is not far away, but he still feels that he is still very young, he still wishes that one day he would see with his own eyes, hear with his ears, and feel his hands on the mossy bricks, where he was born, that these relics will be preserved and restored properly, according to the standards that he thinks any historic preservation and restoration association can accept, rather than having money, instead of restoring it to the old ages, create and mixed the art looked funny.

Hopefully, that day is not far away, suddenly he hears someone say in his ear: "*Sir, the door has been fixed...*" He suddenly woke up, so he had a dream... a dream that he suddenly wished to return and come true more than ever.

Summer 2002

LAZY EYE

Participant number: 3234-832-vb80622

https://vvnm.vietbao.com/a162858/con-mat-luoi-bieng

"Fairy-Destiny, Heavenly Law, Mutual Enlightenment,

Ungainly face puffed incompatibility"

He was born and raised in a war-torn country. The small city where he was born, countless of his friends have died, because of the accidental bullets, the city in which he has many happy and sad memories of his eyes.

Before he was born, a fortune-teller in the village told his mother, she would give birth to a son, it would definitely be a boy and must have a small defect, he said: *"Having talent, later fame in illustrious foreign countries",* but when he was born, his mother did not see any defects, only saw that his left eye was slightly smaller than his right eye. If you look closely, you can see it, she was a bit worried and did not know the fortune teller was telling correctly.

At that time, most of the people living in the village, who had children born, also went to see fortune-telling or get a horoscope to see if they would be rich or famous in the future. In an impoverished country where war is rampant, belief in numerology and fortune-telling or superstition partly makes people feel confident, even though they still know that *"blessed wins over fate".*

When he entered elementary school in the village, his left eye was slightly misaligned. His classmates teased him even more, at the beginning, he felt uncomfortable, and then he became used to it, no longer paying attention to their teasing, just studying hard. In return, he was loved by the teachers because he studied well and wrote the best handwriting in the class, often chosen on the writing board for the students below to copy.

He passed the *"concourse"*, a selection contest that accepted only 200 students out of more than 3,000 to enter the sixth grade of the city's largest and most famous public high school, National

Academy. This is not only an honor but also reduces financial worries for parents. The less fortunate students, if their parents have money to send them to private schools, can't even go back to their hometown to work in the fields or go to the army. The kids used to make fun of him, and most of them *"failed"* to pass the entrance exam because they did not study hard. Less than a few *"enemies"*, in high school, he met a new group of rebellious people, but then he passed the first and second baccalaureates, his grades were high, so he could continue college life, and not have to arrange to join the military as his friends, (his definition of *"friends"* was people who didn't make fun of his little quirks).

At that time, children in the village, in class, when playing or fighting, often used their parents' names to curse, or make jokes about other people's bad habits. Every generation, every time has unruly and bullying children. The place where he was born and raised is not immune to this situation, he is sad but he rarely says it in his heart. His mother took him to a local ophthalmologist and they said nothing. At that time, surgery was a rare thing, there were not many eye doctors, and medical facilities were limited, so he had to give up no matter how much it cost, his mother also saved and earned it, wishing to cure him. At the age of one, his father sacrificed himself for the Fatherland when he brought his army troop from Hue to Quang Tri and was ambushed by the enemy on the *"Avenue of Terrors"*, a great loss for him and his family not only in mental but also in financial terms, he thought maybe if his Dad was still alive, maybe he would find a way to send him abroad for treatment.

The four bad things that the children in the village, in the class often bring to jokes are the first *lazy/cross eyes*, the second *short*, the third *mouth with unaligned chin bones*, fourth *missing or no teeth*. With the medical and financial situation of that time, these defects were often not treated, and those who were born with defects or disabilities had to accept them.

In the US now, missing or no teeth is the easiest thing to treat, even a cosmetic dentist can make it go away. He had an acquaintance who had the courage to eat liquids for 6 months to rebuild her maxillofacial bones. Only dwarfism because when growing up, the body lacks nutrition and bone tonics, calcium from milk, there is no cure. Vietnamese children born in the US are much taller than their fathers born in Vietnam.

Back to his birth defect, medically known today as strabismus (lazy's eye), one eye is born weaker than the other, so if not treated before the age of 6, that eye will no longer see and blind. Because to avoid double vision, the muscles to control eye movement also gradually weaken, some people have one, some have both, statistics show that 4 percent of children are born with this condition.

Since coming to the US, except for the time when he was still poor when he was in school, after graduating from school and having a job, he found eye specialists at many ophthalmology centers. In the US, there are 2 types of eye doctors, one about eyeglasses called an Optometric doctor (O.D.) can only examine and make eyeglasses, but Vietnamese doctors in this industry outside the store also say they are eye doctors! The second is an Ophthalmology doctor (M.D.) who specializes in eye diseases and can treat or operate on eye diseases.

First, he went to find American ophthalmologists, because there were no Vietnamese doctors in the cities where he lived. The advice of these people is almost the same that there is no pain why fix it, nor can it be said that nothing wrong with his eyes, after being diagnosed when he was a child, he was exposed to sunlight, so his eyes were blurred and deviated.

After more than fifteen years of searching, on the occasion of the company transferring him to work in California, he sought out Vietnamese eye specialists here, hoping to explain in Vietnamese that they could find a way to fix it. Or they might refer him to other doctors. After searching, making an appointment, and having an examination, the result is still the same, nothing more than the answer, medicine has no means of eye transplant, etc.. sometimes he thinks it seems that most of the doctors here don't pay much attention to their patients. Going to the doctor's office sometimes takes a whole day to wait even though you have an appointment, if you go to the mental hospital to see some psychiatrists, you come in not sure and you come out and get sick!

He had a friend, and his wife was a bit psychotic, the doctor gave her psychotropic drugs and she went crazy, he was so angry that he moved to a country town, and he didn't give his wife anti-depression drugs anymore. After a period of discontinuation of the drug, she returned to normal. Another friend's wife, who was sick with a mental illness, but didn't know what was wrong, went to an internal medicine doctor in his city, couldn't find a cure, he gave her psychiatric medication, the husband was so angry that he thought his wife was not sick. Then, without medication, he happened to meet a Vietnamese family whose son graduated from medical school, who sent his wife to the University hospital in Miami for a biopsy, then discovered his wife had hepatitis C, currently, there is no cure at the time. From the time the disease was discovered, the couple knew that there was no cure, but as if they were relieved of their burden, from now on, they only care about treating the disease, not looking for it as before.

The other doctor has a wife who has no education, and goes to the clinic to make an appointment and to help her husband, every time she calls to ask for an appointment, she answers, so that I can *"insert"* you go see a doctor. Very angry, his friend once shouted to her: *"I am a human being, not an animal, I go to the doctor to pay properly, not for begging. Please don't treat me like that."* After stopping for a while, with this disorder, people still see her continuing to *"foist"* the patient's name in her husband's appointment book.

Determined not to give up, he kept looking, until one day, his daughter got pink eyes from school. His wife had to urgently take the child to see the family pediatrician. The doctor introduced a friend doctor who is a pediatric ophthalmologist, who after the referral was received, examined and treated her right away, but he said that after she recovered, she let him have his eyes tested, because he suspected she had one weaker eye than another.

The next month, he and his wife happened to take their young daughter to see the doctor, when he looked at him in the clinic, he said only a short sentence: *"I can cure you too"*. He did not expect that this child's eye doctor would be the one he had been looking for for nearly 50 years. When taking to ask for a next appointment, the secretary said that this doctor also treats adult eye diseases! He remembers fifteen years ago when his dentist pulled out two wisdom teeth and asked him why, until now, when he was over 40 years old he never had extracted these two teeth, not earlier, in America, with advances in medicine had the opportunity to discovered and often cured at an early age.

The first time he met at the clinic, after taking out the prisms to measure the angle, he told the nurse to make an appointment for the patient to have surgery. Surprised, I replied: *"I wish I had met you 45 years ago"*, although it is late and incurable to make his left eye seeable, if he had done this before by the age of 6, not only was his eyes normal, but his vision was also corrected.

He found that in the US, there were few adults with eye defects like his, or cleft lip, just because they had the opportunity to cure them at a young age, that's also why he kept looking for specialists. In terms of adults, they only treat diseases such as torn retinas, cataracts, lasik... Remember when his wife gave birth at the hospital, in the first few days, many pediatricians came in to examine the baby, about the body, skin, ears, eyes, nose... to see if there was any disease, referred go to the specialist doctor right away, since birth until 18, visit pediatrician's office more often to have vaccination, annual checkup, nutrition, they measured weight, height, check for abuses...

In the United States thanks to abundant and advanced medical facilities, parents with low income immediately give WIC programs (Women, Infants, and Children) to help with nutrition problems for babies because malnutrition also affects intelligence. Later on, children of school age had to submit all required documents, lack of immunizations would mean being late to school, schools would not accept them, diseases such as paralysis, and smallpox had gradually disappeared, and other birth defects were common but doctors would treat them early.

The results of the surgery were exactly what he expected. His second homeland gave him the opportunity to have a pair of straight eyes, normal like everyone else, no one dared to poke fun at his little quirks. Although the results of eye treatment are nearly 50 years late, he feels more confident and confident than ever.

Since the old days, his wish has been just to be a normal person like everyone else, always happy and satisfied with what he has, not clingy, and always hope, never ever give up, if fate has not come or not, he thought. If his daughter didn't have pink eye, the doctor didn't refer a friend, and he didn't follow her to the clinic, to see the doctor, he would probably still be looking somewhere far away. He also hopes that those who have the same disease as him, have hope because there is a cure. Those who have children, before the age of 5, even though they see normal eyes, should bring their children to be tested with pediatric ophthalmologists for their eyes to be sure rather than wait until old age and that is too late.

When he brought their daughter to the clinic to give gifts to the ophthalmologist after surgery, he gently said: "You don't have to do that, it's my responsibility and that is my job."

The doctor said that, but he knew that this American doctor was very touched in his heart, there were patients who thanked him after being treated, even though it was more than 45 years late. More than forty-five years ago, if he had been destined to meet this doctor, he thought, he would not have been born at that time yet!

2003

MEMOIR OF A TRIP

Participant number: 393-702-vb70104

https://vvnm.vietbao.com/a162730/hoi-ky-mot-chuyen-di

Viet Bao: Mr. Hoa Ngoc Hoang is one of the authors who was awarded the honorary prize for Writing On America in 2002, for the article "Preserving Ancient Relics". Mr. Hoang's job works as an Assistant to the City Manager, and with the Community Redevelopment Agency (CRA) in a city in the South of Florida. Living far from California, he stays busy, but Mr. Hoang still doesn't mind putting in hard work to fly back to California to meet and write about America, not just to receive an award that is not enough money to cover the cost of the journey, but just because he wants to "contribute to keep the tradition called 'Common Flame...'"

The following is a memoir of his trip.

I did not plan to go to South California to attend the Vietnamese Newspaper Awards ceremony on December 27, 2002, for many reasons. The cost of the trip is higher than the prize received, and it is the holiday season so there are not many seats left for flight, and there is no time to buy tickets in advance.Thinking about it for a long time, in my heart, I still see that something is not right.

Going to the Write On America awards gathering is not to brag about or to have dinner at a restaurant, but to contribute to something worth doing. With the Writing On America award, the Vietnamese brothers and sisters who have lit the torch, perhaps we, the participants in the game, must contribute to keeping the common flame from dying out. Thinking like that, I found that if I was afraid to waste time and money, I missed the meeting, my heart would be uneasy.

Last week, Ms. Quyen of the Viet office reported contacting me by phone and left a message, just wanted to call Ms. Ngoc back for more details to receive and attend the award ceremony. When

I returned to the office, I called Ngoc again and said that I could only attend for one person, because I couldn't buy a plane ticket for the whole family to go to California, my family couldn't take a leave because at the end of the year, the bank very busy. Going to the Internet to look for tickets, I found a pretty cheap "package" that included airline tickets, hotels, and cars. At the end of the year, I don't want to bother anyone, pick me up, and stay with them, so in my opinion, self-sufficiency is the best. I'm in the US, anything can be done if you want and are prepared.

FLIGHT TO CALIFORNIA

I left South Florida on Thursday afternoon, the day after Christmas, and it was warm and sunny. As planned, after changing flights in Newark, the plane would arrive at Santa Ana airport that evening, so I had a Friday, walking Bolsa Street before going to the party. But the airline, it is not as good as planned. The flight from the sunny city of Florida to Newark Airport in New Jersey was just in time for the Christmas blizzard to start, causing many flights to be delayed. When the plane was still 45 minutes from the airport, the control tower ordered it to fly around in the sky waiting for the arrangement of the landing area. After an hour of circling in the sky, the pilot gave a prediction when I arrived, which was also the time my connecting flight took off!

I signaled to the flight attendant that I needed her to notify the pilot so they could call the other flight to "wait" for me for five minutes, she replied that when I landed, a tram would take me to the other gate, so don't worry. By the time the flight landed, I had reached the gate, and I found that it was over five minutes for the connecting flight to California. Met the airline staff at the gate, and he told me the flight had taken off. The American couple sitting next to me going to San Diego had the same fate. When we got to the counter for customers who *"missed the flight"*, we were told it was the last flight of the day to California, including to the Los Angeles airport. I let them know I needed to get to California the next Friday, before 5 pm for the event.

Flights were mostly full, but finally got a seat for me the next day, a seat in the middle and rear seats of a Boeing 737-700. This type of seat is so narrow that even a small Asian like me would not expect to have a place to move. Thanks to the Eastern time 3 hours ahead of the west, my flight to South California the next day would have to arrive at John Wayne airport by 2 pm. They also told me that the plane was late because of the control tower's fault, not the airline's, so they didn't pay the cost of the hotel for me to stay overnight, even though I took the time to ask to meet all their *"supervisors"* there to complain. Not get into an argument because they point fingers at the tower. I had to take the metro and take the bus back to the hotel.

Because the airport was delayed, the two hotels next to the airport were full, so I had to choose a place farther away. It is true that it's commercial in the US, the hotel is so affordable, guests *"missing"* the flight like me have no other choice. I don't know where my luggage is lost, with only a set of clothes and a small handbag, entering the hotel to take a bath, put on my old clothes, have dinner and go back to my room, I feel better and happier than any homeless people. The American hotel is fully equipped and convenient, I washed my socks, hung them on the heater, dry the next morning, not afraid to disturb the sense of smell of passengers on the next day's flight.

So tired, I didn't know when I fell asleep, I woke up at 3 am, because there was a quarrel from next door. I don't know if the couple was arguing because of the flight delay, because of the hotel expenses, or for many other reasons. Hearing them raise their voices, I hoped I wouldn't be on the same flight with them in the next morning. Trying to get back to sleep but could not, I decided to wake up, take a shower make a cup of hot tea, and then check out and go to the airport early. If there is another blizzard, being stuck at the hotel is miserable. When the hotel bus entered the airport, I was surprised to see a lot of traffic and people, maybe the same fate as me the night before, and couldn't sleep, afraid of being late for the next flight. The airport, it was only 5 a.m., was already packed with people.

The flight to California took off more than half an hour late because of the control tower again, but the pilot said he would shorten the flight time in the air. After more than five hours on the air, the plane landed at the airport on time, plus an extra hour waiting for luggage and rental car, when I got to the hotel and checked in, in front of the South Coast Plaza, there were two hours left to prepare. Fortunately, my luggage was not lost, the hotel had room and there were no lovers next door like the night before.

THE AWARD CEREMONY

As promised to Ms. Ngoc in Viet Bao, she told me that it would be 5 o'clock when I parked in front of Seafood World restaurant, I looked at my watch, and I arrived 15 minutes earlier. The brothers in the organizers are preparing the banner in front of the shop, the receptionists are standing in front of the newly printed books. After chatting briefly, buying some books and *"cassettes"*, and going back to put them in the car, when I went back to the restaurant, I immediately met a woman with a file in her hand. It turned out that this was Ms. Quyen of Viet Bao who was looking for winners to fill out the tax paper for IRS.

Quyen and Ngoc set me up to sit with other winners, and everyone introduced themselves, including Ms. Phong Lan, the author of *"Mobile Americans"*, Mr. Tong Minh Chau and his two children, Mr. and Mrs. Hoang Ngoc Hien, Mr. Le Hien and a young girl, Faith Linh Ngo, are studying at university and learned that she is a vegetarian. Particularly, Ms. Phong Lan had the courtesy of bringing a bottle of *"Remy Martin"* still in the box, saying to meet another winner, Bo Tung Ma, the author of *"Mr. Ba Anguish"* to *"drink"*. A representative of the Viet Bao Award, Mr. Nguyen Minh, came to sit at the same table, happily "supporting" us together before accepting the award. Later, I learned that Mr. Minh was one of the two signatures on the checks of the *"Viet Bao Award"* awarded to the winning authors. Thank you, Phong Lan, and thank you Mr. Minh and his friends for discussing this unforgettable memory.

I couldn't count the number of people in attendance, but the restaurant was full. The winners and their family members occupy most of the left side of the restaurant, where blue balloons hang. Both American and Vietnamese guests sat on the opposite side of the stage. Ms. Nha (I heard her employees in Viet Bao called this to Ms. Nha Ca), then went to greet each table. Asking Mr. Tran Da Tu where was he? she said that he was still at the editorial office, taking care of the next day's newspaper. So is Mr. Phan Tan Hai. Unfortunately, everyone is busy, so I didn't have the opportunity to talk about her family house next to mine in Hue.

The award ceremony took place in a very cozy atmosphere. The food is also delicious, with all seafood except for the tofu dish, which is favored by little Linh Ngo because she is a vegetarian. There are many people like me, even though they don't know anyone at the party, they still feel an invisible bond with everyone. The atmosphere was very touching when the organizers introduced Mrs. Trung Quang, an author who, despite being 92 years old, still had an article about America and also flew back from San Jose to attend the meeting. 20-year-old student Faith Linh Ngo who sat at our table also flew back from San Jose.

The two authors have an age gap of up to 70 years, showing me more that the invisible thread of the Writing On America award is indeed powerful, connecting generations of Vietnamese in the US. I also feel that this bond of affection is being extended even more when I hear the organizers announce that there will be more Awards for Writing On America in English. Thus, the children who were born and raised in this second homeland will have the opportunity to write and read, share their experiences, failures and successes so that generations of their fathers can see and see them together provide for each other.

Mr. Tu introduced when presenting the awards to the authors, he summarized the details of the article and the author's biography in a concise and touching way. Poet Du Tu Le as well as Mr. Do Ngoc Yen of Nguoi Viet Daily News expressed their enthusiastic opinions about writers and readers. Except for author Nguyen Ha, who was not able to attend the final final due to a traffic accident last week, thanks to his brother, musician Trung Nghia, who received the award on his behalf, most of the award-winning authors reside in California attended.

I see the spiritual and material hard work of the employees of the Viet Bao daily news for the program Writing On America. As a Vietnamese come to this multicultural homeland, I often dream of Vietnamese people having the opportunity to create a cultural center that not only preserves traditional culture but also develops cultural heritage. multifaceted in this free land. Although Vietnam has experienced many ups and downs, life changes and bans, this free country will give us the opportunity to create, preserve what we have. First Amendement give us freedom of speech will give us an objective view and way of speaking that has not been found in our first homeland until the day when *true freedom* comes.

The party ended when my watch, which was still Florida time, was just over one o'clock in the morning. I went back to the hotel and slept well. When I woke up, I saw that California's clock was still 6 am (9am EST), so I took my car to Bolsa Street to buy some gifts back to Florida. Early in the morning, even though it is Saturday, no shops are open yet, so I have to go to... Pho for a big bowl of hot noodle nicknamed *"aircraft carrier"*.

The Pho restaurant was already crowded early in the morning. After eating a bowl of hot pho, I found it not only cheaper but also more delicious than the pho usually eaten at restaurants in Florida.

FLIGHT BACK HOME

The plane took off from the runway at John Wayne Airport at 6:45 am. I changed back to an earlier flight. The night before, I went to bed at California time after listening to the radio talk show hosted by Thai Ha's on Little Saigon radio about cosmetic surgery, but woke up Florida time, and got to the airport too early. Had a delicious bowl of pho to fill my stomach, returned the rental car, and got on the plane, I didn't want to eat breakfast but fell asleep.

When the plane landed at George Bush Airport in Houston, Texas to connect flight to Florida, the airline employee made it difficult for me, refusing to let me take an earlier flight to Florida even though there was still room. She used the excuse that the luggage had to be accompanied by a passenger. Knowing that begging could not be because of the new law after 911, I had to find a corner, chat on the phone with some friends in Houston, and wait 7 hours for my flight. When the plane went to the runway, he was ordered to wait because of bad weather, strong wind, and heavy rain. Finally, after waiting another hour, the plane took off, but I feel 10 minutes after takeoff I was swinging like Tarzan because the plane shook violently due to bad weather.

The pilot announced that the airport had decided to close due to the weather after allowing him to take off. I almost got stuck there. Looking back on April 75, I remember that I too had left my homeland on the last flight.

Although the plane was more than an hour late and had to fly in bad weather, it also reached Florida before the *"airport curfew"*. When I waited to receive my luggage, I did not see my two suitcases anywhere. Everyone on the flight had already left, and the luggage machine had stopped working, I went to the counter to complain about lost luggage, frustrated to see people lining up. The clock was past midnight, I finally managed to get in to see the staff, when in the corner of the room, I saw my two suitcases lying there. The staff member said that it had arrived in the morning and no one had received it, you must have been *"late"* for the flight! I didn't waste time explaining at length to her either. Dragging two suitcases to the parking lot, remember that the airline employee in Houston insisted that she respect the rules of traveling with luggage. Turns out it was her airline company that was the violator.

Although the trip was short, I really learned a lot from my eyes and ears. As a construction official of a city, having worked on many projects, I know the difficulty is not in the beginning, but in making the project successful or reaching the destination and maintaining it.

My wife picked me up at the airport, the car came home, the lights in the neighborhood were off, and everyone was asleep. Opening the door to the house, our daughter ran out and hugged her father. Even though it was late at night, the little girl was determined to stay up and wait for her father to return. Her loving arms have melted away all my fatigue in the days away from home.

First day of the calendar year 2003

Viet Bao Daily News award Writing On America 2002 - California

CHAPTER VII
LEARNING AND PRACTICING A SCOUTING LIFE

ONCE A SCOUT, ALWAYS A SCOUT...[33]

CUB SCOUT – BACH DANG SCOUT GROUP[34]

Cub Scouts consisted of young (Wolf) Cubs (ages 6-12) who could not ride bicycles by themselves, so they often followed their siblings or parents to the weekly meeting place, at Vuon Doat, a local park behind the Hue Central General Hospital or sometimes the campus of the Hue Girls High School. Personally, my brother asked Akéla (Cub Scout Leader) to pick me up every Sunday morning and take me home after the meeting. Ms. Akéla lived in the Van Van Tomb area, so she only went a little further to reach my house. She drove a Velo-Solex with white cap, which was a luxury at that time. She worked for the Library of Hue University, so the Wolves could borrow books to read from the library. This was also an incentive that helped me a lot later because at that time it was not easy to secure good books or novels to read by Nhat Linh, Khai Hung, or Thach Lam in the *"Tu Luc Van Doan"* group. So I passed the essay I took for the entrance exam at National Academy High School for the sixth grade, thanks to books from the Hue University Library: they helped me understand a lot about Literature. The Tintin comic books with the spiky hair boy were also liked by the Cubs because the pictures and the simple French in cartoon style made them easy to understand. We loved them because they were all hard-cover and the prints were beautiful. Watching comics also helped with foreign language skills and books on translation were also not lacking there. There were so many good books here

---

33. *Scout Chief P. Jacques Sevin, Secretary General of the International Bureau of the French Catholic Scouts Association, wrote on page 158 of "Le Scoutisme" published in 1933 that the author of the above statement was Lord Kitchener. During the Boy Scouts' meeting in Leicestershire in April 1911, Lord Kitchener proposed the slogan. Lord Kitchener was a Field Marshall in the British Army, who served as Britain's Chief of War at the beginning of World War I; In addition, at one time he held the position of President of the Scouts of North London. (According to documents of Vietnamese Scout Leader Thuat Van Nguyen - Australia).*

34. *Bach Dang is a famous river (White Wisteria River) located in North Vietnam near Ha Long Bay. Famous because the Vietnamese won all the battles and pushed back the Northerner (Chinese and Mongolian) invaders in 938, 981 and 1288 to become independent.*

that were not available in Elementary or High School, including martial arts novels by Jin Yong.

The Wolf Cubs had to record their *"good deeds"* in a small notebook called the *"Good Work Book"* every day and submit it to the leaders at the end of the week for review and criticism. Some Wolfs didn't write anything; some wolves just wrote a simple task, such as spotting a banana peel in the middle of the road, being afraid that someone might step on it, slip and fall, picking it up, and throwing it in the trash bin, or helping parents and siblings with small things around the house, the purpose is to teach the children beyond the real-life slogan: *"Try your best"* and *"Help yourself, help the world"*, also get used to honest expressions, and familiarize yourself with honesty and trustworthiness by writing: *I have no good deeds today to write down.* No *"made up"* story to lie about (prohibited in the Scouts) and that practice taught me to start writing.

By looking back at Hue, my hometown, I see how the means of borrowing and reading books should be encouraged early for students to help them in later life, as I have personally observed. While elementary schools have no library and high schools have a library, it is so limited. The library is pretty much lacking materials. When I came to Saigon, I was surprised to continue studying at the Vietnamese American Association: students there had a lot of incentives to pursue books and culture, especially foreign languages. They had literary discussion groups after reading books. Although my basic command of foreign languages is not that bad (because I had studied English in Hue), compared to the level of students in the capital, it was far different, as Saigon was less affected by the war than the other parts of the country, and they had more incentives and facilities.

I remember the day our group left the Cubs to join the Boy Scouts. The Cub Scout leaders stood on the right bank of the Perfume River to see us off, taking a boat across the river, a transitional Scout tradition. Every one of them cried; our group transitioning to Boy Scouts was the largest, with about 7 or 8 of us including 2 of each in 4 Den groups: White, Gray, Brown, and Black. Most of the Cub Scout leaders have been lost. At that time, Akéla was Ms. Tran Thi Bich Huong, and Baloo was Ms. Nhuan

[35]. Baghéra was Ms. Mui (who died in the fiery red summer of 1972).

In the Cub Scouts, the motto was *"Effort"*. The leaders took care of everything: we couldn't do a chore even if we had wanted to, because we were so young; when you are going to camp, the leaders even feed you. When we went to sleep, they also surrounded us; going to Thuan An beach to bathe, they would build a fence around the Cubs; each one left his hat on the beach before jumping in the water. On shore, when going back, whenever they happened to see any hats left, the leaders would panic in their attempt to find the missing Cub, until they were sure that none of the boys were still in the water; then they fed them fully, feeling happy like a fairy. Every Sunday morning, I was picked up by Akéla to go to the meeting on a Vélosolex [36]. The meeting place every week was the park inside Dong Khanh Girls' High School.

BOY SCOUTS

From the Cubs of Bach Dang Group with four Dens of White, Gray, Brown, and Black, the leaders took care of everything, from cooking to clothing; we were very happy, so the day we joined

35. *During Scouting activities, she held the position of Baloo (Bear), names were taken from the Jungle Book. The Cubs scout, although still young, knew that she loved an ARVN officer, for unknown reasons, his family did not approve, at that time she was not normal, sometimes she was talking by herself, she loves the cubs very much, so she often takes pictures during meetings, only to find out that there is no film when she opens the camera. A short time later, I realized that the two of them were so close, they really loved each other, so the family had to let them get married and I saw that her spirit returned to normal. I don't remember how long it took to hear that he was killed in battle field and at that moment she became truly insane. The whole group went to his funeral without seeing her cry. After that, I never saw her again. A love, a sad story for the tragedy of the Vietnam war.*

36. *My Akéla, volunteering to drive me to meetings at the youth group every weekend, she is also the Director of the Hue University Library, where I have been able to use and borrow the books here even though I am only a elementary and high school student. The book that I had a chance to borrow and read from a University of Hue Library has helped me a lot academically, including this book. She worked in Saigon and immigrated to the US in April 1975, settled with her family in Miami, Florida and now retired to Southern California.*
The VéloSoleX bikes, manufactured by Dassault, Renault, Motobécane, France, has a small engine in the front, when the engine is started, the lever is pushed forward, and it can be pedaled like a bicycle if needed.

the group, I also thought there would also be other big brothers taking care of us all in Boy Scouts, probably not too bad. The Cub leaders said goodbye to us, as we departed from Thua Phu pier; when the boat got to Phu Van Lau pier, on the other side on the left bank, we were blindfolded by the Patrol, using our scarves. Tuan and I were told to sit down by the Lions Patrol, the leader said I will let you drink coffee, and eat cakes, told you to open your mouths, my nose could smell "*coffee*" and "*gateau*" cakes, so we liked it. When we open our mouths, who knows that they had put in a handful of burnt rice, let you drink a glass of fish sauce, later learned that the tradition of joining the patrol is "*burnt rice with fish sauce*", that's the tradition with the Lion Patrol for novices to join the group, but for the other three patrols of Bach Dang as Nightingale, Crocodile, and Wolf, the ceremony was a secret of the patrols so I didn't know anything at all about it.

We didn't have flags in the Cub Scout Den, so when we saw that the Lion Patrol flag was for our group, I was impressed: the stick was formed from a hardwood tree and varnished, carved beautifully with a lion's head on top. In addition to the patrol flag, there was also a badge and a few small flags below, which were the winner's flags for the games, passed on from Vinh Pho's time, when the patrol group let us visit the Patrol office, a garage near the vice patrol leader's house, which had been remodeled and was spacious. After rolling, I later learned that only a few *"rich boy"* teams could have that honor. In my Lions Patrol, after Mr. Loc and Trung went to Venture, Mr. Tung received the Patrol leader's position. There were seven people, three of whom had Trung as their first name; so we added three words next to Trung's first name: in order of age, the oldest was Trung Ro, the next was Trung Bi, and the youngest Trung Hung.

In Boy Scouts, everything has to be done, according to the method of an "*autonomous patrol*", doing it yourself, like cooking. eating, washing dishes, or setting up a tent, from which to learn from the leaders and others. The Scout Motto here is also *"Be Prepared"*, so learn to be self-sufficient. Each patrol holds separate meetings every weekend, then there is a group meeting once a month or a meeting in Nam Giao Hill. Then, every once in a while, there will be a local *"all-group meeting"*. Every time I had a chance to go to the *Red Fire Center*, my heart was always hung up on it days beforehand.

When the gathering was crowded and serious, Bach Dang's group consisted of Cubs, Boy Scouts, Venture, and Rover Scouts, that is, a full Group. My family had three brothers, all in 3 groups; I was the only one who participated in both Cubs and Boy Scout activities; my brother transferred from Chi Lang Cub Scouts, my sister worked as a leader with the Me Linh Girl Scout group and the oldest brother was in the Rover Scout led by Mr. Anh Gia Phan. The Boy Scout leader was Mr. Hong Van Tran (Quoc Hoc Professor). At that time, there were many families in Hue who were Scouting, but now I only remember the Ly family near Dong Ba bridge, the Tran family, the Ai Hoa bookstore family on Tran Hung Dao Street, the Uncle Xang family or Nguyen Huu family but there were certainly a lot more I did not know of.

In addition to the team activities every week, we went to camp. The situation at that time was no longer safe in areas such as Hon Chen Palace and Gia Long Tomb, so the furthest we went was Thien An Hill or Linh Mu Pagoda, where there were trees, and where nuns even gave us salt to eat with figs. Then there was the Duya-ra (Jerard) Building, the Nam Giao Hill or the Tu Hieu Pagoda, and the closer places like Tinh Tam Lake or the Citadel; every time we went camping, the bicycles of the teams were full of things and more bamboo stick *"spike handles"*, and the patrol leader had a team flag, erected in front of the bicycles, or tagged on the side of the bikes. Each stick was covered with conical spikes below to set up a tent; every time a bicycle was *"missing the slug"* it was miserable: the whole team had to stand around and wait, or they helped each other fix it.

The meeting place was not always certain, so before the meeting, the students had to take turns delivering the news to each other; they had to cycle to each house to announce it. This was also the penalty task assigned to the patrol member who was late to a meeting. or failed to go to meetings regularly or accidentally uttered bad words. At that time, communication was not like now, with phones and cars, but even if it was just a bicycle, our information system was not interrupted.

The tents bought or obtained from the military surplus at that time were very poor, inverted V-shaped, thick canvas, sticks at both ends; on the ground, there was no lining like modern tents today, and the whole patrol of 8 people huddled together. Good luck, with how happy you were when you were in the Cubs; when you eventually graduated to the Boy Scouts, you had to learn to do everything yourself. Although we had dug trenches on both sides of the tent, each time when it rained, we were dry in the middle, while both leaders on the outside got wet. Memories that I thought I would never have again, because life was different for each generation. At that time, we used military leftovers, tents, parachute cords, khakis, boots, outdoor cooking utensils, or backpacks… it was easy to find or buy anything at the flea market. There were also MRE canned foods, which were light but not damaged, but the hardest thing was to bring duck eggs because they were easy to break; if boiled first, only eaten with fish sauce, but we wanted to pour egg rolls or stir fry with vegetables – it had to remain the same, but the field dishes with rice were so delicious, because of hunger, because of fun or for some other reasons, I don't know for sure, but the big brothers prepared all kinds of food when we went camping together, which later helped a lot in daily life, the Bach Dang Scouts later were all famous good cooks, and learned to wash dishes when they got married.

ESCAPE, A SURVIVAL COURSE, AND THE MANUAL RICE COOKER

After I enrolled in school, I listened to the foolish advice of my oldest brother who told me that I needed to enroll in an escape course, survival in the woods in Santa Fe, taught by a Mr. McCullough. He said: we don't need to learn to write English, but only *"practice"* our conversation, which was beneficial later. It was also good to listen to, and to rely on myself having Scout family roots. It was probably not that bad. He also registered me in the course to bolster my confidence, because he had more experience in Scouting and Air Force training. After studying for a week, he said he had to relocate to Tallahassee because he had an FDOT job offered there. I was left alone with some 15 American students: *"It's good to leave, it's bad to leave"*, I stuck with it and had to continue with limited resources and without my brother. My teacher gave me 3 journeys; I had the right to choose 2. The first trip involved canoeing down a waterfall like in the movie *"Deliverance"*, then staying overnight in the forest. I declined that choice because I didn't have a partner for canoeing – tough to find a lightweight partner like me. The American students did not choose me, and besides, they were traveling as a couple.

The second trip was a hike up into a place called Great Smokey Mountains, Georgia. The teacher used a large van to bring his students to the foot of the mountain. It was then that I knew that the trip would be 20 miles (32 km) long. Before that, he only said to prepare 3 days of meals; the group consisted of 11 students plus a teacher, totaling 12, but later I found out that the other 10 were divided into couples, or they were lovers, or husband and wife, or they share the same hobby of *"smoking marijuana"* and getting into wild sex in the forest.

The teacher gave each person a map and told everyone to open their backpacks to check before leaving. I saw a lot of canned food and noodles with drinking water; my backpack had nothing but a bottle of drinking water, water purification tablets, dehydration medicine, a personal first aid bag including a snake bite kit, bags of rice, a packet of *"dried shrimp lice"*, cotton balls in a Ziploc bag. The whole class, except for the teacher, laughed. A student came over and lifted my backpack with one of his index fingers; he lifted it over my head easily because he was taller than six feet. I said because of was a small man, I could only carry that, and the teacher informed me that there was no shortage of spring water in the forest: just drop in the pack of purification tablets and/or boil it. When he asked me to lift his backpack, I gave up, because it was too heavy, probably full of canned food. The whole team departed at 10 am from the foot of the mountain; at first, the teacher was still following me, but then he also disappeared; on the trail was only me, because I knew everyone had gone before. I kept walking, singing: *"The road is far away, thousands of hooves fly ..."* [37].

According to the map, the trail sometimes had huts with maps and numbers to make sure people didn't lose their way or have to shelter from the rain. I wandered alone, drinking water or eating from a packet of beef jerky snacks when hungry or thirsty. Along the way the scenery was beautiful but I didn't pay much attention because I was afraid I would be stuck alone in the forest overnight. sometimes I saw waterfalls falling along the mountains, reminding me of Dalat. I met two pairs of classmates bathing in a waterfall;

37. *The song of the South Vietnamese Army by Musician Van Giang.*

they stopped, so I was able to pass. It took a long time to catch a glimpse of sunlight in the forest, but you only knew what time it was when you looked at your watch. I passed a point where there was a short pole, which was said to be the boundary of the three states of Georgia, Tennessee, and North Carolina, located at a point: a special landmark located on a high mountain. I am proud to have been there.

Arriving at the rendezvous around 5 pm, it was still light, because of summer. Being the 7th person, couples came later because they were acting playful, hiding in the bushes to do something, or bathing in a natural waterfall. But if they went on without stopping, I am sure I would have been the last to finish. Setting up a tent and resting, I chose a spot near a stream; the water was clear enough to see the bottom. It was beautiful; the teacher and some students were building a fire in the fire ring, and people prepared to avoid setting fire to the forest; the group of students and the teacher sat around the fire, I asked if I could use that fire to cook rice. They allowed me to use it, so I went to the stream, washed the rice, and put it in the pot, using two wooden sticks to support the rice cooker horizontally. Two students were cooking a pot of spaghetti noodles, working together at night [38]. Just as they were getting finished, two students carried a large pot to the stream to rinse with cold water; when going up one of them stumbled on the roots of a tree, tripped, and splashed the pot of noodles on the ground, I heard screams from afar,

After the guy fell and got up, he immediately went back to the batch of noodles and pulled the top back into the pot. I heard voices from afar: *"Oh No...I am not going to eat that sh--!"* The guy who fell kept saying *"Sorry..."* repeatedly.

The teacher asked whether my rice cooker was done. I showed him how to turn it upside down for it to cook on top. I explained the *"three-tier"* concept of rice to him, then told him to be careful since I didn't want to spill it like the other guy. He told me to let him do it; after ten minutes the rice was cooked; I took it out of the tree, and put it in a hole in the wet ground. He asked me why. I told him it was to cool it down so that the burnt rice would

38. *Before leaving, perhaps the whole group discussed whether to cook together, either I didn't know, or because I was the only foreigner in the class, they didn't know if I could eat shared food, so I bring my own food enough to use as the teacher instructed. They also went in pairs like lovers, only the Master and I were single people.*

peel off under the pot…He said he had never seen anyone do that before until now so I told him it was a synergistic experience in the Scouts.

After spilling the spaghetti pot, a few students took out more canned food; some ate the rewashed noodles on top. I looked around and saw I was the last one, so I opened the pot, took out a pair of wooden chopsticks fashioned from a tree branch in the forest to stir it, put the bag of shrimp lice and cooked meat into the mix, then scooped out a cup and politely invited the teacher and some students to try it, because I was hungry all day, so instead of cooking 1 cup of rice, I was cooking 3 cups. The teacher finished eating the rice bowl and told his students: *"He is the best rice cooker in the world!"*. He told me to sit down and give a lecture to the whole class on the process and how to cook the rice as well as I did in camp or at home, so I started to tell the story of going into the Scouts, rice cooked in a bamboo tube, then chicken wrapped in clay…with the campfire, the faster, the more convenient, whatever materials are available, the topic of living in the forest, survival technique – so the whole class listened attentively to my broken English presentation. The day we went back, I saw the teacher getting up very early; he said he then drove the van around to the other side of the mountain so that we could get back easier, not hiking so far when we came. The whole group went together; I noticed a few students waiting for me to go with them to talk intimately, instead of going ahead with the group; from time to time I saw a few people hiding in the bushes, later I found out that they had escaped from the group to smoke marijuana or do something together.

On the last trip of the course: the teacher told the class *"I want Hoa to come with me"*. This time he took us to a forest called Ocala National Forest, Florida, near the school and southeast of Gainesville. After wading through a muddy forest, we camped on dry land, this time I fed the whole class *sticky rice* mixed with *shrimp and meat lice*; everyone praised it, because Americans cooked rice both raw and pasty, they boiled the water first and finished it by pouring rice over it instead of using their fingers to measure it as we had learned in the Scouts. On the way back home, I saw people acting itchy and uncomfortable. I thought it was because I didn't shower with soap for two days, so when I got home, I went to take a clean shower, putting all my dirty clothes in the hot water washing machine... later the whole house complained of itching, and later we learned that there had been bedbugs in the forest, nowhere to be spotted because they were mixed in the clothes: when put into the washing machine, they did not die but spread to some of my friends. I washed up several times afterward, and the whole apartment pointed fingers at me; at that time Vietnamese students shared a house to share cooking sessions with cheaper Vietnamese food. The house had two rooms and could accommodate up to 5 students, but in the school dormitory, you had to eat American food every day; the room rate (dormitory) was more expensive than renting a house to share the rent.

On the way back, the group stopped at the foot of the mountain, in a small town with the beautiful name of Helen, Georgia. Here the Bavarian-style houses like in Europe were very cute. Stopped at a buffet *"all you can eat"* BBQ restaurant, and right in front of the entrance were two restrooms, for Men and Ladies. I read the words in English: *"Once you come in here, you must not return to the dining room, even if you have washed your hands"*[39]. After spending days in the forest, we all ate a meal that was *"worth the money"*.

A memorable course; some American students took it because they liked dating, having sex in the woods, and escaping to smoke marijuana – which was forbidden at that time. When they were young, they liked to go hiking and camping outdoors and share the same hobbies and many memories of natural life.

The next quarter, I met the instructor in the school again. He told me, you know, so far I have only given two people an "A" grade; you are one of those two because my students only went to the forest to secretly date or smoke weed. They relied on their strength for a solution, not their wits or experience like you, except for those with ambitions to join the Navy SEALs (SEa Air Land). In the United States, they had to go through tough living challenges and practice before performing their missions. I told him that if I joined the SEALs, I would dive and never emerge.

---

39. *"When you are here, you are not allowed to go back to dining room, even your hands are washed and cleaned". Their purpose is to limit diners who use the excuse to wash their hands or go to the bathroom to continue eating without limits. They only let them wash their hands once before eating.*

Later, when I had the opportunity to go to summer camps, as well as training camps in the US, I found that the camp here was large and fully equipped, such as the Tung Nguyen 4 course, Tanah Keeta Scout camp in Tequesta, Florida with thousands of acres, able to serve more than a hundred people, with air conditioning and a screened-in cafeteria. This was a special course where the majority of Vietnamese trainers let more than 70 Vietnamese students eat all the Vietnamese food they liked, and this was also the course with the most Vietnamese people bitten by American mosquitoes.

WOOD BADGE TRAINING STAFF FOR BSA SR-430 *TÙNG NGUYÊN IV 2001*

The World Scout Movement originated at the initiative of Lord Baden Powell (1857-1941), a former British lieutenant general famed for leading the battle to defend Mafeking (South Africa) with an army of about a thousand when the city was besieged and surrounded by eight thousand enemy Boers who had rebelled against the colonial regime. The Scouting movement was born in 1907 and was eventually brought to Vietnam in 1930.

As mentioned before, my entire family was devoted from an early age to Scouting in Hue, so when I went to the US, my brother was the one to reconnect with the movement, in 1983, after a meeting of veteran Vietnamese leaders in Costa Mesa, California, the overseas Vietnamese Scout Movement was reactivated, mostly in the United States, Canada, France and Australia, with the motto: *"Once a Scout, always a Scout"*.

Vietnamese Scouting units were established and operated under the auspices of the Boy Scouts of America (BSA) in the United States, after 1975 and 1983, along with the Girl Scouts of the USA. However, without a homeland, to preserve their cultural traditions, they are still allowed to hold activities together, under the auspices of the International Central Committee of Vietnamese Scouting (ICCVS).

To educate youth for leadership, as well as maintaining

traditions, the Canadian Scouts sponsored training, with senior courses called "Tung Nguyen" for Vietnamese leaders in Canada and at Gilwell School (UK). They then came to the United States BSA to sponsor training in the US. Tung Nguyen Course IV (BSA SR-430) was held at Tanah Keeta Scout Reservation Camp, Florida from June 2-9, 2001. This camp was in the Gulf Stream Council, 20 miles north of West Palm Beach, which is world-famous for the *"butterfly ballot"* of the November 2000 US Presidential election.

WoodBadge (WB), or *"Tung Nguyen"* in Vietnamese, was the most advanced training course of the Boy Scouts, involving leadership skills meant to guide children in the movement. Campers had to have had previous training and active time, as well as other mental and physical preparation. Particularly for the trainers, in addition to having a Wood Badge, they must also have been selected by a Course Leader and the Training Board and invited to *"volunteer"* to serve in the group. I passed this training course of WB in Atlanta (BSA 92-38), so I am fully qualified. Because the place of training was in the locality where I live, Course Director De Tan Nguyen perhaps needed a local man, assigned to the position of kitchen assistant, to provide food that could be purchased locally. It should also be added that this was the first course under the new program of BSA: the training staff had to provide all students with three meals a day, so that they could focus on their studies instead of the way it was before, where trainees had to take care everything, including daily cooking for patrols. Each way had its advantages and disadvantages. Here's what I wrote about this two-week trip, as a kitchen assistant.

Trainers and trainees: a total of more than 70 persons to feed with the limited finances of the Course; we did not expect that the kitchen would have enough staff. The two main chefs, Hong Bich, and Thuy Lan, decided they would feed all with delicious and exotic Vietnamese dishes, not American dishes (which are easier and quicker to prepare).

On the first day, Friday, May 25, 2001: Scouter Toan from Maryland asked us to pick him up at Palm Beach Airport (PBI). I'm sitting in my office, carrying my walkie-talkie right into the airport. He was the first to arrive, as a trainer.

The second day, May 26, 2001: After breakfast, Toan and I went to pick up Course Director De Tan Nguyen, coming in from Texas. De went to get a rental car and made an appointment to meet at the office of Bob Katz, a local Scout leader whose address De had used before for deliveries. Twenty-two baggage boxes filled up my Toyota minivan to the brim. Go to the camp to temporarily, stow everything in the Scoutmaster Lounge. It may have been called a *"room"*, but the area was only about 10 x 15 feet. After that, go back to the Airport, and welcome the first staff member from California, Ms. Tran Hong Bich. Her suitcase was full of things, and I saw all the kitchen stuff… Pho noodles, dried vermicelli, even a few bottles of soy sauce, all for the Vietnamese dishes that she had bought, carefully packed in boxes. Perhaps she had prepared *"nostalgia food"* for the staff and trainees, to bring back memories of their former lives: eating and sleeping were the basic elements...but in the Scout camp, there was little sleep, so they had to make up for it.

We go home. Called *"home"*, these are the 5 acres of land that I bought and haven't built on yet; only a *"double-wide"* mobile home that I call *"my farm"*. The Staff jokingly labeled it a *"ranch"*. When Scouter Long arrived, we invited each other to South Beach, Miami. When we got there, there was a spectacle of crowds, people wearing two or three layers of clothes, people with skimpy clothes, and even naked. Sorry for those who have never visited this place at night.

On the way home, there was a sound of hunger in the car, so we stopped at Denny's – open 24 hours – only Staffer Bich was faithful to the promised rule: *"No eating after 7:30 pm"*.

May 27, 2001: We waded into the nearby woods, cutting sticks from Australian eucalyptus and rose apple branches from the farm. Those will serve as walking sticks for Staff and participants.

May 28, 2001: Starting today, we go into the agenda called *"Staff Development"* for the actual course. We count six in the kitchen staff (Quartermasters): Steinmetz, Thuy Lan, Hong Bich, Nhan, Thang, and Hoa will have to take care of 70 hungry souls for 1 week. Mr. Steinmetz, an American and Tanah Keeta's camp manager, would find it difficult to work with Vietnamese cuisine.

May 29, 2001: The previous night, when we had returned to the Staff tent, someone nearly had to call 911, because Chief Cook Bich couldn't breathe, probably because of Florida's summer climate, which was very hot and humid. I assumed the duty of going to the market, one that the Cooks should logically have taken up, but in the end, I just followed the list and bought whatever they wanted, making bulk purchases at both Vietnamese and American food stores.

May 30, 2001: Scouter Toan returned to DC, and Nhan replaced him as a staffer. Today, the kitchen fed vermicelli noodles with split water spinach. It should be remembered that going to a camp with Vietnamese-flavored food was already good, but it became even more difficult to meet the standards with a large number of people and limited time. Today looked like being in thirty-six streets in Hanoi. Only Scoutmaster leader Hui was unable to eat; later we learned that he could not swallow noodles.

May 31, 2001: Let the kitchen team rest, especially the two main chefs, Nhan and Hoa, who were responsible for preparing the American breakfast: Waffles, Cereal, and coffee. We were asked by a Scoutmaster to pick up a male Venture Scouter of the Truong Son Group, arriving from California. Go to the Airport to find out that this male Venture has turned into *Sister* Thuy Tien, a girl's Venture. This was an early arrival, so the exception was usually the trainee, and the coach only met after the opening day of the camp.

June 1, 2001: This was officially the beginning of the *"hurricane season"* along the East Coast of the United States, especially in Florida, and also the last day for staff development, to prepare incoming participants for the opening of the camp. The ceremony of the staff at Charter House was very cordial: the two guests, Mr. Ranger and Ms. Sherri from the local Gulf Stream Council, had a touching meal together with us. An unforgettable day for those who had joined the Scouts to step into the path of helping themselves and others.

June 2, 2001: Today, the staff only took care of participants returning from far away. The number of 48 students was almost exactly as planned; there was one student who paid for the course but volunteered for the next course, asking for help from the culinary department. After seeing the kitchen, he changed his mind and applied to be a student again! This speaks to the harsh truth of *"We want to hide"*. At the opening time, a participant phoned in, saying that he had missed his flight and had to fly to Miami Airport

– quite far from the camp. Nhan from the quartermaster staff went to pick him up and both of them returned to the camp at 3 am the next morning.

Chicken noodle soup was planned for the evening, but the culinary department, when going to the pier to get supplies, saw that fresh fish had been brought to shore so they planned to make a braised fish dish the next day; the fresh fish should be eaten immediately – the other dish can wait; so the mackerel got fried up. Ginger fish sauce, including chopped mango… it was Southern style!

June 3, 2001: Six patrols gathered at 6:30 a.m.: Beaver, Bobwhite, Eagle, Fox, Owl, and Bear. Too bad for the participants coming back from the West; now their *"body clocks"* are half past three in the morning... After the spirit, gathered at Gilwell Field. We found out that Father Tien Loc, a veteran leader of the movement, would also attend from Vietnam. Surprised by his reuniting with some of his young men, after more than 20 years of separation: the *"fire of miles"* tradition once again lit up a Scout camp, similar to Dalat: the chance to meet. Once again, the songs he had composed resounded in the quiet forest, half a globe away.

June 4, 2001: My schedule today was to teach a training class on High-Performing Teams and Nhan took care of the rocket launch, so the kitchen was short of two people. Fried chicken with lemongrass was for lunch.

June 5, 2001: I was tasked with bringing Father Tien Loc (Camp's Catholic Priest, arriving from VietNam) to the Ft. Lauderdale airport, more than an hour's drive to continue his interstate journey. Singing: We are together today… resounding farewell. I took the priest along the coast, the famous street here of houses that even millions of dollars can't buy.

June 6, 2001: Today, some staff and participants set out for Brown Sea Island. This was a plan the students suddenly thought up for themselves, even though they had to eat, cook, study, etc. They are provided with the necessary food in the tents of each team. They arrived at the rendezvous, not knowing that swarms of hungry mosquitoes were waiting to share the food they had enjoyed these days. Everyone will be given a mosquito medal before leaving the island; the campsite was as beautiful as Dalat, as poetic as the lamenting lake because of the lament of the students: Oh why are there so many mosquitoes, hungry and loud like in the forest U bright. As for the quartermaster's team, because of a lack of students, sad or tired, had a day to recuperate and eat the leftovers from the previous day.

June 7, 2001: Some of the students, when they saw me handing out food to cook today... each team got a chicken, asked to find a "*magic potion*" to *"light the fire"* [40], lack of nicotine, heard that there were people who felt like fainting, but because of the rules of the course, they were afraid of "*forest fires*", and had to wait a few more days for their smokes because the staff was told that fire would be *"off limits"* in this area.

June 8, 2001: After two days and nights of being preyed on by hungry mosquitoes and *"no-see-ums"* [41], the graduates were taken to Florida beach, on a bus, while the kitchen prepared for the closing party that the two ended. The main female chef had carefully prepared a beautiful decoration, with flowers, fruits, and pine needles, mixed on a beautiful white tablecloth. Someone joked that it looked like her wedding.

In addition to the faculty and students, Tr. John Alline, class advisor, and George Randall returned from the BSA central office in Texas. Ronnie Oats, Chief Chau, Bob Norwillo, Lowell White of Gulf Stream Council, and my Akela Bich Huong from more than 40 years ago also attended. What an honor this training had been.

The training course went well, but the trainees still had to make a *"ticket"* for what they had learned. This was an obligatory duty and required for the candidate to wear a Gilwell scarf after the theory part.

---

40. *Scout leader slang for smoking while in camping.*

41. *In Florida, in addition to mosquitoes, gulls also have a small creature, invisible to the naked eye, so called "no-see-um", shaped like a pacman on a microscope, mouth bigger than their body, cling to people and sting. Because we can't see it, when it is bitten, it only feels a little pain, hands or feet, it likes people who wear perfume or allergies, hives arise and itches after being bitten by it, usually in dark places, humid and reed areas close to the coast, only the wind can cure it because it is small, so when there is wind, it hides or is blown away, high-rise buildings also cannot fly high, only low. This camp won the record for Vietnamese dishes on all days of the camp and was the camp with the most Vietnamese people bitten by American mosquitoes.*

June 9, 2001: A week had passed for the trainees and two weeks for the training team; today was the day to leave the airport for the majority to return, all of whom were scheduled to meet again, 7 years after 2002. Two weeks with many memories, busy to forget our summer afternoon sleepiness. Looking back at the deserted school camp, even though the night before an *"Order of the Arrow"* ceremony had taken place. Say goodbye to Tanah Keeta and Tung Nguyen 4 camps to see a future Tung Nguyen in a peaceful homeland, when the Scouting movement officially rejoined the WOSM [42].

Leaving, I still heard a singing voice behind:

...Back to Gilwell, Happy Land...

Scouting Story – Vietnamese Scout 7th Jamboree – Texas 2002 – Memoir

Our family set off to attend the 7th Vietnamese Scout Jamboree (called *"Thang Tien 7"* in Vietnamese) meeting camp on Thursday, June 27, 2002. On the way we visited the family of a retired acquaintance, in a coastal city of Northwest Florida, and by the way, we celebrated our first daughter's birthday, as she was just 5 years old.

Saturday morning; we stopped at the city of New Orleans, where there was a lot of French architecture and culture, the way, to visit a family of acquaintances we had not seen for a long time, then set off to go directly to Boy Scout Camp Strake in a direction north of Houston. I thought the camp was probably far from the city, in some remote place, but after crossing the highways, we noted the camp was not so far from the city, with most services not more than a mile from the camp gate: restaurants, hotels, shopping centers.

At the camp gate, we saw quite a few Scouts in Staff guiding

42. *The Scouting Movement of Vietnam (HĐVN) after shutting down at the end of April 1975 in South Vietnam, banned from domestic activities by the New Communist government, has since been moved to organized overseas according to other countries that had Vietnamese settlers under the name International Central Committee of Vietnamese Scouting (ICCVS). After 44 years, in 2019, the World Organization of the Scout Movement (WOSM) officially accepted the Vietnam Scouting Organization as the 170th member.*

in the parking lot. The registration office at the entrance was quite busy because there were a number of registration units on site, nameplates, and meal vouchers given out; then we boarded a white van of the organizers, to be taken to see the camping sites. The first was the Press tent, the Canteen, then the sub-camps of the units; then there was a camp for elders, with an air-conditioned meeting room, quite far from the main activity area, so a shuttle bus was required to get to the Canteen during the day.

On Monday morning, the first day of the camp, early morning we saw many guests visiting the campground; leaders and patrols were busy with procedures at the registration tent, then dispersing to the divided campgrounds. Houston's climate is quite hot and humid; we had come from Florida, a place that is also hot, but there is always a sea breeze or a thunderstorm in the afternoon to relieve a bit of the sweltering heat of the summer afternoon. Although the Camp had lots of trees and shade, many leaders had to "sweat it out"; maybe that is why at the last minute, the organizers postponed the opening ceremony to 7 pm, instead of 2 pm as planned.

The stage and the opening ceremony of TT7 camp

Lunch at the 2800 square foot "canteen"

The opening ceremony took place solemnly on the main stage. Many units from the United States, along with countries such as Australia, Canada, France, and Germany ... were represented, the hot Texas weather did not stop anyone, but some leaders and families, because there was no space at the seniors camp, or since they could not stand the sweltering heat of the Texas summer, had to rent a hotel nearby, in there, or go temporarily "wandering", because their place had been taken... such as Scouter TCH who came from Florida, or the Senior Scouter Tuyen Thuy from the San Jose golden flower valley...

After the opening ceremony, all went through the main campfire, a campfire with the colors of Texas cowboys performed by local units.

On Tuesday morning, the second day of the camp, activities took place at the press tent, the dining hall of the American Scouters, including a souvenir stall, which was attended by many patrons. This morning, a meeting for senior Scouters was held to vote as well as draft the program of activities for the next 4 years. Scout leader Thoai handed over the jade seal of the flag back to Scouter Chau and Nhan; then, the Deputy at the Office of the Board of Directors was approved by the General Meeting. Tr. Chau wanted to pass the main responsibility to Nhan after 2006, but Scouter Nhan only asked to be the "third crown prince" instead of a prince. Excited discussion with the decision to hold a seniors' camp in the summer of 2004 in Orlando, Florida was approved. After lunch, the General Scouter Conference was again held in the meeting room of the Senior's area, where there was an air-conditioner, so it was more comfortable. The conference, led by Scouter Chau and Nhan, took place with a large number of participants, and two parts of 14 points were concluded for submission to the General Assembly for approval the following evening. The meeting ended; the rain had just stopped, creating a cooler and more pleasant atmosphere.

Scouters Nghiem Van Thach, Nguyen Trung Thoai, and Nguyen Tan Dinh received North Star Medals from Chief Scouter Mai Lieu. All four chieftains are gone.

After dinner, there was a musical program by singer-songwriter Nguyet Anh, a Scout and a leader who held a one-day Scouting activity, to become a lifelong Scout. She came from Washington, D.C., and the Hung Ca Viet band in Texas, the program run by Rover's sub-camp had attracted seniors, parents, and some leaders without units. Unfortunately, the units and youth groups had their campfires, so they did not attend the events. The lively and exciting performance, which lasted for more than two hours, brought the audience back to the beloved Motherland of Vietnam through eloquent songs of national love. Thanks to the afternoon thunderstorm that made the climate quite comfortable, the concert ended with the Vietnamese version, Vietnam, Vietnam composed by Pham Duy, sung together in harmony by the whole group.

On Wednesday morning, the day for seniors and rover groups a trip to Houston was organized, visiting NASA, strolling through the Vietnamese Hong Kong 4 shopping mall, and especially the Youth group and all units held competitive sports games of the day. After dinner, the General Assembly was held in the main meeting room of the Seniors' area, with many leaders attending.

General Assembly session

INTERNATIONAL CENTRAL COMMITTEE OF VIETNAMESE SCOUTING

The main part of the meeting was the re-election of the Chairman of the ICCVS for the 2002-2006 term. The meeting took place with enthusiasm and excitement with two nominees: Leader Vinh Dao from France and Leader Nguyen Van Thuat from Australia, who had proposed a program of activities for coming years. As a result, Leader Nguyen Van Thuat was elected Chairman of the International Central Committee of Vietnamese Scouting (ICCVS)for the next term, replacing Leader Vinh Dao. Scouter Pham Ngoc Que Chi was appointed a Member of the Financial Supervisory Board. The last part of the AGM decided to vote for the 8th International Jamboree camp land in 2006; it took rather longer than planned, with three locations, Germany, France, and Southern California proposed. Two countries in Europe volunteered to organize; however, most of the leaders wanted the 8th Vietnamese International Jamboree camp to be held in the United States because of the number of campers attending, mainly because they could not afford to attend a camp in Europe. After more than two hours of discussion with many ideas and suggestions, including a proposal to organize in 2007 in France to be able to visit Gilwell Scotland on the occasion of the 100th anniversary of Scouting, the Assembly voted for Southern California to organize the 8th Jamboree. However, France will be an alternative in case of obstacles in Southern California for whatever reason. When I went back to my room to go to bed, I saw that the clock was already past three o'clock Thursday morning.

Today is the Independence Day of the United States; since the day of the Proclamation of liberty in 1776, every year, the citizens of the United States consider this an important holiday to mark and celebrate the day the United States completely dedicated itself to independence. After the September 2001 terrorist attacks, Independence Day became even more important. Particularly at Camp Strake, the American Scout volunteers who took care of the camp were surprised because the number of people visiting and attending the camp for the traditional day was so large; they never had to park their cars at the main gate, as well as the activities area, packed full of people, sitting or standing, especially the evening party, more than 1000 campers and over 3000 guests attended, a resonance in the Vietnamese community in Houston that benefactors directly or indirectly showed their strong support for a successful meeting.

Vietnam Scouting song before the opening ceremony of the General Assembly

Mr. and Mrs. Vu Tran, the parents of Deputy Camp Chief Kim Thoa Tran, and musician and matriarch Thang Tran contributed a lot to the Texas beef dish. Perhaps after the camp, the units operating here will not lack students to register, because the parents who attended noticed that many families brought their children along, "not yet wearing the Scout uniform". At the end of the party, in addition to the seniors or parents talking, a very Texas cultural program took place right on the main stage, including local singers and musicians. Before the party, leaders who had passed the Wood Badge training course in different countries met as a group reunion for the second time behind the press tent.

Friday morning, the last day of the camp, it was already hot in the morning. That morning, after breakfast, senior Scouts returned to meet to say goodbye and take souvenir photos; meanwhile, near the press tent area, the US group leaders were invited to attend the establishment of a representative group in the United States.

We departed for Houston again, after saying goodbye to those of the leaders we knew. Friday afternoon Scouter Huong, one of the sponsors of the 7th Jamboree, a former Bach Dang Rover group member in Hue, invited us to attend the meeting of Bach Dang and Dao Thua Thien at his house. The dinner was full of Hue specialties such as filter cake, wet cake with shrimp lice, beef vermicelli ... everyone enjoyed themselves after days of eating unlimited dry food and instant noodles at the camp. Even Senior Leader Thoai also attended, thanks to Scouter T. Lan the last minute: she took care of transportation for him and returned to the camp to await the flight the next day to go back to Canada. (He passed away on October 8, 2005 in Montreal, Canada).

Bach Dang Group reunion in 7th Jamboree 2002 – Lập, Lâm, Hòa, Châu, Luyến

Bach Dang group: Cub, Boy Scouts, Venture, and Rover reunion 2002-Bach Dang former scalf.

Front from left: HHHương(d), DPLuyến, HNChâu, TVLâu (Rover) HTLập (Venture)
Behind: HNHòa (Boy Scouts) MVDũng (Venture).

Leaving Houston at noon Saturday, we returned to Florida on Sunday night, after driving through five states: Texas, Louisiana, Mississippi, Alabama, and Florida.

A trip with a lot of memories, leaving a sunny area to go to a warmer and more humid place, a week of camp, quite long but time passed quickly, in a moment, and then we would meet again in the sunny summer of Florida in 2004, a place similar to Vietnam's climate, near the ocean, tropical fruits and especially famous tourist destinations will probably allow the seniors to reunite and have fun together during meeting days, especially the General Assembly Conference.

CHAPTER VIII
FAMILY AND FRIENDS

FAMILY TRIP
TRIP TO FIND COLLEGE...

Summer 2013

This is my little family memoir of visiting Universities in the East of the United States, from South to North, before visiting Florida State University afterward.

Sophia entered the 9th grade (High School) in 2011. After leaving the 8th grade, the last grade of junior high school, students who go on to the 9th grade often have to change schools. Where I live, there is a famous American oil billionaire named Bill Koch. This year he decided to spend $50 million to establish a private high school called "**Oxbridge** Academy", a combination of the names of two famous universities in the UK: **Ox**ford and Cam**bridge** University. The school, located at 3151 Military Trail, West Palm Beach, is a massive facility that had been acquired and remodeled to include sports fields like football and baseball. Here, in addition to the majors that they want students to familiarize themselves with, in an autonomous learning program like a University, each class had only 15-25 students, organizing and studying according to the University framework, not like other public high schools.

In order to be admitted to the school, in addition to exceptional high school transcripts, students must also have high-income parents to pay annual tuition of more than $30,000 per student. In the first year (Inauguration) they only select 25 students for the 10th grade and 100 for four 9th grades, including the founder's children. Excelling students are required to undergo an interview with the School administration.

When we applied for Sophia, we had to fill out complicated paperwork that required proof of both her parent's income; we were invited to present ourselves to the professors and administrators of the school during an open house, thinking it was just a high school, but when we arrived, they arranged greetings probably to make a good impression on the parents. Looking around, I didn't see anyone familiar. The person who came to greet us was a very friendly lady, and after talking to us, we learned that she was a Harvard Alumna and had come down from the North. Seeing the credentials of the future staff and faculty of the school, we thought perhaps this was a school that would train students who could succeed in entering university or even beyond. Sophia was called in for an interview and they talked to her for quite some time. When we were notified of the acceptance letter, we looked at each other: *"Now, where do we get the money to send our child to this school?"* Annual tuition: over 30k dollars.

When we went back to the school to meet the Admissions Director, who was the one who had interviewed and accepted Sophia, we met a Professor named Fred McGaughan, who had come from Princeton Academy of the Sacred Heart in Princeton, N.J. *(he passed away in 2016, at age 59)*. He said that Sophia had been selected and this was *an interview for parents*. Turns out that parents also had to be interviewed!

Did they choose so carefully? We informed him that our finances are not like those of the school founders, so the decision to send our child here or to public school would depend on many factors including money/cost. He looked at us and said after interviewing Sophia, he wanted to accept her to study here, because he appraised her ability above what he expected, so he could help. He brought out all sorts of papers and told us to fill them out. Having become a *"professional"* in filling out financial aid forms, I did it as fast as *lightning*. He read it and said, *"Your handwriting is so beautiful. I have never seen anyone fill out forms so quickly."* I looked at him and said, *"When I applied to go to UF in Gainesville, I didn't have a dime in my pocket, I had to: I applied for a four years scholarship; everything to fill in having to do with income or finances was zero!"* He said that if Sophia was approved, it would also be for 4 years, but the condition was to maintain high grades throughout the years. When Sophia was informed of her full scholarship, we decided to send her there instead of public school. For 4 years, the school had its cooking chef/staff in the kitchen for breakfast, lunch, and snacks during the day for students, free of charge. Each student when entering the school was provided with a brand new *Apple MacBook* laptop for free and they say that after graduation, you do not have to return it: it is a *"rich family"* school. Taking care of school lunches for their children when they go to school early in the morning was a concern for many parents; we comfortably did not worry about this for 4 years at the school. Many American parents complain that the food at school is too delicious so when the children come home, they criticize the dishes their parents cooked at night...

The school also does not choose a *valedictorian* after each year of the 12th grade, because the administration says that doing so would upset the good students who are not selected. Each student was selected by an office worker or professor to advise and guide as a mentor. This was the way of working at the university level or higher at the professional schools that they introduced very early to the high school level.

At the end of the 10th grade, before entering the 11th grade, in June 2013, we decided to pay an exploratory visit to universities for our daughter, in the East of the United States, on the occasion of visiting my brother's friend in Canada, Niagara Falls and the places where Sophia would buy wool for her knitting hobby. All the planning for the trip was prepared by Sophia in advance: my wife and I were just mentors.

The trip started from Florida, on **Wednesday evening, June 12, 2013**. After coming home from work, I stopped by to pick up a rental car from Hertz near Palm Beach Airport: a new Altima with *"Never Lost Navigation"*, satellite system, and internet, so I was not afraid of losing my way; before that Sophia had entered all the data into the computer, just downloading it. The whole family loaded up the car; it was almost 8 pm so we only targeted driving to Melbourne Beach and would spend the night there, two hours' drive to the place, all our belongings still in the car.

Sophia was so excited, for this *"exciting"* trip, that she set the alarm clock for 4:30 am. The clock was an iPad left in the living room, so it was impossible to snooze a few more minutes, everyone had to wake up, take a shower to wake up and hit the road. Just stopped to fill up at Eau-Gallie on I-95 and it was almost 6 am.

Thursday morning June 13: I-95 North freeway was empty in the early morning, no traffic jams, only when entering I-295 in Jacksonville to bypass the city did traffic slow down a bit. Expected to stop at Santee, South Carolina at Exit 98 for lunch, because in 2010 while on our way to D.C., we stopped here to get gas and discovered there was a Bojangles Fried Chicken restaurant that sold delicious dirty rice. Arrived at noon, filled up with gas and a picnic portion of dirty rice for each person. To save time, we decided to eat in the car, with passengers feeding the driver after eating, to reduce drowsiness and shorten the time. Santee was about halfway from Florida to DC and also about midway through South Carolina.

At the South of the Border (NC and SC), there was no reason to stop, so continued to drive to the border of North Carolina and Virginia, then stopped at Welcome Center for stretching; then onward via I-95 and bypassing the city of Richmond, via I-295. At this point, the weather changed: rain and strong crosswinds made it unwise to run quickly.

From Fredericksburg to Washington, we've seen traffic jams, southbound more than Northbound because people were coming home from work in the afternoon, and the road from Woodbridge was full of traffic. In the 1980s, Springfield was far away, but now the areas around Washington, D.C. had expanded further, so traffic jams could not be avoided.

Since we did not plan to drive to DC, instead of spending the night in SC or NC, Sophia didn't reserve a room in Northern Virginia; she got on Expedia through her iPad in the car and found that there was room at Homesuites Hilton, a location right in Falls Church, for only $90. When we came in, I could see how the hotel was newly-built, and fully equipped, with free breakfast and dinner. Unfortunately, by the time we arrived, they had just closed the dining room. The bedroom was large and clean with a big refrigerator and a kitchen.

Carry all the luggage up to the room on a big trolley; it was still light because it was only 8 pm in the summer. We just went to the *Vietnamese Seven Corners* area to have dinner; when we got there, some shops were closed, but I spotted Nha Trang grilled spring rolls. Although it was closed, there were customers, and when asked, they said OK, so we came in. The grilled spring rolls here are no longer served to customers like a few years ago, but they made them ready to eat, not by yourself, and the snail noodles are not that bad. The snack shops were closed, so we had to go back to the hotel without any snacks to eat at night, as was our usual custom.

Friday morning, June 14: After a long sleep to regain my strength, when I woke up, the hotel had just finished breakfast, so the whole family stopped in the Arlington Boulevard neighborhood to eat Pho: bowls of noodles. In this area, there is a quite a crowd of Pho 75 restaurants and a Vietnamese bakery. The Pho here was passable, had a proper aroma of pho, but probably cooked with oxtail. They only accepted cash – no plastic cards.

The next stop on the program was the home of Mr. and Mrs. Ray Scarboro in Darlington, Maryland. Ray and Shirley are winter guests of Sandgate (SG); have been in SG for more than 30 years, but because we ran out of rooms, they stayed in our house. They are a very nice couple, so last year, if we planned to go north, we would stop by to eat crabs. Darlington is a small city north of Baltimore near the Pennsylvania state border, where the broad Susquehanna River flows into Chesapeake Bay. They also invited their sister, with her spouse and daughter Cricket, to take half a day off to help cook and welcome guests. She often comes to SG in the winter with her parents. Her husband is named Joe, a Valedictorian of the Navy Seals. named in the National Museum of the US NAVY SEALS at 3300 N Hwy A1A, Fort Pierce, FL 34949. He had died the year before (2012); she cooks crab cakes because she knows that Sophia loves this dish the most and only eats it in Maryland.

They show us their gardens, all the things he made himself, such as the dome house, the glass roof covering the swimming pool opens automatically, in the garden blueberries were luxuriating but not yet ripe. He covered them with a net to prevent the birds from eating them; cucumbers are ripening, only to see all his old car collection that they used to park in a corner of the garden. he said he would not sell nor give one to anyone.

After showing us around the garden, he drove us to pick up the crabs that had been ordered from the restaurant, winding and winding through empty streets. The local restaurant was a small house located in an open field, surrounded by cornfields. They sell a dozen (12) medium-size crabs for only 6 dollars; he ordered 4 dozen. When the table was ready with all the food, we noticed only Shirley, Cricket and the Hoang family joined in: the rest did not eat crabs because they said it would take too much time to crack them open. Mr. Ray was afraid of embarrassement caused by his hands shaking, because of his Parkinson's, so he did not eat either. Really good crab with special bay seasoning from Maryland.

Mr. and Mrs. Ray and Shirley Scarboro visited Hoa's project at Palm Beach - on February 16, 2008 (she died in September 2015 and he passed away in October 2022).

He also let us taste a cake and a fruit cocktail he had made himself. Our stomach was too full; the conversation lasted until 4 pm, so we said goodbye and proceeded to continue our trip. My wife asked for a small tree – a Japanese Bloodgood – which grew wild beside their house, and he put it in a pot to take with us.

From the Scarboros' house down the I-95 highway is a small road running along the river. As soon as I approached Exit 93 on I-95 and Highway 222, I saw a crab restaurant right there; my wife told me that when we came back, we had to stop by to eat if it was convenient. Directly on the 95 North freeway to Delaware is a toll road but the New Jersey Turnpike is worse: both traffic jams and a steep toll fee. Passing through New York is the same: just cross the bridge and pay up to 14 dollars! This is also a place where we did not plan to stay overnight, so Sophia went to the Expedia site to find a Marriott hotel in Milford City, a convenient base for visiting the school tomorrow. The hotel room was spacious and comfortable, and our stomachs were full, so we just ate snacks.

Saturday, June 15: Waking up, feeling well because I didn't drive that much the day before, departed for New Haven. This city has the famous Yale University, although the surrounding neighborhoods are not very good. Around the school are green leafy roads, with numerous pedestrians strolling down sidewalks.

Yale University

Quinnipiac University

After visiting Yale, we went to Quinnipiac University, located in the city of Hamden, north of New Haven. This is the school that many people know of because it is famous for the national surveys they do every election, but few people pronounce its name correctly. The school is located on a hill, the trees are green, and all the entrances are guarded.

On the main road of Prospect, we happened to see a very neat little school named Albertus Magnus College, majoring in Liberal Arts, so we went to take pictures. The beautiful little school with charming scenery is not far from the famous Yale.

Albertus Magnus College

Albertus Magnus College

Proverbs on the school entrance and exit gates at Harvard University.

It was still early. We decided to continue onward to Boston, where we arrived in the afternoon. We strolled down the streets and went to Cambridge to visit the famous Harvard University. Located on the campus are ancient buildings with libraries underground and walkways above. Two maxims on the entrance and exit gates caught everyone's attention: ***Enter to grow in wisdom. Depart to serve better thy country and thy kind.***

Going around and then driving past Northeastern University, we couldn't find a parking space and Sophia didn't see anything special about the School; her stomach was also empty, so we went to Chinatown. Visit Pho Hoa, this place is OK to eat and Chinatown is too crowded, and narrow, but cleaner than New York's Chinatown. The hotel was quite expensive and Sophia didn't like Boston very much, so she decided that we should drive straight to Portland, Maine. Right into the hotel next to Maine Mall is the largest shopping area; dropped our luggage in the room and went down to the street along the beach. This is a neighborhood with many restaurants; because we had watched Food Network TV Dinners, Drive-in and Dives, Sophia suggested dinner at Becky's Diner, as featured on this program. This is a small but crowded restaurant, of course, especially Lobsters and New England Clam Chowder, the second is only $10 more, so twin lobsters were appreciated by everyone. Lobsters were nice and fresh.

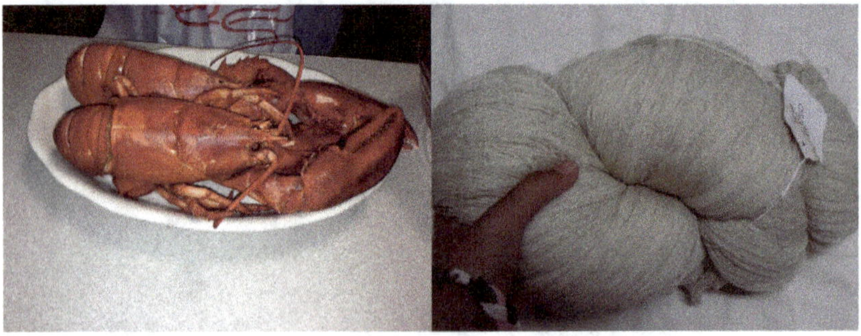

Twin Lobsters and yarns of Sophia

Back to the hotel to rest, because we planned to stay here for 3 days, eat leisurely, and peruse Sophia's wool shops (Yarns) which we found are not open on weekends. The first Yarn store was located in an old neighborhood, far from the city, just over half an hour's drive, so Sophia was shown the machine room upstairs by the owner. The next day, we visited another shop, located in the same small city. The warehouse belonging to the yarn factory had been moved to South Carolina years earlier for economic reasons. The showroom was small and didn't have much wool, but when given a round of tours, we saw that the back was a place to dye wool, using all-natural chemicals, and they provided quite a few domestic agents.

The next day, we visited a university located in Biddeford, on a hill, overlooking the very poetic Saco River. The school is called the *University of New England;* there are not many streets around, and only a few small cities nearby.

Running along the city of Portland, we saw a park overlooking the river which was very beautiful, surrounded by stones that are rarely found in Florida; so we went to collect a few for our garden, as souvenirs.

Sophia pointed to the north, where the city of Freeport hosts L.L. Bean, specializing in selling outdoor, camping, fishing, and hunting items, open 24 hours a day and never closed. Seeing the North Face shop in front of the street full of people, Sophia told me to go there to shop before returning to this shop, because she was confident it would still be open. The North Face store here is an outlet, and it was early summer, so all ski jackets were on sale, marked down 50% off, so each person selected a winter coat, saving it for Alaska! Beautiful warm coats in the North that are rarely sold in hot states like Florida; her mother goes for *black*, she picks the *white* and her father chooses *yellow*, technicolor for our family, so we are not afraid of getting lost.

Anyone who loves camping, fishing, or hunting must love L.L. Bean: nothing is missing here, tents, outdoor ovens, guns, fishing rods…or clothes are nothing short of complete, and there is a Starbucks cafe right inside the shop, for you to take a break.

LL Bean shop and the pier, with a floating restaurant.

My wife wanted to find a lobster restaurant, but when she searched on the Internet, such restaurants were no longer available or had been closed for a long time. There was only Lobster Shack, south of Portland in Cape Elizabeth, offering Lobster Twins with the second only 10 dollars more. So we headed south to visit the Fort Williams lighthouse. This belonged to an old garrison but has now become a place to visit *free of charge* only a small gift shop is run by volunteers, so we had to buy some items to support the free entry.

Fort Williams and a souvenir from gift shop.

The Lighthouse

Leaving Ft. Williams with dreamy photos, we climbed the mountain by car to Lobster Shack. The restaurant on the mountain was crowded, more than half the patrons sitting outdoors; right next to the checkout is a lake containing lobsters, customers were lined up out the door - the shop is only open in the summer.

Monday morning June 17, Before leaving Maine, Sophia wanted to visit Yarns, but they weren't open on weekends, the owner had a house on Peaks Island and had to take the ferry to the shop and walk to the shop every day, the shop had special wool. But this shop seemed special and could not be ignored by Sophia.

Around 11 am, we left Portland, stopped downtown, and had lunch. Thai food is okay but the service was unacceptable, maybe they hate Asians or something because they served some other people differently. We did not feel welcome there. From Maine, the road that follows the mountain slope through the White Mountains is beautiful, the stream with many large pebbles running alongside the road; the scenery is hard to criticize. We stopped at the Vermont state border, which was also full of hills, on both sides of the road cliffs had been split open.

The cliff was split into rubble to build a highway - Vermont

Following Highway 91 North, the road was empty; there were no cars in front of us or behind us. We stopped right at the Canadian border, it only took 30 seconds to check our passports; we entered the territory of Quebec Province, directly to Montreal – but the Vietnamese people called *Mong-Le-An*. We hadn't been to the city but the traffic was snarled; my wife studied the road signs but only saw how all were in French, so she didn't know which way to go. Luckily, the GPS in the car was so smart that, crossing the border it immediately changed to metric, counting kilometers (km); although the number is high, it is faster than miles. Cars in Canada are allowed to run at 100kph (60mph) but the fine is very heavy if you are speeding, so it seemed that cars with Quebec number plates were slow, only sometimes a few cars passing by; they looked like American license plates. To the hotel located in a downtown area; parking here costs 20 dollars a day, so we put all our things in the room to go find Vietnamese restaurants. there are a few close ones, within walking distance, most of which are Pho restaurants, but the Pho shops here must be doing pretty well. When you see the owner, the diamonds are glittering on her fingers; her husband is replete with gold on his body, and if they happen to be the staff of the restaurant, the owner must be up living in a high castle somewhere.

Returning to Montréal after more than 30 years, the city had changed a lot, the sidewalks were full of pedestrians, and the city looked old and dirty; parking was a problem.

Tuesday morning, June 18: In the morning we went to eat Pho near the hotel, near the shop the night before, and then stopped at Yarns Downtown after buying a Canadian-style bagel for Sophia. Shops that don't have washrooms have to use a nearby store; then we visited Mt. Royal Park and the famous St. Joseph's Oratory.

Towards the West along the 401 Freeway, we went directly to Toronto (nicknamed *Big Dragon Nest* in Vietnamese), out of Montreal, the streets are quieter but many trucks are loaded down. Police on both sides of the road are waiting to fine speeding drivers. Keeping to the speed limit of 100kph, we arrived in Toronto around 4 pm. Traffic was stuck, so we had to change our program to go straight to the hotel and then call my brother's friend [43] to come pick us up at the hotel, instead of going straight to their house as planned. They came by to pick up around 7 o'clock, and we went directly to Chinatown.

Two buildings are connected by a bridge.

43. *Mr. Trai is my brother's Scout friend in Hue, went on a USAID scholarship in 1968 to California. After graduating from school, he returned to Vietnam, got married and got stuck when April 1975 came. They settled in Toronto, Canada and have two sons, now retired. His bachelor's degree was very special, signed by the Governor of California and later the famous 40th President of the United States, Ronald Reagan, two terms (1980-1989).*

Canadian National
Tower Toronto, Canada

It is true that when you come to any place, you need to have a local person show you around. My brother's friend drove us to Chinatown because they heard that Sophia likes mangosteen; here tropical fresh fruit comes from Vietnam, mangosteen costs CAD$5.99 while in the US it costs US$8.99, and two dragon fruits sold for 1 dollar, so my wife bought them. Mangosteens and bon bons. They took us to a Chinese restaurant where the food was delicious; the lobster was made in an Asian style, unlike in Maine, it was only boiled and dipped in butter, deep-fried tofu, and sautéed cabbage with mushrooms, and a dish. The fried rice they make is delicious, white in color, not black and yellow because they put a lot of soy sauce like most Chinese restaurants do. After dinner, we went home to watch Thuy Nga 108 and ate fruit and cakes; their house is in a quiet area, and the external architecture looks like a small castle; the basement had a kitchen and entertainment center as a private apartment. The house is not small for just 2 persons, so it is very neat and elegantly decorated.

When he drove us back to the hotel, it was already past midnight. Went to bed and slept until morning.

Toronto, Canada Chinatown

Wednesday morning, June 19: Loaded our bags and headed to Chinatown to buy more fruit, checked out CN Tower and downtown before heading straight to Niagara Falls. The road from Toronto to Niagara Falls is not long: only about two hours by car, so when we arrived at the Sheraton Hotel, it was around 3 pm. The sun was very warm; it was good to go to the hotel to eat the foods that my wife bought in Chinatown – and prepare the camera for waterfall views. From the hotel you can see the waterfall; this is a hotel shared with the Hilton, that has a crosswalk across the Casino and shopping facilities; visitors come here to see the waterfall and perhaps gamble.

The two waterfalls look more beautiful from the Canadian side than from the US; tourists go along the two banks, and the water flows down the river and shoots up water droplets reflected in the sun, shining like diamonds.

Father and daughter.

The sky is clear blue without a cloud, the scenery is as beautiful as a watercolor painting. Going back and forth, taking pictures, we went to the gift shop, where there were souvenirs for visitors to buy as gifts or to take home. Going back to the hotel is a steep slope, but the pedestrian walkway is quite wide, so people keep climbing uphill. Arriving at the hotel early, Sophia didn't want to go because she could not get in yet; my wife and I went to see the Casino opposite the road, outside shopping anyone could enter, but inside is only for people over 19 years of age, tables for ordinary guests and VIP guests have their rooms. Behind is the Grand Buffet restaurant; each serving is 20 CAD, the cost is 45 cents more than US dollars. They limit food to 1 hour and stay open until 5 am.

Seeing nothing special, the computer systems in the dim light only made me dizzy, standing and seeing that there was no way to beat the house, more chance to lose, so maybe my wife and I were the only two who went in and out without losing a penny. When standing in line to pay for meals, an elderly couple recommended the restaurant, they go there often; when they learned we are from Florida, they said they often come back and relax with their friend's family in Cocoa Beach. I asked if it was Xanadu and they said yes, the 10th floor is right on the corner overlooking the sea. My brother's condo is also here on the 10th floor next to their condo – it is a small world.

Returning to the hotel, I slept until morning, then took my luggage to return to the US border. The GPS locator just goes over the Rainbow Bridge; at the end of the bridge is the US customs and they check the passport, the staff member with a serious face compares our picture on the passport and then lets us through. All passing vehicles are photographed and cameras are everywhere. The highway is wide; New York state is a place to pay a lot of tolls, follow Highway 90, then continue down 81 until Harrisburg in Pennsylvania, then change to 83 South until reaching Maryland. Since we estimated the arrival time would be evening, we changed the program to go straight to the Residence Inn Hotel and then to a Vietnamese restaurant instead of eating crab as planned. We planned to stay there for 3 days, so no rush.

Saturday, June 22: According to Sophia's program, we will visit the Library of Congress and Botanical Garden. Sophia planned to take the Metro, but I said that it is a long walk and since it is a weekend, maybe driving is more convenient. That's right: DC on weekends isn't as crowded or congested as usual, and parking near Capitol Hill isn't as restricted as it usually is.

The United States Congress is now as difficult to get to as it was in the past.

In the afternoon, we drove straight to Bethesda crab restaurant. A few years ago, we ate and bought spices here, next to a Spanish food spice shop, so my wife bought 10 more packs. She loves purple myrtle (Japanese myrtle) so she had to visit the nursery to buy it. There is room in the car only for one tree because it is already full up, so I have to send it back to them to take care of it until the day I return to pick it up.

Ornamental trees and stones commemorating the trip to North America

Departing back home after making a big bowl of pho at Pho 75 and buying snacks along the way for the driver, not forgetting to stop by to pick up the myrtle tree, we left DC at just over 10 am, got stuck in traffic near Woodbridge, stopped to eat Dirty Rice and refuel at Santee, SC and since the departure was later than the time planned, we reached Sandgate near midnight. We did not bother to unload our luggage, but slept until almost noon the next day, and continued on to Palm Beach around 5 pm.

Luggage, trees, and rocks are carried out and the rental car had to be returned by 6 pm, the number of miles traveled is 4,214 miles equivalent to 6,782 kilometers and there was no empty space left in the car. A trip full of fun and memories.

MY MOTHER...1920-2019

"Mother's heart is as vast as the Pacific Ocean..."
"Mother is like a ripe banana...like sticky rice with honey, sweet like sugar cane"

At first, I planned to write about my Mother in English, but thinking back, I wouldn't be able to write everything I thought in my second language, so I had to use my mother language to describe her, who I think is probably like thousands of other Vietnamese mothers, who love and sacrifice for their children, except that some of us in Hue call our mother *Mạ* instead of *Me, Mẹ, Má, Vú, Đẻ...* or even in French: *Maman or Măng*.

The same word *"Ma"* I use to describe my mother; but when I came to the US to take my first English course with Professor Carnell, I used to describe the rich Vietnamese language with six accents to my first English teacher at Santa Fe Community College, Gainesville, at the beginning of learning, the difficulty was expressing what you wanted to say, the more you tried to talk, the faster you became good at listening and understanding, so when she asked about Vietnamese, the English professor just wanted to know the stories of Vietnamese refugee students; none are alike, both letting them learn English by describing their mother language in English and real stories are a very practical way of learning a new language, so I rambled on about the accents of the Vietnamese language, a wrong accent imparts a different meaning, only one word Mạ, but if the accent is wrong, there are 6 different meanings, unlike Mom or Mother in English.

1920-1945- My Mom was born and raised, even married during turbulent war times. Her family and my Dad's (we call him Thầy), were the product of an *"arranged marriage"*, negotiated by two families, even though they did not know each other. At the time of the wedding, the groom was still busy with his military duty and away. After World War I, the world economy was in crisis, *The Great Depression was the worst economic downturn in the history of the industrialized world, lasting from 1929 to 1939. It began after the stock market crash of October 1929.* At that time, the French still colonized Vietnam, but the most remarkable thing was still to come: World War II, the period between 1939-1945, when the entire world was in a war fever. Right in Vietnam, countless innocent people died unjustly, the Japanese fascist army only occupied Vietnam for a short time, but killed pro-French citizens, at the time of execution. When the French army retook the country, they captured others, killing those they thought were on the Japanese side; there was a famine in the year of the Rooster (1945), which was also the year Mom gave birth to my sister. She had to take care of the whole family, while my father had to avoid all three sides: the Viet Minh and the French, also the Japanese army. Mom had to send her whole family back to the city, but when she was evacuated, it was not easy, so many stations to check in and watch us, even relatives did not dare to trust each other. Mom told me that year people died of starvation, their corpses lying on the road, not yet buried. Some people were so hungry that they caught typhoid, or they had to eat banana roots or bran *(the remaining flour when grinding rice left, usually just for pigs or animals to eat, not for human consumption)* to keep from dying. The year of the Rooster left horrifying impressions in the hearts of Mom and the people of Hue at that time.

Mom and her children were still young and couldn't be of much help, her husband was mostly away on military duty. She alone dared to complete all the work, including having to deal with her husband's brothers and sisters flexibly, on the one hand, taking care of her own children well; on the other hand, she could not let people know that her family had enough to eat, because they might kill the family, even though I was not born at that time, just listening to the stories made me shudder. While the war ended around the world, it was not so in Vietnam, because on all sides are your enemies. It must not have been easy to face that negative reality: during the day the French army controlled the land and forced villagers to fill in the pits that were destroyed by the Viet Minh (VM) who had forced them to work the night before. Mom was three months pregnant with my brother and still had to dig tunnels or destroy railways under Viet Minh orders until the French planes dropped bombs. Everyone ran to avoid bullets, everyone tried to survive, not to mention how the VMs cheated and told people to give money and gold for them to use to fight the French. Then Uncle Ho's banknotes were really just a piece of waste paper, many families' property was lost through this period. It may have been easy to get over it physically, living with this fear of spiritual terror and mentally unstable, but it was not easy for anyone to pass, after the French-Japanese period, the situation was a little brighter. My father, during his long military mission trips, had a *"mistress"*. Mom patiently endured this until one day my Dad died while leading his army through what later became known as the *"Boulevard of Terror"*. He died, and the Communists took with them our money and valuables that Mom had saved up to build a house (see the Report in the Appendix). I was less than 1 year old at that time, and Mom was widowed at the age of less than 32. My dad left only his wife and four young children, three boys and a girl with a National Honor certificate and a "Vietnam National Order 5th Class Medal". When occupying Hue city in March 1975, the VCs rubbed them in the dirt and tore them to pieces when they entered our family's house, even the picture of a deceased man wearing a majestic military uniform on the altar was torn up by them to take revenge.

February 24, 1954: My Dad died just a few months before the Geneva Agreement, to divide the country into two (July 20, 1954). Fortunately, the 17th parallel was only a few dozen kilometers north of the city, or otherwise, Ma would have had to bring us to the South; the days of being a little comfortable would not have lasted long. My mother had painfully lost her husband, and then sadly saw the country divided into two; not long after that, my paternal grandfather passed away... bad things came rushing in. The small, long-enduring body of my Mom, who could not afford to carry all the finances in the family, sold the house in the inner city to move to a house in An Cuu, next door to the former family house of Nha Ca *(VietBao Daily News founder and famous author of the book: Mourning Headband for Hue in 1968)*. In order for her children to have the opportunity to live as they did in my father's time, Mom went to work, sewing in a tailor shop at Nguyen Hoang bus station to An Lo, Sia, for just enough to live. She bought beans, rice, or other foods other things from the villagers, and then resold them in other seasons; that extra money, plus the pension paid by the government when my father died temporarily gave us a pretty decent life. The thing Mom feared the most was the lack of a father in the house. Children can be spoiled easily, so she always paid attention to her children's friends, confirming that they had come from good families; besides, she allowed us to join the Scouts, also helping her a lot in our educational work, so Mom had time to take care of making a livelihood at home, until one day while sewing, she fell ill to the point of vomiting blood badly and was admitted to a local hospital. Except for me, we were still young, so thanks to the life of the Scouts, we found ourselves able to take care of ourselves. However, after she recovered from her illness, we lived on her widow's and children's allowance (up to 18 years old) from the government and the extra work she did was enough: we barely made it. What she wished was that we would be successful, or at least finish high school or college.

1963 Coup D'état - The war was escalating more and more, in addition to the tension between the government and the Buddhists that rendered Hue politically unstable. My brother was studying at Hue University, but the arrests of student demonstrators frightened my mother even more; then the coup on November 1st, 1963, escalation of the war, students in Hue kept taking to the streets, protesting again, going on strike. I know Mom feared the most for the future of her children if this situation was allowed to continue.

1968 Mậu Thân Tet's Offensive- At the end of the Year of the Goat, on the 30th day of the Lunar New Year, our family was all at home. Before that, my eldest brother had just returned from the US and was residing at Da Nang AFB, flew to Hue to celebrate Tet, my older brother had returned from Saigon, and my older sister had also come back from Quang Ngai, where she is teaching, her new job after graduating from a teachers' training school, this was the happiest family gathering. After Tet, my older brother would go to Saigon, before leaving to study abroad with a USAID scholarship; the eldest brother would return to work in Da Nang AFB, my sister would also teach in Quang Ngai before transferring nearer home, and I would continue toward completion of my high school studies. I saw Mom was very happy, Mom had made all delicious food, her children's favorites; a few days before we had all gone together to the flower market, I had never seen the whole family so happy and full, after worshiping as traditional in the afternoon, the whole family invited each other to play cards, including my cousins, waiting for New Year's Eve worship time.

Year of the Monkey...The sound of the guns that I thought was like a firecracker to congratulate family reunions, but it only took a second when everyone realized that the gunfire sounding like an AK-47 this time was not like a firecracker, but a cry of pain, separation, destruction...everyone was scared. looking at each other, going down to the bunker to hide, did not know that Hue city had changed hands, the new owner was a fierce god, a cannibal devil; the next morning, when we went out to the street and verified that the city had collapsed into the hands of the Communists, Mom's life experience through 1945, 1954, 1963 saved our lives. The days here were days of panic, living in fear; she had all her children, but worries mounted more and more, there was only one mat for the whole family in the hallway of the Catholic Church, we stayed together here until one day, about late morning, there was the sound of people running fast through the corridors, shouting loudly: *"they (VC) come, run, run..."*, in less than five minutes, they forced us all go outside, male and female, young and old, including babies. Separated from men, the women walked in two different rows, and looked around, Mom held my hand tightly, although I was 13 my body was small and my sister walked beside me; I did not see my two brothers with us, later I heard a brother had come over to the Sao Mai printing shop next to hide, oldest brother ran home, Senator Dien Tran, a known Scout leader, blatantly proclaimed his true identity, only to be taken away by them, buried alive, when I ran past the place where my brother's black Suzuki motorbike was parked near the wall, it was burned by a rocket that had landed right on the saddle. Mom said: *"Don't worry, material was lost in place of human life"*, we ran away to the Model School the following days because the Church was no longer safe.

My brother was supposed to return to Saigon around the 7th of the Lunar New Year to study abroad, but he didn't return to Saigon until the end of the month. Fortunately, the government had postponed the trip because of the general attack around the South. Personally, after the school reopened, it took time to repair and clean up the rooms that had become shelters for the people, but the sad impression that I will never forget is that day by day, the students were lined up in front of the school to say goodbye to innocent victims whose bodies had just been found in mass graves; few people had documents to identify their families, students, men in blue pants and white shirts, girls in white "ao dai" dresses stood along in two lines next to Le Loi Street. Then, together, we walked along in a mass funeral ceremony to the final resting place, including my friends, our teacher, and even the leader of our Scouts...all buried alive in shallow graves they had dug themselves. A massacre that we shall never forget.

1971-1972- The year of *Operation Lam Son 719 or 9th Route – Southern Laos Campaign* (named by the American Military) and also the year of the *"Avenue of Terror"*. I passed the first part of the Baccalaureate in 1972; this was also the time when my classmates parted ways to join the army because the government draft had dropped one year younger, if you failed the exam, off to enlistment you go. There were still a few acquaintances, the other part were students who had transferred from Nguyen Hoang and Quang Tri schools, north of Hue. Because the border area was no longer as safe as before, the School was mostly occupied by refugees as a place to evacuate. We tried to study at home.

One day, when Mom was in the backyard, I was standing in the front yard playing, when suddenly I saw two strange Air Force officers, wearing flying suit uniforms (I had never seen them before), coming into the house, asking me: *"Young brother, is your Mom at home?"* I answered *"Yes"* but had a bad feeling through my backbones, I rushed out of the house and called *"Mom, Mom..."* When Mom entered the house, two officers who were sitting on the couch stood up to greet her, I saw her face turn pale; she was the one who spoke first: *"When did he die?"* She guessed that when they showed up at our home in full Air Force uniform, they were there to report bad news. The officer replied: *"Madame, we were ordered by the Squadron Commander to take a helicopter to pick you up to go to Da Nang Air Force Base, because Captain Chau's chopper was shot down and he was seriously wounded near Southern Laos, is in the hospital aboard a US Navy warship"*. I saw her let out a light sigh, saying quietly, only loud enough for me to hear: *"So he's not dead"*, then she went in to get her clothes, burned incense on the altar, and followed the two air force officers, after telling me to take care and stay home. My brother later recounted, that when his helicopter was hit by an anti-aircraft missile, it exploded above the main rotor blades like fireworks; it also shut down the aircraft once it got hit. From the high hill, he let it fall in *"auto-rotation"* mode, because the rotor blades were still spinning, tried to make an emergency landing if possible, but when the copter was near the foot of the mountain, luckily, the engine started again, and he brought it back to the base at Khe Sanh. He had fainted because he had lost so much blood; he didn't know that at that time, Airborne General Luong Quang Le came for him to be specially promoted. The US Air Force took him to the US Navy Hospital anchored at the port of Da Nang for treatment because there was too much shrapnel embedded in his face, knees and legs for them to remove.

Six months in hospital and my Mom thought after this, *"He will retire"*, go work in an office, no longer flying because of his serious injury, but in fact after recovering, my brother would continue on his outlined path, returning to the helicopter squadron but more than half had been sacrificed; the wrinkles and anxiety on Mom's face I had seen again...

1973-1974 The war in the central region was increasing day by day, even though the Paris Agreement of 1973 stipulated a cease-fire to allow the US to withdraw, one side continued to violate it. After finishing the 12th grade, I had to stay with my brother in his airport dormitory to study for the Second Baccalaureate exam. Every evening, when the sirens sounded to warn of artillery shelling, the jets took off, the first few times I still *"jumped"* out of bed and went under shelter, but then gradually got used to sleeping deeply. After this exam, I packed up and went to Saigon to continue college life without any budget.

Did not want to burden Mom's pension, because a poor student from a small city like Hue moving to Saigon needed a lot of money. My textbooks were quite expensive at that time, even though I went to the library every day, study materials from college professors were not available in the Library and students had to buy them. Some of my college friends borrowed and copied material by hand, as no photocopier was available and would end up more expensive than an original. My older brother was studying abroad; every month he provided me with 50 USD through the Manhattan Bank; this was quite a large budget for a student, as my brother's scholarship money was only 200 USD per month, he portioned off part of it for me, so I didn't dare to squander it. At the end of the first year exam at Law School, Mom came down to Saigon to visit me, staying at my cousin's house. I went to school when they posted the results, and when I came home, I only told her the words *"I passed"*, I saw her breathe a sigh of relief, but I knew she was very happy inside.

Beginning of the year 1975- The war did not slacked off after *"Vietnamization"*; the Americans withdrew their troops back home; although I was in Saigon, the Capital city of South Vietnam, I could still see the intensity of the war increasing, day by day. Some of my friends had died, some were still training in military school; those who were lucky enough to still go to college – like me – had to work hard, because no one wanted to fail the exam and go enlist in the Army.

March, 1975- I still remember the first time my friends at the College of Law celebrated my birthday – the first time in my life; then there were a series of days that I will never forget. Mom and my sister packed into Da Nang when Hue fell, a friend of my brother's was able to safely bring Mom and my sister to Da Nang AFB, Mom's older brother was evacuated by boat, the shipwreck which only my uncle survived, thanks to a plastic bag, on the last day when Da Nang was about to fall into the hands of the Communists, my family friend Mr. T. was in Da Nang AFB and brought my sister and Mom to Saigon. He was from the South and had no relatives, served in Da Nang AFB but picked up and followed my uncle's instructions, hiding the story of my uncle's family; otherwise, Mom would refuse to follow him to Saigon, only the next morning Da Nang AFB fell into the hands of the Communists.

I continued to go to school, until one day, April 8, 1975, in class, we huddled under the table after several explosions from the direction of the Presidential Palace, bombs from an F-5 jet fell not far from my school. Professor Mau Vu was giving a lecture in Civil Law to allow students to leave, I just had time to say goodbye to my friends, a motorbike right to where Mom was staying temporarily, my brother had just arrived at that time of the day, we packed up and headed for Tan Son Nhut airport, if it hadn't been for my friend who was a security officer at Phi Long Gate, my brother wouldn't have been able to take us inside the Airport. At my friend's temporary dormitory, we knew this may have been the safest place, but it may also be the place targeted for the most shelling, the haunting of the Lunar New Year is still there. A small city with such a tragic short period in 1968, now losing the whole South, will surely be hell on earth. Mom's experience through these times: she said to my brother: *"Mom and your sister are female, but you boys have to find a way to get out of this place by any means possible",* she knew that if we had to take care of the whole family, he and I would be trapped, an even more dangerous predicament.

Monday, April 28 Evening into Tuesday morning April 29: We lay in a bunker near the dormitory, listening to the shells, knowing this was about the time to change hands, the most dangerous period in the war, the bombers, fighter jets taking off at night due to shelling, but my brother said no planes landed after they supposedly ran out of fuel, the Vietnamese Air Force could not refuel in the air, so maybe they were all shot down? Another theory is that the planes escaped to another place to avoid shelling; I later learned that it was the U-Tapao airbase in Thailand. It was early morning; the shelling had just stopped, my brother and I took a motorbike, along with his friend, the 233rd Squadron Commander to the gate, he had come in the night before to check out the situation because his wife had just given birth a day ago. Seeing that the situation was tense, he asked for a ride to the gate to return to his family, but before we reached the gate, we saw the Military Police pointing a gun (M-16) in the air, firing several warning shots telling us not to go out at this time; I sat in the middle, Mr. Thanh sat in the back, my brother turned back, and directed to the runway, after a while of searching, there was no fuel left, we ran past Air America, the blue and white helicopters parked neatly, each one was full of fuel, my brother asked an American Lieutenant Colonel in full pilot uniform standing nearby: *"May we use your chopper?".* I remember him answering in English: *"Help yourself!"* My brother and Mr. Thanh looked at the chopper, quickly checked around and got in the front two seats, I sat in the back, wearing a headset; when I went to a helicopter, I knew what the person in the back had to do before the engine started, I looked around and shouted: *"clear!"*, they started the engine (the helicopter must start with the battery first, then the engine had momentum and could run itself), and then I heard my brother say: *"Thanh, well, if we took this chopper, even with permission, nobody would know about it so either side could shoot it down"*, because the CIA uses Air America as a means of transportation. They decided to turn off the engine and we climbed down, continuing through the helipad with motorbike; when we saw a Chinook CH-47 full of people, the pilot, who was my brother's friend, said the plane did not have enough fuel. Knowing that we could not get a chopper with fuel, the purpose was to pick up Mom and my sister back in the barrack, the three of us passed the C-130 parking lot, jumped into a running plane, took off right from the *"taxiway"*, the main runway having been damaged by artillery shells the previous night. When the cargo plane left Saigon airspace, I heard someone crying bitterly; I looked at my brother, with the same thought, said goodbye the last time to the city, my beloved homeland including Mom, my sister without saying goodbye and also no chance to bring them along.

1976- We were able to contact Mom by letter sent to my future sister-in-law in Australia, using only our family's language we could understand, telling Mom that we had safely arrived in the US. Mom and my sister… at that time the new government forced everyone to return home. In my old hometown, my sister thought that since she was a woman, a teacher, she would not be expected to have to go to a re-education camp for more than a year at the Ai Tu, Binh Dien concentration base near Hue for the crime of *"escaping from office"*. Mom, although all her sons were now far away, now had to take care of her daughter. Several bad people told Mom they were sure she would never have the opportunity to meet her children again. Mom went up to the temple to pray and shaved her hair, she almost went into the monastery after giving birth to my brother, once again she had to endure the detractors. My brother tried to transfer money to Mom through acquaintances because there was no longer the old government pension like before, all the sons were gone, and the only daughter was also going to a re-education camp. Her life was much more difficult, not physically but mentally.

October 1, 1991- After more than 16 years of separation, Mom and my sister's family came to the US, under the O.D.P. (Orderly Departure Program) guarantee by my brother. We persuaded her to leave, to save the future for her children and grandchildren. When I returned home in 1988 to visit, Mom didn't want to go abroad; we couldn't sponsor my sister's family alone, although I tried to find a way with Mr. Bill Flemming (d) at the Southern California New Year market organized by Ms. Nam Tran, to help the refugees with their documents; immigrant settlement had not been approved. Tet market was held for 3 days but you had to get a number and wait until the last day to see him, just enough time to give him a letter that said: *"Please read the letter I wrote to you and your wife when you returned to your office in Bangkok to bring my family's* *file to review"*. At that time, he was in charge of this immigration program for the US government in Thailand.

Coming to the US at 71 years of age, when she heard that people without citizenship would not receive Social Security benefits, she was also determined to take the exam and became a US Citizen in 1998. From 1954 to 1975, Mom had received a pension, a monthly South Vietnam government-issued allowance under the family of a military officer and my National Adoption category until the age of 21. After March 1975, that income was no longer available and it was not until 1998 that a US government benefit was resumed for her.

2000 – We celebrated an 80th birthday ceremony for Mom, and at her request, made it simple, so it was only in the family, through many wars, her birth certificate papers, parts burned, parts lost, and redone. On her new birth certificate, Mom was allowed to be born on the first day of the year, so we also celebrated the first day of a new century, on the occasion of thanking the person who gave birth and raised us, although her husband had died at a young age, staying single to worship her husband and raise children, with a rare generous heart, a Vietnamese woman with the virtues of patience, endurance and sacrifice.

2001 – 9-11. She witnessed two buildings collapse, war right in the peaceful country of her second homeland; her eyes were red, and she just shook her head and said nothing, but I knew in her heart she was very sad when an unexpected massacre occurred in her second homeland. Tolerating and fortunately surviving through the Japanese, French, and Viet Minh times until the day she reunited with family in the United States, a devoted Vietnamese woman sacrificed her whole life for her children and grandchildren. Please give her a rose, every season Vu Lan comes *(Vietnamese Buddhism Mother's Day in the full moon of the month July-Lunar year)*, I am proud to bring a ***ROSE*** for her because it is also the beautiful name of my Mom, ***Hong Hoa***.

2010 – At the 90th birthday of my Mom, we met at a vacation home by the Atlantic Ocean, cooked together, fished, and reviewed old stories because our children and grandchildren had worked all year and rarely had the opportunity to meet. A New Year's Day reunion on her 90th birthday.

Celebrating the 90th birthday of Mom with her children and grandchildren – 2010

2017- Because my mother's health was getting worse and worse, we took her to stay with us temporarily in Palm Beach at the end of the year. On this occasion, my sister and her children decided to move to a new house to have more room for the whole family. The two elders are Mom and my sister's husband; neither were in good health. At the beginning of the year, we just bought a *"99-year-old birthday cake"* for her and ate banh beo (rice cakes), which was Mom's favorite dish. When she returned to Orlando, she said she was tired; when asked if she needed to go to the hospital, she just nodded slightly, so we took her to the hospital and took turns staying the night with her. A few days later, the doctor sent her home.

Mother's Day 2019- Her health was getting weaker and weaker, day after day; all the time she is tired; she goes to the hospital to get an IV, and when she feels better, they let her go home. The last time she went to the hospital was in May, 2019 and after two days in a hospice at DeBary Hospital, Mom passed away, with her children and grandchildren, as well as a great-grandchild, surrounding her bed, right on the weekend of Mother's Day in the US.

2019-2022: After Mom died, we asked people in Vietnam to build a mausoleum for her, and her ashes to be temporarily held at Long Van Buddhist Temple, Orlando for two years. While she was still alive, she had set aside funds for this, not wanting to bother her children and grandchildren. I drew up plans for the family to approve, and after a few months of construction, the work was completed, before the Covid pandemic. When going to the temple on Sunday, a lady whom my Mom had met before told my sister about her dream the night before: she saw her face was bright and happy to tell her that a mausoleum had been built in Hue, very beautiful, when my sister showed the picture to the lady, she was shocked because she said it was the same thing she had seen in her dream: the lotus was round. While Mom was still alive, she used to go to the temple with my sister every Sunday and meet friends, including the one who told her dream story.

On September 16, 2022, my older brother and my sister-in-law brought Mom's ashes to be placed in Mui Bac, Hue next to my Dad's grave. Relatives in the family, including her adopted daughter, came to see and say goodbye for the last time at the house, as well as at the mausoleum. The family fulfilled her wish, as she had instructed, before her death.

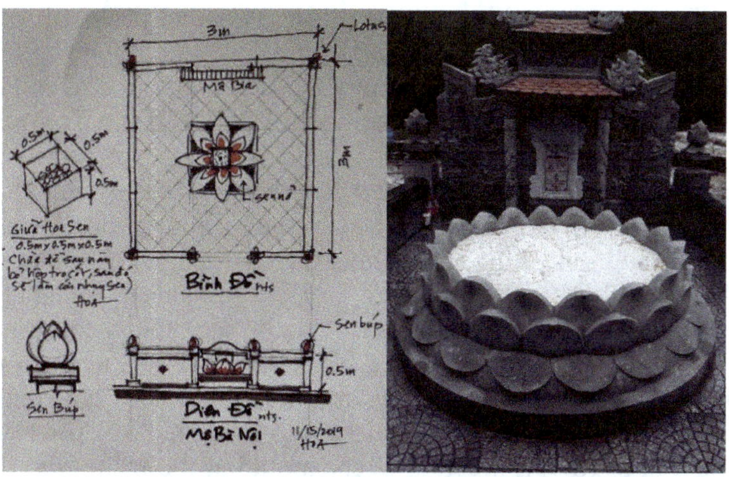

Drawings and mausoleum, tombstones were built at the end of 2019.

MY ELDEST BROTHER AND HIS AIR FORCE STORY.

My first brother was born in the year of the Snake and was thus exactly 12 years older than me. Because my father had died when I was only 1 year old, and since he was the eldest brother in the family, the younger brothers considered him as *"the rightful brother, the father"*; everything in the family regarding foreign affairs or study should be under the control of the older brother.

Maybe he thought: *"Love for the whip, Hate it for the sweetness"*, so it was very difficult when I was a child. I was also agitated, so whenever my younger siblings were playing and one of them was crying, he would tell us to go to bed, which was the size of two thick pieces of hardwood lying on two logs, and swept our butts with a whip, but intentionally favored me in the inner arm because I was the smallest, the person on the outside would be hit the hardest because it was the tip of the whip.

When we were older, the first thing was that he let all of his younger brothers participate in Scouting activities; then he was an adult, so he was in a Scout Group of Bach Dang, a Rover Scout of Van Kiep. My sister was a member of the Me Linh Troop, and my next brother at that time was in the Chi Lang Cub Scouts with Akela Quynh Hoa (d). But when he went to the Boy Scouts, he was in the Wolf patrol of the Bach Dang Group, and I was the youngest, so I joined the Bach Dang Cub Scouts, under the control of Akela Bich Huong. Usually met in the same place, but the big brothers had their program of activities, and the means of transportation at that time were bicycles or Velo-Solex, so they changed their weekly activities and meeting places unless there was a large meeting or the whole group consisted of Cubs, Boys, Venture, and Rover, meeting every month at the Nam Giao Hill, on the campus of Quoc Hoc, Dong Khanh or Vuon Doat ...

In 1963, after the 12th grade, he passed the Second Baccalaureate, Math Division B; at that time students had to take an Oral exam after passing the written exam, so it was very difficult. Some candidates only failed the oral exam and had to retake it. I just remember my brother's friend was very good at studying because he kept repeating: Mr. Huy Khac Le was able to study in Canada, I heard that he studied best at McGill, Montreal. And Mr. Van (the late Lieutenant Colonel) was joined after passing the entrance exam at Da Lat National Military Academy. At that time, the number of students who passed the Second Baccalaureate was small, but the number of students entering the University in Saigon or studying abroad was even rarer. One of his friends, Mr. Trinh Mau Nguyen, went to the University of Saigon, the College of Pharmacy, so when my brother applied for the University of Saigon, Mom approved the move right away, because he said he went to Saigon to live with his friend in Minh Mang Dormitory.

After the *coup d'état* of November 1963, the political situation was no longer stable, so high schools in Hue were also affected, sometimes when they were studying, they heard the class was canceled, and the students rushed out to protest. In 1965, I passed the entrance exam to the National Academy High School. The two words, "*strike*" and "strike", were normal in the curriculum at that time. Our class of young students kept hearing that there was to be no class, we were happy to go home, but we didn't have much concept of politics or awareness of someone pulling the strings from behind.

Just remember that Mom received a letter to report to the mandatory military draft for him to be sent home; she was worried, trying to find a way to contact my brother in Saigon. He later told Mom that he had been selected for the Air Force but did not dare to tell Mom when he accepted. Although she worried, she felt more relieved, because choosing a military career is better than going into the Army, but most likely it would be the Infantry after completing training. He also said that the reason he volunteered to join the Air Force was because he felt that continuing to study at the University in Saigon would be too costly for Mom, and would greatly affect the future education of the other children. Mom also didn't wonder much because the paper calling for enlistment was lying there; there was no other way. *(Military service was mandatory for all boys above 18 years of age except those exempt because of their health or the only boy left in the family, similar to Private Ryan. Most ended up in the army infantry, apart from those volunteering for the Air Force or Navy).*

He entered the Air Force Training Center at Nha Trang and then was selected to go to the US to train on the types of aircraft that the US would support Vietnam with later. American advisers saw that the Vietnam War would require quick helicopter support, so his team was chosen to learn to fly H-34 helicopters and train at Lackland Air Force Base, San Antonio, and Fort Rucker, Alabama. The H-34 is a helicopter built by Sikorsky that has two front wheels and one rear wheel under the belly, unlike the Huey UH-1, which only has two landing gear. This is a heavy aircraft, so sometimes it has to run to gain momentum on the runway to take off or land because it is transporting operations, more than attacking, so there is only one machine gun on the side, not on both sides. My brother said the Vietnamese pilots gave it the nickname *"the mill"*. I went up in one a few times and found it heavy, noisy, and not as agile as a Huey later on.

When the US started moving to the Huey, refurbishing it for the Vietnam battlefield with two more miniguns and rockets on both sides, my brother was one of the first to volunteer to switch over to an armed UH-1 to support army troops on the ground, unlike the H-34 which just moved troops and was fitted with a machine gun for self-defense. A UH-1 Gunship can both attack and defend. The US did not support the RVNAF with the AH-1 Cobra as an attack helicopter, so the RVNAF had to refurbish some of the UH-1 from troop transport into an armed helicopter, which was very effective and a perfect match for the infantry and armor tanks of the Viet Cong. Later, they modified the exhaust, pointing up to the sky to dissipate heat when flying, to avoid the Viet Cong's Russian-provided SA-7 heat-seeking missiles, because the original exhaust blew backward, so the heat was much easier to track by surface-to-air missiles.

After training at flight schools in the US and graduating from school, depending on the aircraft they learned to fly, helicopters, cargo planes, fixed wings, or fighter jets, they could not be selected but by instructors randomly; if they failed flight school in the US in both English and technical matters, they would be sent back to Vietnam to join the army infantry.

After graduating, he returned to Vietnam in 1967 and chose to serve in the First Air Force Division, 51st Tactical Wing, 213th Twin Spiked Maces Squadron, Da Nang AFB, at first using H-34 but later switching to armed UH-1. 213th Squadron was a famous squadron in Da Nang because the pilots bravely supported the field troops but never left their comrades behind with the slogan: *"Don't leave your brothers, don't leave your friends".* Because of superstition, thinking that the number 13 was unlucky, there was a time when the superiors tried to change it to figures like 216 to reduce bad luck *(Vietnamese helicopter squadrons all started with the number 2 and had odd numbers at the end)* but because of wartime, bullets could not avoid people, so the number of crew members this squadron sacrificed was more than the other squadrons and was formed first, attack helicopters also targeted by the enemy more, so, of course, it was not strange that more members ended up KIA, because of anti-aircraft weapons – Surface-to-Air Missiles or SAM/SA7 for short, were provided by the Soviet Union for the North Vietnamese faction to become more and more advanced.

A few days before the Mau Than Lunar New Year (1968), he asked for leave to return to Hue to visit family, because at that time his main squadron was stationed in Da Nang, but there was still a small support squadron of pilots who stayed in Hue at the small airport of Tay Loc inside the citadel. At Thuan Hoa Hotel on Duy Tan Street, this section of the road is closed to local traffic for security, and US military advisors (MACV) were also located there. The squad in Hue near Tet returned to visit their family in the South, so at the end of that year, Mr. Khanh left a Suzuki to lend to my brother to use for a few days of Tet. When he left it on the side of the Disciple Institute of Catholic Church, it was destroyed by a VC rocket, so my brother had to pay his friend to buy another motorcycle while he didn't even own one. This passage I recounted in the part of running from the Tet Offensive with my family.

He returned to serve in the 213th Double Spiked Maces Squadron, but later this squadron was armed with Helicopter Gunships, and in 1971, all Helicopter Squadrons in Da Nang AFB were ordered to support Lam Son 719 *(Operation Lam Son 719 or 9th Route – Southern Laos Campaign)*. With a military life that did not know when to expect to die, pilots who returned became more superstitious; many true stories are told: a fortune-teller told a pilot not to do anything that day because it was taboo; he asked for leave that day, but at home felt sad with nothing to do; he drove into the squadron office, which was unexpectedly short of pilots that day; he took a flight, got shot down and never came back.

Here, I recall the positions of Chief of Flight Security and Chief of Operations that my brother held. Both are important positions in the squadron, but it is a position that pilots call dangerous because it schedules flights for the crew, if there is a shortage of pilots for missions, such as an emergency, he is often the one who has to replace it, but in the squadrons, substitute flying is not favored because many people leave and do not return, and *"no one looks for fallen bodies"*.

When my Mom and I went to the airport to visit, during the unstable time in our hometown, Hue, he was at the single dormitory for Tran Van Tho residence. This area had two building blocks facing each other; every 2 single officers shared a room, but there were 2 double bunk beds and if necessary, they could be increased to accommodate 4 people. Most of them are in the squadron waiting area, scheduled to fly any time because of the war situation, so they just go back to their dorms to sleep, waiting in the office was more comfortable with air conditioning, a game room, entertainment, and recent war news. Some of the pilots decided that would be the best place during the day and night.

My brother's room had two double beds, so in 1971 and 1972, before I took the year-end exam, the school was occupied by people evacuated north of Hue. Here, I often went to the next room to meet with Major Tu Duc Trinh, flying an A-37 Dragonfly[44], of

44. *The late Major Tu Duc Trinh of the 516th Flying Tigers Squadron, formerly known as the Destroyer II Squadron, of the 61Tactical Wing, First Division Air Force, at Da Nang Air Force Base, was right next to my brother's dorm room. He flew the propeller A1-H Skyraider until 1968, then changed to the A-37B Dragonfly jet, built by Cessna. At that time, students like us kept seeing Air Force Officer wearing flying suits, sometimes black, sometimes orange, wearing Walther P-38s, daggers dangling from their hips like Mr. Tu, Mr. Du, Mr. Thuc... we felt "cool". Where do you know that life is like a passing wind, when you go to war, you go, without setting a date to return, but slogan: "no one is looking for a dead body of the pilot". Now they were at peace in another world without hatred and war. An incense stick for the pilots who sacrificed for the country.*
On April 30, 1972, during a mission in Quang Tri, to support the ground troops, Major Nguyen Du (528-Scorpion Squadron) was shot down by a rocket, he parachuted out of the A-37B, wounded and captured alive after rescue helicopters were also shot down by VC fire. (my brother also came tried to save him with his chopper gunship but failed due to heavy surface-to-air missiles fire from the enemy). Air Force Major Du Nguyen was brought to death by the VCs, stoned to death in 1972, he was only 32 years old.

the 516th Flying Tigers Squadron. I also often met a person I call Uncle Tu, journalist Tu Nguyen, a war correspondent of Chinh Luan Daily Newspaper in Saigon[45], often following military aircraft of the South Vietnamese Air Force of all kinds to send reportage from the battlefield. He often carried a leather handbag for his belongings. He has a beard, so if you look at him from afar, he resembles a foreigner. Major Trinh is also tall; he is a Vovinam master, so he looks like a samurai who has gone down the mountain after completing training. His room didn't have a roommate, so every time Uncle Tu came here, he stayed there. I ran over to greet him, or asked him why the newsroom gave him the nickname called *"Fast as Lightning"*.

Today, if you see him with the pilots of Flying Tigers 516th (A-37), then the next day you could see him sitting in the helicopter squadron, waiting for a flight to the battlefield area to do his reportage, because when he was in Region I, the next day was in Zone IV, not staying in one place for long, true to his nickname. I found him always looking serious, rarely smiling, but he was actually very gentle. Major Trinh asked to take a leave of absence to go back to SG to marry his girlfriend; his prospective mother-in-law made an excuse to stop them from marrying, although at that time his girlfriend was pregnant. He was sad, returned to DNAFB, and went to the squadron office to fly to support army troops in Quang Tin. When the plane pulled in after dropping its bombs, it collided with a Cessna L-19 observation plane and caught fire. My brother and the crew flew into the war zone to find

---

45. *Reporter Tu (Dinh) Nguyen of Chinh Luan dailynews in Saigon, whom I call Uncle Tu, is a war correspondent, he often follows air force pilots to battlefield including my brother's chopper to report and send to the editorial office. His reports are always completely true, on the battlefield, under the gunfights that the ARVN, RVNAF soldiers are fighting, especially the Air Force. When he went by helicopter to Hue to do a reportage, he visited my house a few times with my brother's crew to eat the rice paper rolls made by Mom. The funny thing is that every time he meet my Mom in the dormitory, he calls her as his Aunt, but I also call him Uncle because he is only 4 years younger than my Mom. Few people have had the opportunity like him to go with them on military aircraft without knowing if they will return safely or not. In April 1975, although he was able to leave at the last minute due to many acquaintances in the air force, including Americans, he was stuck because he was worried about helping journalists in the newspaper's office whose families were trying to evacuate stayed and imprisoned for 12 years. He successfully escapped by boat to Hong Kong in 1988 and then settled in the US.*
He remained single until his death at the age of 86 in 2010 in Alexandria, Virginia.

Major Tu's body, even though he knew that his life as an Air Force Flight Officer meant *"No one is looking for a pilot's dead body"*. He died that year, never seeing his unborn daughter's face. When Ms. M. went to Major Tu's funeral, she stayed at my house and I saw that she had shaved her head.

After the years 1971-1972, the war situation got worse day by day. I often asked permission to take a helicopter from Hue to Da Nang; when I went, I always saw a helicopter parked in front of our high school or the Tay Loc airport, looking at the tail number, whenever which squadron was familiar, the pilots let me go along, I knew most of the officers and helicopter squadron commanders in DN, because I often met them at the staterooms of the squadrons. Most of them were my brother's friends so if you say it right, the pilots will also know that they are Air Force family members and they let us take a ride. The 213th Squadron, named Double Spiked Maces, was commanded by Lieutenant Colonel Khoi from Hue; I knew it was easy, Major Ta Thai, deputy squadron commander was also from Hue, and the 233th Thien Ung Squadron was trained with squadron commander Major Thanh, nicknamed *Thanh Mosquito*. He landed his chopper like a mosquito on the body (this is a training squadron for officers entering the airfield who later did not go to the United States to train when there was a Vietnamization program) so Mom liked to go with him. The deputy squadron commander was Major Nguyen Trung Hieu; he should have been the senior of in the force, but because of *"smashing the ship"*, he was demoted to lieutenant; from that time, he did not wear a badge until he was promoted to Major again. Major Hieu was the one who brought my Mom and my sister to Saigon around March 27, 1975, and back to DN to finally fly out of the DN airport in a helicopter on the morning of March 29 when the airbase fell to the VC. The 239th King Hawk Squadron had Lieutenant Colonel Toan from the North as the squadron leader, also from the 213th. By knowing most of the commanders in the Da Nang AFB, I did not have any problems flying from Hue and vice versa during my last two years in high school. My brother's dorm was quiet and safer than in my hometown.

My brother used to practice the game of *"spiral approaches/divergence"*, drop holes or *auto-rotation* with a rumble like autumn leaves, so he was nicknamed Chau Cowboy, during the Vietnam War, you cannot follow the manual for your helicopter, he survived because of a gunship, fast and surprising to avoid SA-7 rockets from the enemy because helicopter speed was not as fast as that of a jet you cannot fly high, but only above the trees as low as you can. Later, when my brother changed to the 257th Rescue Squadron to transport the nightly wounded, the squadron commander was Lieutenant Colonel Binh, nicknamed *Milk* (because of his young face), and Captain Nguyen Hoang An (I told the story of his noble sacrifice in this book).

Captain An and my brother were two pilots in Da Nang Air Force Base (DNAFB) who were assigned to the South Vietnamese Navy ship before the 1974 Tiger New Year. When I returned to DN from Saigon by means of a C-130 on January 12, 1974 (December 20, Buffalo year), I went to the reception room of the 257th Rescue Squadron and waited to go to Hue with my brother, because he had asked for leave to return to Hue to celebrate the Lunar New Year with his family. He just waited for me to come back from Saigon. I happened to see those pilots playing cards and chess when they suddenly disappeared into the conference room, leaving me alone as a civilian sitting there. About more than an hour later they appeared, and my brother asked me to follow him. I took my luggage with me, thinking that he was going to fly his helicopter to Hue with me, but he came to the 213th squadron, told me this was the last mission flight to Hue that day and he did not want me to wait until the next day, he asked the captain of the chopper where to drop me and told me: *"I have a special job to do urgently now, can't go to Hue to celebrate Tet with you and mom. You let Mom know; that is all I can tell you now"*. I followed the crew of the 213th squadron this time as a gunship, only two pilots and two gunners went by Tam Giang lagoon, they signaled me to cover my ears since I was the only one not wearing a helmet or headset; it turned out that they wanted to test their rockets, two miniguns, a few bullets exploded, the chopper jerked back and forth each time the rockets flew forward and the howl of two miniguns released 6,000 rounds a minute. Sitting between two machine gunners, this was my first time to witness a gun test on a helicopter gunship, something rare for civilians.

Arriving in Hue, the two pilots dropped me on the soccer field near my house because I knew they had to go on an urgent mission; they had not expected a special passenger. I walked home, and Mom asked *"Where is your brother?"* I told her that he was busy with work at the last minute; her eyes looked sad, she did not say anything more but she looked at the jams and cakes she had prepared on the table, this year she expected my brother and me to celebrate Tet with the family. I later learned that he and Captain An volunteered to take a helicopter to the warships of the South Vietnamese Navy. The purpose was not to support an attack because it was not by gunship but by ambulance helicopter belonging to the 257th. The two pilots of the squadron are two famous pilots who are good at flying during the day as well as at night, in good or bad weather, and at sea. The purpose was only to save (defense) but not to hit (attack). Called *"the Battle of the Paracel Islands"* between South Vietnam and China. If the war with China at that time was about the Air Force or Navy, it would be just an egg fight with stones, because the United States did not support it. South Vietnamese Navy HQ 10 Nhat Tao resisted and sank on January 27, 1974. (This was the old USS Serene that the US Navy had transferred to South Vietnam in 1964, called HQ 10).

My brother often said that he was a witness; he would write about this battle as two RVNAF pilots docked on a South Vietnamese warship to fight China without any help on the part of the United States. The air group sent two so-called best helicopter pilots to volunteer, but before he could write anything, he suffered several strokes and now is considered to no longer be able to write. His recollections as well as the witnesses of the last days of the Buffalo year when he was about to pass the Lunar New Year at the 257th Squadron, I rewrote it out, even though I know that if he had written it, it would be more complete because he was on that Navy Ship. The intensity of the war was clearly seen and China took this opportunity, to take the two islands of Vietnam for the sake of the Americans, with a tacit agreement with the other side; they had been withdrawing, while the ARVN soldiers fought in vain, just like *"The hero is disarmed waiting to be exhausted before the thugs"*.

Returning to Saigon not long after the 1974 Tiger New Year, my brother announced that he was moving to Bien Hoa Airport and working with a helicopter squadron there. He worked 2 days off shift, so he sometimes went back to Saigon to visit me while I was at school, temporarily staying at Tran Quy Cap Elementary School. At this time, he was promoted to Major, but he lost his entire country before the ceremony could be carried out.

When Mom and my sister entered Saigon with Major Hieu, 233rd Squadron on March 26, 1975, they temporarily stayed at Ms. Dung's house at 8/1 Thieu Tri until the day we got to TSN Airport, after Nguyen Thanh Trung bombed the Presidential Palace on April 8, 1975 morning. We decided to go to the airport.

When we arrived at TSN Airport, he was afraid that when Chanh couldn't bring me to go under the DAO; he told me that if we had to use a helicopter to escape, he would fly to Vung Tau, then there would only be enough fuel left for about 30 minutes of flight. If there are no large ships, he would set the landing gear for everyone to jump off and then *"ditch"*. This plan failed and Mom and my sister had to stay with the VC for another 15 years, but this is the method many RVNAF pilots employed to get some families and soldiers to the VN Navy fleet or the US fleet at the end of April 1975.

In a "ditching" scene in the East Sea on April 30, a small boat came to pick up the last pilot who jumped out because there was no place to land. Fortunately, there was a clear spot on deck and the chopper was pushed into the sea to make room for another plane to land. The image on the Web.

After coming to the US, we settled in the same city of Gainesville, Florida. He and Mr. Thanh went to get a helicopter license; at that time, it only cost $500. Major Thanh is the flight squadron commander for training, famous for his light landings – like a mosquito, so Thanh *Mosquito* is a nickname because he landed as light as a mosquito, not knowing that the plane had landed. When the two of them took the exam, the examiner saw two flight books, more than 10,000 hours, he commented that they had more flight time than he had (South Vietnamese pilots because of the war, day and night on the ship, flying a lot, so the number of flight hours was high). We joked that most of them slept in a chopper, ready for a mission at any time. Of course, both of them passed easily, because they were so familiar with the Bell Helicopter.

Most of the Vietnamese helicopter pilots were brought to Savannah, Georgia, or New Orleans, Louisiana because there were American advisors here who sponsored their Vietnamese pilots and some got their flying licenses back in the US like him, then applied to Helicopter services companies like PHI (Petroleum Helicopter International) based in Lafayette, Louisiana. These services are for oil companies; they specialize in using yellow-painted helicopters to transport employees to drilling rigs in the Gulf of Mexico. When I went to work on the rig that summer, I was also transported by this type, faster than taking a long boat trip – and no seasickness. Thanks to their training during the war, Vietnamese pilots returning to fly in the US is not difficult. Mr. Thanh was admitted right after the interview and test flight with the airline, so they let him know that if he wanted to go to Louisiana to apply for a job, he could. Mr. Thanh is studying at SFCC and he is doing very well; he has a job as a shuttle pilot for an accounting firm boss but he is thinking about his wife and young children stuck in Vietnam. He needs a stable job, coming to the US to find jobs, it is easy to get a job that they are already familiar with, don't have to get more training, also familiar with the chopper and the sound of the propeller engine.

My brother went to Louisiana and also interviewed with PHI, in this company, besides flying, a pilot had to know about Navigation because they flew at sea and of course, he passed. They accepted him immediately, but suddenly a few weeks later he returned to Florida. When we ask why he did not accepted the job: *"They don't like your cowboy style of flying and let you retire early,"* he said, *"Flying that chopper is as easy as getting stuff in a bag, but "I don't feel safe because it doesn't have rockets and two miniguns under its belly!"*. It turned out that because he was used to gunships, he could not get accustomed to a non-war scene; his specialty was both defense and attack on the RVNAF's modified UH-1 Gunship.

Deciding to return to Florida, he took a job with the State of Florida Department of Transportation (FDOT) to measure roads; he was recommended by my other brother. The group consisted of three people riding an RV (Recreational Vehicle); arriving at the location, they stopped to tie a line on the road for cars to pass; each time a car passed on the rubber belt it registered twice, and was counted as 1 unit. It could be used to collect data, so that civil engineers could calculate the number of vehicles in traffic, to avoid traffic jams, or for road safety. The job was not difficult, but perhaps after visiting those of us studying at UF, seeing that it was not difficult for some kids older than him to study, he decided to go back to school. When I graduated in March 1980, he re-entered UF and asked to stay in a school family residence; at that time, he had just married.

He studied in school the old-fashioned way, with a bunch of index cards, and formulas... and he graduated with a degree in Electrical Engineering (Bachelor of Electrical Engineering, University of Florida) in 1983. Before he graduated, he got a job. Many places wanted to interview him because of his military background. He easily passed many challenges and got a security clearance. But it is true that many places chose him, so it was difficult for him to decide. First, he chose to work for the Navy, at a submarine base in Panama City, Florida, but then he chose to return to Macon, Georgia and this small city was so sad that he ended up being transferred to the Naval Center in Orlando, Florida until his retirement. After the first breakup, he returned to Vietnam, remarried, and brought his wife and her son to settle down and retire in Orlando, Florida.

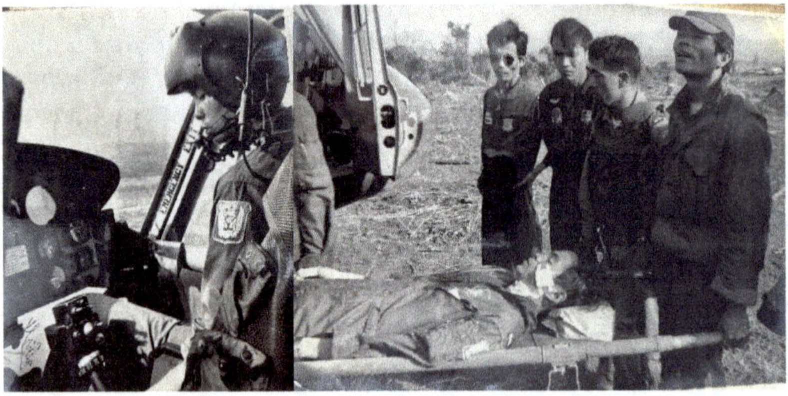

Lam Son 719-Southern Laos campaign[46]. The picture on the left shows my brother Mr. Chau on a flight to prepare to go to the front battlefield. The picture on the right is when he was shot down by VC's anti-aircraft defense, the copter shut down due to the heavy damage, but he finally brought it back to the base in Khe Sanh; he had lost a lot of blood, fainted, and had to be taken to the emergency room at the US Navy floating hospital in Da Nang. He still has bullet fragments in his body that have not been removed.

Miraculously enough, while his helicopter (213th Double Maces Squadron) was badly damaged, it managed to land at Khe Sanh's base. Notice that the windshield cover on top of the pilot's head was destroyed by the air defense explosion from above. The two landing gear sank deep into the ground [47].

---

46. Operation Lam Son 719 or 9th Route – Southern Laos Campaign was a limited-objective offensive campaign conducted in the southeastern portion of the Kingdom of Laos. The campaign was carried out by the armed forces of South Vietnam between 8 February and 25 March 1971, during the Vietnam War. Sources from Wikipedia

47 *In the Vietnam battlefield, the captains sat on the right, co-pilot on left when*

Khe Sanh Helicopter Base in 1971, ready for Lam Son 719-Photo Courtesy AFP

A mission to support and release the Special Force of H-34 Artist Co Khai Vu

---

they were on the mission, but when they were in training, the instructors sat on the left. When it comes to battle, sitting on either side is equally dangerous with enemy air defense.

A-1H Skyraider 516th Flying Tigers Squadron by artist Co Khai Vu.

A-37B Dragonfly 516th Flying Tigers Squadron by Artist Co Khai Vu - 2012.

SISTER BỢT

This is an adopted sister, one who holds a special place for me and my family. Her family is in the countryside, too poor for her mother to be able to feed the whole family with a normal life and get enough food and clothing, so she had to let my Mother raise her, partly to help her in her daily work, and also to have an independent life later, not to be so poor she would have to beg. Many families are poor, but they try to survive, maintain their dignity, do not have to ask for help, just like the slogan: *"Torn paper must keep the margin"*. She came to my house when we were still living in the inner city. My mother made an agreement with her mother to stay until she was 20 years old and then return to get married, but seeing that my Mom really needed help and no one could help her, she stayed, and Mom didn't forget this, so she saved money to help her to buy more rice fields later. We called her Sister Con until she got married (1963), then called her by her husband's name.

My Dad died when I was not even a year old, so she was the one to take care of me; she was about 15 years older than me, she carried me to play in the garden, went to the front gate because the house was big, she took care of me and fed me because I was still so young. When I was a child, after my Dad and my grandfather passed away, my Mom was depressed and did not have time to take care of us like before. So Sister Con was like a real sister, a young mother taking care of her younger brother. At that time in Vietnam, there were no diapers for children; every time I went to the toilet, she made me stand up on my butt, and pour cold water from a ladle to wash; sometimes the water was too cold, so I ran away and she had to dash to catch me. That I still remember. When she went to An Cuu's house, she helped Mom with housework, from cooking, washing dishes, and carrying buckets of water from two public wells to fill in two *"concrete containers"* and a few *"lu"* for use gradually [48], she still had to go to An Cuu market every day if Mom didn't go; besides all the errands are carried out by her, especially the food for the pigs to grow up quickly to sell [49]. I was 6 or 7 years old at this time, so she didn't have to worry much about me.

My mother only lived on her government widow's pension, which was not nearly as much as when she was still with my Dad; so she had to raise more pigs to make a profit, after selling them, she saw the customers coming to catch the pigs, who screamed so much they were so pitiful... so she gave up of investing this way. Thanks to Mom, she raised pigs so I knew how the process was; first, she bought a small pig, with white or black hair, and waited for a few days or weeks; there were a few men on the street, holding a rod like a fishing rod and a bag containing tools including needles. thread, cutlery, a grindstone, and a jar of betel nut lime. As they walked around, they shouted "*Who needs to castrate pigs?"* The boar *(castrated)* or the female pig *(spaying)* so that it only eats, and animals are routinely castrated in order to reduce aggression. These men (called *neutering guys*) performed surgery very quickly, when they finished sewing up the wound,

48. *My house has a shallow tank made of cement, reinforced concrete, rectangular in shape of about 1mx2m with four legs, about 1 meter high, with a "hole" on the side so that all the dirty water can be drained when cleaning if needed. Used to store rain water or well water, with a lid on the top. When needed, just take the "dipper" above the ladle to use. Dirty settles to the bottom, once in a while, we have to clean up the moss by draining all the water, climbing in and scrubbing.*

The jar is a large clay pot, the middle is bulging, so people often parade fat people like a jar. May contain liquid or dried foods such as rice, beans or cereals. If water is stored for drinking, the water in the bowl is clean and cool. When I came home from school hungry in the afternoon, I often took a baked rice paper, dipped it in a bowl to soften it, then added the granulated sugar, rolled it up, chewed it deliciously, scooped up water in the jar and drank until dinner was served.

49. *Food for pigs is usually bran or some banana trees in the garden, cut down the banana tree, peel off the hard outer shell, leaving the young core, chopped, mixed with chopped spinach, and cooked for them to eat.*

they applied lime to the wound, so it would heal up in a few days. This is the pigpen that is in my memory; when I was not satisfied with something and started to cry in protest, my eldest brother picked me up and threatened to put me in the cage with the pig crawling inside, scaring the little boy even more, crying hysterically. Shouting, he did this many times, but this method did not cure my *obscene nature*. Later, in the US, they brought a breed of *boars (Vietnamese potbelly pigs or mini pigs)* from Vietnam, sold quite expensively, more than several thousand dollars; they make good pets in the house because this breed is very intelligent.

Since my mother is aware of how poor Sister Con's family is, every year she contributes money to allow her to go back to her hometown to visit her mother; every time she goes, she hides a package of clothes in front of the alley to avoid us finding out and not letting her go. Her mother can sometimes afford to visit her daughter every year, sometimes even every few years; every time she returns to the village, Mom sends clothes and food with her. At that time, I was too young to see that I did not know how poor I was to be pitiful, but I still knew that I was luckier than many others, not having to work as an *"osin"*. Mom got a birth certificate for her, and declared that she was like an adopted child; she is older than my oldest brother Chau but he always calls her *"older sister"*. Mom also lets her go to a night class called *"Popular Education"*, which was open to illiterate people who yearned to learn to read and write at that time. Maybe she didn't like it, so Mom didn't force it on her either. Every day we grew older and went Scouting, so she had to take care of us less and less. Mom knew that there was a daughter in the house is like having an atomic bomb. At that time, if there was an unmarried daughter who got pregnant, the village people would still have to kick them out of the village, smeared with a bad reputation for life, so Mom saw when she met her boyfriend Mr. Bot, his family was also poor, so he had to work as a blacksmith in Ngheo Dan Xay with Uncle Dich, working on aesthetic Wrought Iron Gates and Fences. She met him when she came to collect water from the well on the weekends. There was a summer drought when the public well near the railroad had no water to take home. Mom let her get married in 1963, then she gave birth to her first son in 1965, named Ty (older) in the Year of the Snake, 12 years younger than me by the correct zodiac sign. After getting married, her husband had to join the army at the rank of non-commissioned officer (from Private to Sergeant), so she still stayed at my house temporarily. I often played with her youngest son and gave him some of my old toys. I invented and instructed him to make his own toys: back then there were no ready-made toys like now. One day while playing behind the kitchen, Ty suddenly started crying and crying; both my sister and I ran over, saw a red stain on his cheeks, and looked up at the roof to see a hole. On the ground was the head of a bullet from an unknown source. He had fallen down, but luckily he was okay. During the 1968 Tet Offensive, Mr. Bot returned home to visit and was also arrested when he took refuge in the Catholic Church in town, fortunately for him, he was crowded in with the soldiers and non-commissioned officers, so they didn't notice him. He untied his ropes and escaped back home, or else he would have died in Phu Thu or Khe Da Mai.

The family was poor; they knew that living in the city would be difficult to make ends meet, so they moved to a village. The eldest son, who got married, also found a way to work, to help both small and large families; he went to cut wood in the forest and unfortunately, while transporting it back in 2013, the car flipped over and he died. When Ms. Bot suffered a ruptured appendix and had to be taken to Hue Central Hospital, if not treated she would have died, but she had to pay in advance per hospital policy there. Mom, when she heard about that - her children and grandchildren informed her on the phone - money was sent to her urgently, and so she could be sent to surgery in a timely manner. Perhaps she has also seen Mom and us treat her like sisters and children in the family, not like servants. Mom later called her *"Grandma Bot"* because she surpassed her in terms of the number of grandchildren, including *great-grandchildren.* She called my Mom back *Grandma.*

Life in her hometown after getting married with many children was also very difficult, but she never complained or asked for anything, because she was always grateful to Mom for helping her a lot.

Mom told us, that when she visited her house in the village, the meals were rice with only grains of salt. Mom asked if she needed any help, and her husband asked for a threshing machine to process rice faster and easier. Unlike other people who often ask Mom for money to live, they only asked for a rice-making machine to make a long-term living, so Mom gave it to her immediately. Mr. Bot is also a very gentle, honest, and industrious person, so the couple is loved by many people around them.

In September 2022, when she heard that my brother Lap and my sister-in-law informed them that they would bring Mom's ashes home for burial, despite being old, she asked her grandchildren to take her to the mausoleum to say goodbye to Mom. Not only did she visit, but she also dressed properly, took off her shoes and left them outside the mausoleum, and went barefoot to pay respects to a benefactor, an owner, and her adoptive mother for the last time, in a respectful and dignified manner. She did not have the opportunity to study and get a higher education like many others, but her attitude and actions touched and were admired by my family. This is a poor family that I must use the following qualities to describe: spontaneity, honesty, uprightness, and gentleness.

Today, although they are still poor, they live happily with their children and grandchildren and great-grandchildren. She has 8 children (*with 3 children having died at birth*), 14 grandchildren and 4 great-grandchildren, living in a village on the Bo River in Co Bi village, Phong Son ward. She is 85 years old this year, but still healthy, which is a good thing.

She bowed and said goodbye to her foster mother at the tomb.

In the picture of the whole family, Bot is the one behind me, with long hair on the left.

MY BROTHER

My older brother was born in 1949, the year of the Buffalo. When he was born, my father had gone through World War II, the famine of At Dau (1945), the French, and the Japanese adding to the Viet Minh's seizure of power, so his dream for Vietnam was expressed in naming his two sons, taking the two main words out of the four words to express the wishes of the majority of people at that time *Independence* and *Peace*. The wish is so small, but more than half a century later, it has not yet been found in the beloved homeland of Vietnam.

And because *"Ngoc"*, the middle syllable of Hoang's surname, doesn't always rhyme with the first name *Lap (Independence)*, he had another intention when he replaced the word *Thong* in the middle name for *Ngoc*, implying the use of *Thong Nhat (Unified)* in naming, perhaps though the future Geneva accords, but he foretold how the French would divide the country in two. The literal and figurative meaning of both my brother's names is the wish of the Vietnamese people at any time. Our Dad only died a few months before the country was divided into two and considered *Independence* because the French colonialists withdrew and gave control to the Vietnamese people, but after that, civil war broke out in Vietnam. Until 1975, the country was unified, no longer divided into two regions. Thus, his name in a double meaning is considered to have applied to his homeland Vietnam after 26 years *(Unified and Independent)*. My name *(Peace)* is still nowhere to be found half a century from the day of *Reunification*, everyone is still blindly looking forward to *Peace* and *Freedom* for someone's immortal sentence *"Nothing is more precious than Independence and Freedom"* is an obvious fact in life accepted by all people. This is difficult to do if the government is not for the people, but only by a small number of people using their power to force opponents to obey their rules. That is contrary to the definition of the two words *Freedom*, both spiritually and materially.

He was born at the same time as my Dad, because of his military trips away from home, had a *"mistress"* and she was pregnant with his child. My Mom struggled to overcome many mental challenges during this period. Growing up in such a situation, my brother and I tried to learn so that our mother would not be disappointed. When the whole family moved to An Cuu's house after our Dad died, he had to stay temporarily at an acquaintance's house to continue his elementary education at Tran Quoc Toan Elementary School in the Inner Citadel. Uncle Diep was a staff member of my Dad when he was still alive, so it was okay there; it is just that the family did not eat spicy like our family, so when he returned to our family after completing primary school, he didn't like spicy food like the rest of the family. My Mom had to cook less spicy or bland food just for him.

Getting used to spicy foods before my brother joined the group, my oldest brother and I had to bite more chili peppers put in the side because in the cold season in Hue or when we ate a bowl of tuna vermicelli with a whole chili cooked together, it took my brother decades to do that.

He attended Nguyen Tri Phuong High School after he passed the entrance exam for the Sixth Grade. At that time, this school only had grades six to nine, so then he had to move to Quoc Hoc (National Academy) for secondary level 10th to 12th grades. My whole family was in Math B and majoring in French as a second language, except for my sister who chose English.

In addition to the general classes at the school, he also studied French in the evening, at the French Cultural Center. In the first year of the 12th grade, he finished the program of the French Cultural Center in Hue (Centre Culturel Francais), so his French was very good, and later served him well when he entered Saigon: he had to submit to an interview with the Director of the Residence Alexandre de Rhodes in Saigon, who was a Canadian. This was a completely French-speaking dormitory run by Catholic priests, so it was difficult to enter; most people attended French-speaking schools; each year they only accepted about 3 to 5 people. The year before that, there was Mr. Ly Gia Tin (from Hue), and Mr. Le Han, the following year, my brother and Mr. Le Chi Nghi were admitted, all of them were on USAID scholarships and went to the US to study in 1968 [50].

50. USAID: United States Agency for International Development
USAID scholarships funded by the US government for 4-year undergraduate programs

He studied much more diligently than me, taking Math from our cousin Mr. Luyen, because he was a professor of Mathematics. He also read most books at that time, especially the swordplay novels of Jin Yong. During that period, if you wanted to read a book, you could rent it, then return and borrow another book after reading it, since famous book series like Dragon Girl, Water Margin, or Journey to the West each had more than 20 episodes; author Jin Yong wanted to attract customers, so he kept the story moving along for a while and then transitioned into another story so that the readers of that time were fascinated to see where the story would go next. Later, when the movies were filmed, some people loved to watch one episode after another, until going to work in the morning. I was fortunate to be able to borrow a volume from the University Library, thanks to Akela BH as the Director there, so I didn't have to rent books like my brother; every time he exchanged books, he had to ride a bicycle or on the way home from school, rent books right on Duy Tan street. Crossing the An Cuu Bridge before reaching the Mieu Dai Cang on the right were small bookstores. Sometimes, our aunts came to my house; my Mom invited them in to have lunch with the family and saw that he was still eating and reading books. They went home and told their children that they had to *"study well like Lap. I enjoy seeing him eat while still studying: that's why he always passed the exam!"* They didn't know that he loved swordplay, my family had to eat together, but he was obsessed with Wuji who was flirting with his girlfriends or the Sun Wukong monkey in Journey to the West was fighting with the demon in the novel.

He participated in Scouting a lot, learned more martial arts (judo) and was better than me. From the Wolf Cubs, he became the leader of the Chi Lang Cub Group under Akela Quynh Hoa. Must be the leader of the white den to get Akela and the leaders were promoted to be the all-group leaders. Now that I think about it, why are the leaders biased, the black, gray or brown dens rarely won the contest like the white – do you think the white den was superior to the others?

---

at US universities, according to many people, are more difficult than Colombo scholarships to New Zealand. The scholarship is reviewed and interviewed by US staff. The year my brother applied, there were 1000 students, after two exams, there were only 200 left. After interviewing 60 people, my brother was an international student selected from that small number.

When he went into the Boy Scouts, I was still a Cub, but the Wolf Cubs were loved by the leaders. There was also ready-to-eat food at the camp, the sleeping place was on the floor like in the camp, and the leaders surrounded all of us unlike the Boy Scouts, who had to take care of everything themselves: transportation to eating and drinking to training in the basics of leadership, livelihood, called *"the Patrol Method"*.

When I was about to transfer from the Cubs to the Boy Scouts, Mom told him, *"Let Hoa join the Wolf patrol with you to go to a meeting or go camping together for convenience"*. That's what she thought, but I was not surprised when the Cub Leaders transferred 8 Cubs; the Bach Dang Boy Scout group had 4 patrols: Nightingale, Lion, Wolf, and Crocodile. I did not join the Wolf team with him but went with the Lion patrol with Patrol Leaders Loc and Trung.

Hung went to the Wolf Patrol; my brother was the patrol leader; Tran Dinh Tuan became the Lion. Tran Dinh Loc was Tuan's brother, who was the Patrol Leader (died in Montreal, Canada in 2022), Mr. Loc's family lives at the Ai Hoa Bookstore; all family members joined the Scouts; they owned a movie theater; I loved to watch the artists paint a large canvas poster hung up in front of the theater when a new movie arrived: their hands were quick, they painted quickly, the colors were beautiful. After Mr. Loc went to Venture, Mr. Tung succeeded him (later becoming a Doctor at the Central Hospital in Hue). The four Patrol Leaders when I joined the group were: Lion: Mr. Tran Dinh Loc (d)(Canada); Wolf: Mr. Hoang Thong Lap (USA); Nightingale: Mr. Ly Gia Nhan (Australia) and the Crocodile was Mr. Diep Ngoc Tiep.

But instead of joining the Wolf team with my brother being the patrol leader there, I went into the Lion patrol. At that time, Mr. Le Trong Trung was the assistant patrol leader, and Mr. Trung was the son of Uncle Xang, the director in charge of the Youth group in the local government. In Hue, Trung's brother, Hieu, was also on my patrol. My brother was close friends with Mr. Loc and Trung (San Jose, California), and this patrol was known as *"happy"*, the whole My patrol was nicknamed *"the rich patrol"*, since we had a patrol office (the garage of Trung-Hieu's family on Nguyen Thanh street in the inner city).

My brother must have known the saying *"Familiarity breeds contempt"* or *"No man is a prophet in his own land"*, so it would be better to let me learn from another leader. I don't know what it would have been like to be in the same patrol with him then, but not long after becoming a Boy Scout, Scouting opened the new Venture group (1965, for 15-18 year-olds), and all the patrol leaders in the Bach Dang group left their leadership roles and handed them over to younger ones. After the 1968 Tet Offensive, we lost a few leaders and our activities were no longer normal, as the war was getting fiercer, so after the *"red fiery summer of 1972"*, we no longer had the good fortune to go camping far away, but only had meetings at the National Academy Boys or Girls High School, located in the middle of the city.

Talking about my brother, but also talk about Scouting life a lot because in my heart, I personally still think that thanks to Scouting, my whole family is fortunate to live with Mom's support; without a father in the family we had to become self-learning, self-disciplined from a Scout's life. The whole family, whether boys or girls, knew how to cook and sew by ourselves because Mom has a foot pedal Singer sewing machine on which my brother sewed patrol flags. I just know how to mess around with it and sew pillowcases – the easiest thing until later.

After completing his second baccalaureate degree in Hue, he went to Saigon to continue his studies at the University in 1967. Thanks to his fluent French during the months of tutoring in Hue, he was admitted to the Alexandre de Rhodes Residence in Saigon, where he applied for a study abroad program and received a USAID scholarship from the United States. He was scheduled to board a plane on the 7th, after the Tet Offensive in 1968. Returning to Hue for Tet and stuck, but fortunately, the study abroad program had to be postponed, because of the international students, despite the effect on several cities in the South; thus, he returned to Saigon and traveled to the US later.

Along with a group of international students, he went to California and studied for the first two years at California State University, Fullerton, California, before transferring to the University of Florida to major in Civil Engineering. After graduating with a Bachelor's Degree, he applied to continue his studies for an M.S. and should have returned to Vietnam around 1975, because he had sent his belongings back and was actually ready for his return trip. Fortunately, he did not return because he was scheduled to submit his thesis in April 1975. *(In early 1975, USAID prepared, informed, and sent him a one-way airplane ticket for his return, scheduled for August 1975 after a stop for a one-week conference in Washington, DC. On the way back, he was to have made a stopover in Australia. That would coincide with his fiancée's schedule, as Miss. Le Tuong had just finished her Colombo scholarship and both of them would be in Saigon at the same time. Fortunately, April 1975 took place before the repatriation, otherwise, they would both be stuck in Vietnam like his friend, Mr. Nguyen Van Trai (US/AID) who returned home, got married, and could not get out at the last minute. Later, however, they managed to settle in Canada.*

When he learned that my oldest brother and I had made it to Thailand on the 29th and then Camp Pendleton, California, he said to *"Call me Collect"*, anytime I wanted to talk (the recipient pays after the Phone Operator connects). At that time, the phone companies allowed this method if the caller had to use a public phone to call the recipient. I don't know how much he had to pay for the phone while we were in the refugee camp.

After a month in the camp, he asked for help from Mr. Ted Srygley, then a student of Cuong Nhu Karate, who was the Director of the Shands Hospital's UF Medical Library in Gainesville. We went to Gainesville, Florida, but did not stay with the Sponsor for a day; he and Mr. Le Trong Hieu (my Lion deputy patrol leader, Bach Dang Boy Scouts) went straight to the Airport to pick up us and take us to the rented accommodation at Glen Springs Manor Apartment. Mr. Thanh, the 233rd Sky Hawk Helicopter Squadron Commander, also accompanied us, because he had no one and did not want to stay in the refugee camp alone waiting for a sponsor.

He finished his thesis at the end of 1975. Ms. Le Tuong, valedictorian of the best girl's school in Hue, and his fiancée passed Baccalaureate 2 in 1970, while studying in New Zealand through a Colombo scholarship. When I was a student of the National Academy, and I heard that there were students who had studied abroad on a Colombo scholarship, our eyes met, because one had to be very good to get in: the US scholarships were easier, but they were not available for study of medicine or any related subject, because of the lengthy time required for schooling. She graduated from college in New Zealand in 1974, went to Australia to work, then got stuck in April 1975: no country to go to, my brother filed a petition to relocate her to the US in 1976 and they got married in a simple wedding ceremony at the main Cuong Nhu Karate dojo at University Avenue in Gainesville. Those invited to the wedding only included close relatives and martial arts students, the dojo only had a few chairs so everyone had to stand around. Home-made dishes were brought in, so they often reminded their children that their wedding only cost $300 and was still as happy as usual, the moral being that you don't need to spend a lot of money on a wedding.

After graduating with a Master's of Civil Engineering at UF, he returned to the capital city of Tallahassee, Florida, and worked with the Florida Department of Transportation (F.D.O.T) until his retirement as Chief State Traffic Engineer and Manager, Traffic Engineer and Operations Office). In addition, he also held the position of President of the Florida State Civil Engineer Association. Outside of work, he is also a Karate master of the Cuong Nhu and established a dojo in the state capital named Phoenix Center and on the nearby campus of Florida State University.

They had a first son who graduated from Stanford University and opened a specialty restaurant called Freshrolls; the second granddaughter attended UF and worked for the Federal Highway Administration (FHWA), certified as a professional engineer (PE) in civil engineering and holds a position of the State of Arkansas Department of Transportation Administrator. The youngest daughter, after finishing Stanford University, studied and graduated with a Master of Business Administration (MBA) from the famous Northwestern Kellogg School of Management and has been working for famous brands such as Disney, Apple, and DoorDash as Director of Global Strategies [51].

Their success and that of their children is probably partly due to the family upbringing style: she was the top student (Valedictorian) of the famous Dong Khanh Girls' School in Hue, where her mother worked as Assistant Principal. The eldest son and the youngest

51. *DoorDash, where his youngest daughter works, opened in 2013 by 3 foreign students studying at Stanford University, at first only delivered food to customers' homes in PaloAlto, until 2020, with service Covid has become a major global company because of increasing customer demand. The owners have become billionaires.*

also ranked first (Valedictorian) at Leon County High School in Tallahassee and both were accepted, attended, and graduated from the famous Stanford University, California.

He was chosen to be honored through the *"Vietnamese People's Glory"* program organized by journalist Trong Minh (California), whereby successful Vietnamese in the US were highlighted. They retired and settled in Venice, Florida, although their children are still working.

Two brothers - Hoa and Lap

The picture on the left was taken in 1984 with Grand Master Dr. Ngo Dong (died 2000), the founder of Cuong Nhu Karate in Hue (1965) and the University of Florida (1971). Phoenix Dojo, Tallahassee, Florida (1987) (right).

My brother's family.

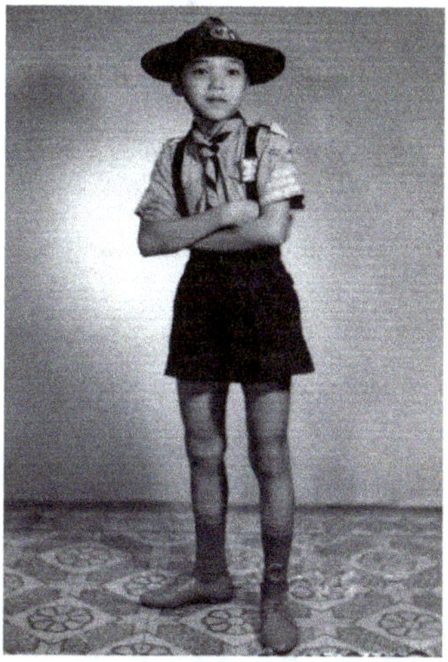

Picture taken around 1960-My brother was the leader of the Cubs

This photo was taken in the summer of 1970 while my eldest brother was still a lieutenant of the 213th Double Spikes Mace helicopter squadron (wearing a flight suit on the right) and a pharmacist friend, a lieutenant in the Airborne, Nguyen Mau Trinh (on the left) at Tan Son Nhut Airport, when taking my brother Lap for his return to the US and his fiancée Le Tuong, who went to study in New Zealand on a Colombo scholarship, after Mr. Lap returned home to visit in the summer.

MY OLDER SISTER - 1945-2021

In my family, the only girl was my sister. She was born in the year of the Rooster, 1945 which is an easy year to remember because of the famine in Vietnam and around the world. Not sure where my parents were but my aunt handled the birth registration for her; she also had a daughter named Gai (girl), so when the document maker asked what her name was, she said that was her name. That is how her name stuck with my sister for the rest of her life. She hated that name because Mom and Dad did not intend to name her that. When she was growing up, she asked how to change her name, but the court's office said there had to be a valid reason, the most common one being holding the same name as another ancestral family member. If there is any evidence, such as the genealogy that must be recorded, they will change it but still have to use the old name for a while, together with the new name for example: The old name and new name Nhu Nguyen.

Finding it difficult and having to write down her name, changing it back in the genealogy, even though it was temporarily taboo for the elderly, so she wouldn't do it later, but if she did, her name would be Hoang Thi Nhu Nguyen, or add a bottom accent of Nguyen. The intention to change her name was canceled until she moved to the US with the whole family. When she entered the country, she changed her mind because it was no longer necessary, people called her Ms. Hoang because she used her last name instead of a name like in Vietnam, and when she came to the US, the US immigration officer who did the paperwork was surprised that no one in her family had the same last name. Her husband is in the royal family, so he has to follow the verse for naming order: the purpose is to know the higher and lower status in the family. Her husband's family name is Vinh, her son's last name is Bao, and her daughter's family name is Huyen Cong Tang Ton Nu... Hoang is her last name, because in Vietnam when she got married, she didn't adopt her husband's last name, like in the US. Although they are Nguyen Phuoc, few people use them because they do not know their hierarchy, so they follow the verse: Mien Huong Ung

Buu Vinh…Bao Che Dinh Long Truong…

Growing up in a war situation, after she finished primary school at Doan Thi Diem School in the inner city, the whole family moved to An Cuu and in 1959 she passed the entrance exam to Dong Khanh High School for Girls, 6th Grade. She chose English as her second language, but all of her siblings chose French, only when she was in grade 10, she also chose Math B, which girls rarely choose because studying Math is difficult to swallow. Remember when the novel by writer Quynh Dao (real name Tran Triet, from Taiwan) was just popularized in Vietnam at the beginning, my sister was such a fan of her books that she always read them. with her, from the *River of Goodbye*, *By the Water to the Empty Hamlet...* which was later turned into a movie, but at that time, you had to read books. She loved her stories; so many people mistakenly thought she used the pseudonym of the female artist to name her youngest daughter later. The name of her youngest daughter was given by her husband, taken from two verses of Kieu's story [52]:

143 Hài văn lần bước dặm xanh,
144 Một vùng như thể cây ***quỳnh*** *cành* ***dao****.*

His figured shoes gently striding in the green,
The environs sparkled like a grove of gems. [53]

Finishing a Baccalaureate Diploma I in 1964, she went to grade 12 in 1965 and chose to take the Quy Nhon Pedagogical Examination (SPQN) after taking the 2nd Baccalaureate exam in May 1965. This is a major belonging to the Ministry of Education, which upon graduation she will specialize in teaching from grade 1 to grade 5 at elementary level. If any teacher supplements this with Baccalaureate II, they will be allowed to practice in Saigon and then move on to teach High School (grades 6 to 9). Starting with the first course, it is only open in Quy Nhon City, so students had to stay in a boarding house if they had come from another province, mostly in Hue. She entered the school in September

52. **Quynh** plant or Scientific name: *Epiphyllum,* Family: *Cactaceae*
Dao plant also called *"The fish bones tree"* in Vietnamese. Scientific name: *Euphorbia Tiricabira*, Family: *Euphorbiaceae.*
Both plants are known for medicinal uses.

53. *"The Tale of Kieu"* by Nguyen Du (1765-1820) a famous Vietnamese poem had 3,254 verses. Even though so many people had translated into English, it would be true to read the original rather than a translation. I have taken these two verses English translation from Phan Huy, MPH.

1965, the 4th class of SPQN, along with a number of registered girls, including Ms. Dong Hai, who was very close and was her roommate during her studies. In 1970, because the number of teachers from Hue was too large, they opened a new Pedagogy class 7 in Hue to study at Quoc Hoc on the next floor, near the Governor's Palace. She graduated from school in May 1967. In July, she chose to work in Quang Ngai Province and at the end of the year she returned to Hue to celebrate 1968 Tet when she met the massacre of Mau Than. Coming here to teach for a while, she decided she would like to move back to Hoa Vang, Da Nang. At that time, my oldest brother served at Da Nang AFB, so he often went out to lunch and brought his Air Force friends with him. My sister, from the family school class at Hue Girls' School, cooked delicious Hue food, so some of the brothers loved it, some of them asked my brother to let them become serious with her, but my brother knew the RVNAF pilots' life and didn't want his sister to be a widow; thus, he didn't encourage anyone to jump in. Later, she applied to teach fifth grade at Le Loi School; at that time, I went to Saigon to study. This is the school in the city center in front of the Treasury Department and the Main Post Office, next to it is the Jeanne d'Arc girls' school we call Rang Da, the boarding girls there are like devils when the crowds of boys were passing by, even though the nuns who were supervising them heard that they were very strict and cruel.

She taught in Hue until March 23, when my brother's friend Thanh followed his instructions to follow Colonel Phuoc's helicopter to Hue to take my sister and Ma to Da Nang Airport on her blue Yamaha motorcycle.

On March 27, she entered Saigon, with Major Hieu's flight from the 233rd Sky Hawk Squadron, and on March 29, we lost Da Nang. My sister and Ma stayed temporarily at Ms. Dung's house until April 20th, then went to TSN Airport and temporarily stayed at the family dormitory near Phi Long gate. When my brother and I left on the morning of April 29 to find a way to go to the Airport runway to find a plane to get out, Mom and my sister were stuck at TSN dormitory and returned to Ms. Dung's house when the Airport was occupied, then had to return to Hue and report to the new government.

She was stuck in Saigon, returned to Hue, and was fined and

not allowed to teach at Le Loi's old school again, but sent to teach at a school farther away in Phu Vang and had to study and be re-educated in *Ai Tu Binh Dien* reeducation camp for more than a year. This was typical of the despicable revenge regime of the new Communist government, only one female teacher, in education, but they did punish her like in the military.

Not leaving Saigon in the last days of April with me and my brother, although staying at Tan Son Nhut Airport in the last days and hours, she had to return to Hue to teach again at a new location and get to know Mr. Quy, the music professor, and Hue theater owner. He is the only son in the Royal family, living on Binh Minh Road right at Dap Da, Vy Da. They had a simple wedding in April 1977 at home. Before the Communists took over the South, rumors circulated that when they entered, they would force Southern girls to take their wounded soldiers as husbands. Therefore, after April, many couples rushed to get married. Although he was a teacher of music and drama, he also had a lot of poetry, including poems that he put to music. At our wedding, he wrote a poem with the first words put together into a sentence. My wife's name is very special, and difficult to incorporate into a poem:

My Brother-in-law Vinh Quy's poem for Hoa-Tuoi on our wedding day:

The pearl from here shines on your home,

In tune with a love song together,

Spring with green the love color forever,

Fresh always means passionate love,

Hundreds of mountains and thousands of rivers, we are together,

Five continents and four oceans, you are with me,

Happiness wishes for the couple,

Eternal happiness blooms with thousands of flowers.

In Vietnamese all the word at the beginning, if you put them together:

Ngọc Hòa Xuân Tươi Trăm Năm Hạnh Phúc.

Ngoc Hoa Xuan Tuoi Hundred Years of Happiness.

When I went home to visit in 1988, I advised her and her family to supplement the application for sponsorship through the ODP, but she said that her husband did not want to go abroad because he did not know whether he could continue to teach music. He did not want to change jobs. He graduated from Hue National School of Music and Drama. He knew how to play musical instruments, namely the Clarinet, but he can play other traditional instruments. I told him: *"America is a free country; you can do whatever you want; no one will force you."*

Immigrating to the US through the O.D.P. (Orderly Departure Program) they went to Tallahassee and then moved to Orlando. They have a son and two daughters. All three finished high school in the US and graduated with Bachelor's Degrees from the University of Florida (UF). The first son graduated with a Bachelor of Mechanical and Industrial Engineering, the second daughter majored in Finance from the College of Business, and the youngest, after finishing her BS at UF, continued her MA in Library at the University of South Florida, but after working for a while, she did not like it, and continued to study at Nova University as a Physician's Assistant. When the children were still studying at UF, if she missed her children on the weekend, she would drive her car to Gainesville by herself, about 2 hours from Orlando, by memory, without a map, as at that time there was no GPS device like there is now.

After the children graduated, she had to take care of Mom because it was more suitable for Mom to live with her daughter than with her daughter-in-law. In 2016, her husband began to suffer from dementia (Alzheimer's), but she decided not to let him into a nursing home; rather, she stayed at home to take care of him. In 2017, she changed to DeBary City for her youngest daughter to go to work at a closer hospital and the house was larger because she had to take care of both the elderly relatives: her husband and our Mother.

Her husband was getting weaker and on Valentine's Day in 2019, he entered the hospital ICU and passed away after a few hours, my sister was disappointed and sad even though she knew that his illness was getting worse.

After her husband's passing, Mom's health degenerated; Mom could not eat or drink much, and she had to have a nurse to help Mom in the evening to ease her burden, until Mother's Day in 2019, when Mom passed away.

In just a few months, she lost two loved ones; her personal health decline was evident when we went to visit. My wife and I intended to visit her more, but in February 2020, I informed her that I would postpone my trip to Vietnam to attend my 50th National Academy High School reunion because of COVID-19. The Covid situation in the US was getting worse and worse; without any vaccine everyone stayed at home, only communicating via phone or FaceTime. Mom's first death anniversary was in 2020 but we could not meet our family until her second year anniversary in May 2021, when my oldest brother and family member, her doctor, confirmed that she had terminal lung cancer, although she had previously reported it privately to us. Everyone was sad; her children came back to meet and visit St. Augustine together as a last reunion. She had planned to follow us back to Vietnam and visit Japan when Covid was over but never had the chance to do it. She also did not have the opportunity to read my book when it came out.

Despite chemo and medicine, no one can avoid Birth, Aging, Sickness, and Death. This is the life cycle of a person, a law derived from Buddhism. She texted me and my brother when she was admitted to the ER/ICU on Friday, August 13, 2021, a week before Vu Lan (Buddhism Mother's Day). The next Saturday morning, the children informed us about her condition. She started to become confused, so I informed Ngan and Dong Hai, her former roommate and best friend in Tampa, that we had decided to drive up to visit her at DeBary Hospital right away.

Halfway to Vero Beach, her children called and said that after the hospital took her to the Hospice room downstairs, because of her condition, she passed peacefully and quickly, and because of Covid-19 the hospital would only let in one person at a time, but in fact they let the whole family in. My family and Mr. Ngan and Dong Hai also came from Tampa, arriving an hour after us because of a traffic jam. She passed away with her children and grandchild surrounding her, friends and relatives, and the prohibition of the

Covid pandemic; everyone tried to come to say goodbye for the last time. Thus, she met her closest people for the last time. I hope she left peacefully. If there is a next life, please let her not have to become a woman again, as she always desired.

Quynh flower and Dao plant

I admitted to ICU tonight. Last will to the kids, let me go.

Can I go to visit you?

Yes.

I will contact your daughter for appointment.

Are you in hospital or at home?

ICU (Intensive Care Unit).

Go ahead and rest. Do you want to tell me anything?

My son just came.

Good, How do you feel this morning?

Tired if sit up.

The original text message she sent was on Friday, August 13, 2021 when the ambulance took her to the ICU (above). No one thought she would be gone the next day, because she was still using her iPhone to text and still wrote all the accents in Vietnamese.

FRIENDS

MY FRIEND'S SEPARATE DIARY PAGE

This is a "loose diary page", briefly written on the back of a cigarette pack at U-Tapao airport, Thailand on April 30, 1975, by Second Lieutenant Chanh Van Nguyen for his lover stuck in Saigon, about his last hours at Tan Son Nhut Airport, where he served as an Air Force Security/Intelligent Officer. Rewritten from the copy with the consent of Second Lieutenant Chanh. Chanh was National Academy Quoc Hoc's high school friend me from 6th to 12th grade (1965-1972) and even when we came to America to study and graduated from the University of Florida.

April 29, 1975: At 4 am, the Viet Cong (VC) started shelling Tan Son Nhut Airport (TSN) with 122mm rockets from three directions: Nha Be, Hoc Mon, Go Vap…and it seemed that there was an inline, so the targets were heavily shelled; they hit the parking spot of F5, EC-47, AC-119K, C-130, A-37, UH-1H aircraft …and some facilities, Office of Air Force Command, Air Force Residences, Air Force Passengers Loading area, Phi Long Gate…

9 AM, I was still at the operating office (Air Force Security Office near Phi Long entrance gate), listening and receiving messages on Motorola System[54] Con Son channel (the name for the highest level officer using communication devices), inventorying the damage caused by the artillery fire last night. Initial raid assessment: Most of the A-37 PKG jets exploded or caught fire (31 of them), UH-1H Helicopters of the 259G squadron burned up (10 choppers), EC-47, F5, and C-130 (6 damaged).

9:15 AM In the morning, there were reports on Con Son channel

54. *Vietnamese Airport Security/Intelligent Division used the Motorola Walkie-Talkie System to communicate each other inside the airport. They used code names that changed and only them know who they were talking about in the communicating channel, avoid the enemy secretly listen to and reveal the codes. As we noticed, they are using the famous land sites, including some in the North.*

C-130 and C-119, large cargo airplanes, a number of passengers, military personnel, and pilots of all kinds climbing onto C-130 and C-119 aircraft, taxiing to the runway and taking off.

9:45 AM there was a report from Qui Nhon 2 (QN2): four persons, namely, Major Mai, My, Quang, Ha plus Captain Loc and Second Lieutenant Nhan, and a lot of Air Force Security branch personnel climbed on a C-130 to go. I presented to Lam Son, Hong Ha (HH), and Hong Ha 1 (HH1) and 2 (HH2) but did not hear back; no one answered.

9:50 AM QN 2 reported HH1 and HH2 boarded to C-130. That's it... Hoang Robert, Kiki cried in the phone to call HH, Lieutenant Tuong and I reassured him but Hoang was still panicking. Lieutenant Nha (Hung Cuong) and Captain Thuan (Victory), Major Thuan called Con Son to ask how the situation was and the evacuation of the aircraft (?). Lieutenant Tuong did not dare to answer the question clearly for fear of people panicking, but in my opinion, now there is nothing left to hide. Thu Duc 1 called Thu Duc (TD) but did not hear back. Earlier, TD had issued an instruction: *"You should find a way to get out to the airstrip and get on a plane ..."*. HC was stuck at number 4 Nguyen Binh Khiem[55] how to get to TSN?. Perhaps Lieutenant Nha and his employees were all stuck down there because of the 24-hour curfew from 5:20 p.m. on April 28 after three A-37s bombed TSN Airport.

10:30 AM Cuong, Vinh, and Chanh got on Jeep 0198, brought enough guns, and carried more staff, served at Bien Hoa AFB, and Airport Security Office staff to run towards the runway. I wanted to run across the dormitory to get some more clothes already in my handbag, but Cuong was driving so he didn't run back to the dormitory, and none of us thought of running this way! When I

55. *This is the main office of Air Force Security/Intelligent Department (ANKQ), located at 4 Nguyen Binh Khiem in the city and at Phi Long Gate is the operating office of TSN airport. The staff of Air Force Security/Intelligent Office, working at TSN, sometimes assigned to work in main office, and on April 29, the move from here (DaKao) to the airport was quite far, and 24 hours curfew make it harder to travel. The American fixed wings that aided the Vietnam battlefield such as C-47, C-119, C-123, C-130 equipped with miniguns and cannons (gunships) were added a model. ending with AC-119K, AC47D-Spooky, AC-123K or AC-130A/E/H Specter or calling ACK-119 nicknamed "Stinger" or "Shadow". The crew had additional gunners to use the guns mounted on the rear side of the aircraft. AC probably stands for Armed Control Aircraft. EC stands for Electronic Control Aircraft.*

boarded the plane, I thought I had left my homeland forever.

The EC-47 plane flown by Captain Tam and Lieutenant Lan, carrying 17 people including me, landed at U-TAPAO airport, Thailand at exactly 1:40 pm (12:40 pm Thailand time). The plane went straight from TSN to Ha Tien and went straight to U-Tapao Airport. Perhaps this was the last military plane carrying soldiers from TSN, then only fighter planes came from Binh Thuy and Can Tho airports. I didn't stop by the dormitory to get any clothes; so I went to Thailand as a refugee but only had an Air Force Security uniform on my body, nothing else, and was too hungry because I had nothing to eat since morning. It was not until 4 or 5 pm that a group of US Air Force (USAF) soldiers brought relief supplies to distribute. Hungry, but not eating at all, bread, coke, chocolate, and cigarettes for a person who has never smoked before. *From now on I am a refugee; I lost my homeland and do not know where my future is going to be.*

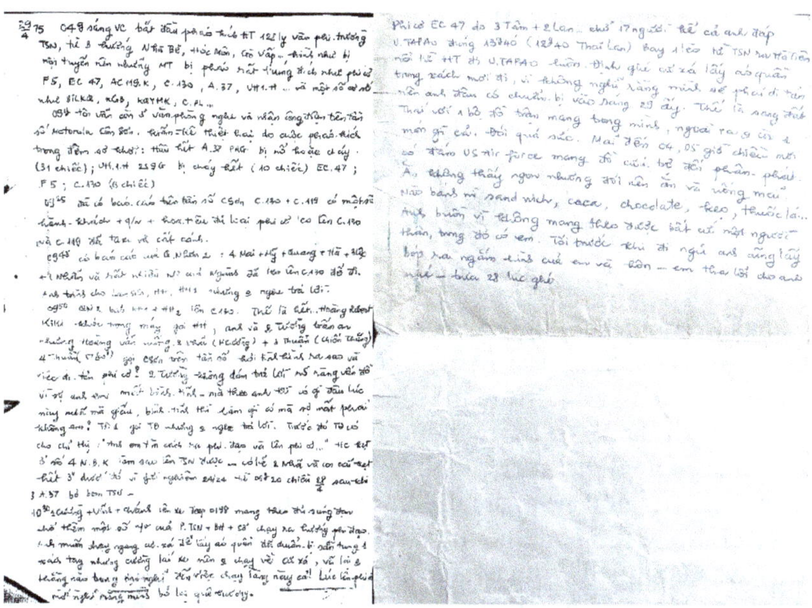

The original loose diary pages of my friend, written on April 30, 1975 on the back of a cigarette pack.

My friend's full month's salary of $26Kvnd, was still with him when he left Saigon.

DIARY PAGE WRITING ON MY FRIEND'S BEHALF

In life, those who have the habit of writing a diary in their free time at night before going to bed to record their happiness and sadness, a way to describe and review their introspection during the day, their inner thoughts – but when you are getting older, you often have more time than when you have to be busy with work and family every day in your youth.

My writing habits have been strengthening since the time I went into Scouting, from the youth group for the daily charity workbook, and also from the time Akéla let me into the Hue University Library to borrow and read books. Not sure about my daughter: when she was a child, writing the Daily Journal by herself was a habit from small family outings, just like me when I was a child, writing on lines of calligraphy at the top of every page, but I was completely unaware of this at first. Writing is also for me to read, but who is lucky enough to see other people's works, because this is a private matter: *"Live to your heart's content, die with it"*.

Talking around a circle, because the diary is written for yourself, no one will write it for you... strange things in life... even though another friend has written in this book and lets me use it when he knows it is related to the subject of the book. If you don't like to write, you like to read books like me, then I will write for your narration – as simple as that.

My friend's family is larger than ten people, so in the last days of April, Saigon was in an uproar: the oldest brother only got one ticket to evacuate with the DAO in TSN airport to Guam. He gave it to his youngest sister to get on the plane. The passengers were evacuated to the US around April 27; the whole family was able to evacuate, even though the first brother-in-law honestly did not want to go: he just wanted to stay and fight, because he was serving in the military Commando unit.

I heard that, in Da Nang, before everyone knew Club Danube, her eldest sister worked there, many soldiers noticed her, he (her future husband) went to the Club, and left a grenade on the table before he talked to her, so few people dared to come near. Then, together, they arrived at the refugee camp. When they were evacuated from home, they hurriedly took the wrong suitcase from their family home because the two were similar, so they couldn't bring anything valuable to support them in the first days of coming to the US. By chance, some students studying abroad at the University of Florida at that time applied to go to a refugee camp; their purpose was to help newcomers; it was always convenient to change visas from *"studying abroad"* to *"I-94 refugee"* to get a job preference in the US. An international student became acquainted with my friend's sister, so they settled in Gainesville. The sponsor was a family who has a pet grooming business, so they thought everyone would learn the profession and work for them, but only after a short time, and not getting used to the job or considering it suitable for them… many Americans considered animals more important than people, so the brothers and sisters dropped out and enrolled in school. Perhaps I was one of the first people to go back to school, so when I went to school, every time I saw a Vietnamese person applying to study, I was eager to help, because I was working part-time at Student Activities[56] at that time. My boss,

56. *This is a small office of Santa Fe College that takes care of the student activity services of the school, later changed to Student Life, including sports or cultural issues, movie screenings, student ID card (SFID). I get paid through Work Study, $2 per hour and 20 hours per week. I had not studied Architecture in the US but was in Vietnam, so I wrote beautiful letters, I was assigned to handwrite posters or banners to hang around the school, sometimes just small posters because at that time there was no computer and printer for this services. All this work has to be written and done by hand.*

Elaine Meade was a native of Finland, had beautiful silver hair and let me work on the new student list and student card (SFID card), and she encouraged me to help my homeland people whenever possible. Helped a lot, but only noticed a girl with dimpled cheeks and especially sad eyes whom I called *"underground charm"*, filled out all kinds of papers, and scholarship applications, and gradually became closer.

We lived in the same apartment complex, and went to Santa Fe College, a small school, at that time only offered a 2-year degree, so we often met at the Cafeteria. When we went to U of F, we studied in two different colleges so we didn't have the opportunity to see each other much. Most Vietnamese students at that time studied engineering. I graduated first and went to work; everyone has a private life, seemingly afraid to disturb others. Not being selfish, I always wished her a happy life. After a while, she got married, a normal thing like everyone in the district because at that time, I was still searching for a *"Dieu Bong's Leaf"* for her.[57]

Studied well, graduating with a Bachelor of Science in Computer Engineering, a degree that is not easy to get, was accepted by IBM, then got married and both worked with the same company. She had four children, and at the same time when her husband was laid off, he went to find a job in construction/renovation with Vietnamese people. Being away from home, having fun all night with new friends, and avoiding the responsibilities of being a husband and father led to unhappiness. The disadvantage for both men and women when there are many followers is how to choose the right person. A lot of people do not appreciate what they have, *"dropping bait to catch the virtual ball"*.

A friend of mine in McLean had an aunt. When I went to her house to visit, she told me that when she was studying at Hue Girls' High School in the 1950s, she was a pretty person in Hue at that time; she ignored one of her boyfriends. and he loved her and kept pursuing, *"planting sycamore"*. When she refused, took *"two pan covers"* to beat his chest repeatedly, afraid that he would harm himself, she felt *"pity love"* for him. After a few years and bearing children, he also got involved with mistresses;

57. *Vietnamese Poet Hoang Cam composed the poem "Dieu Bong's Leaf" in 1959. In 1990, musician Tran Tien put it into music "Why should you hurry to get married", everyone knows that this leaf is never real.*

she said *"Among most men, there are few faithful people... it is rare, my dear!"* Her voice sounded sad but funny, so we often went to her house to listen to her tell her old love story, because her husband had many wives. The two important factors of a man are *duty* and *responsibility*, so the pursuers are not necessarily faithful after getting married. At that time, even today, many men don't appreciate what they have, using the excuse of having many wives and concubines, the law was not restricted at the time. For some women, when there are so many people pursuing them, no one is perfect; it is time to choose, sometimes because of predestination, they choose the wrong person.

Now that she is retired, she is happy with her children and grandchildren, and when she has free time, she goes to the temple and does volunteer good deeds to earn merits later.

MY HERO, CAPTAIN NGUYEN HOANG AN

Has it been 38 years? 38 years since that dark day, I keep thinking about you; should I write about you? You are my brother's most trusted junior officer, part of the 257th Rescue Evacuation Squadron of the 51st Tactical Wing, Air Force First Division in Da Nang Air Force Base, whom I only happened to meet a few times. The first time, in 1973, I knew that Captain An had returned to Saigon to take a new helicopter to Da Nang for the 257th Squadron; I was studying at the University of Saigon. I didn't have any way to go home to celebrate Tet, the Vietnamese New Year, and staying in Saigon without family was sad because I had no relatives; everything is closed. He showed up and took me on his Honda motorcycle, straight to Tan Son Nhut Airport, a new helicopter filled up with fuel, we stopped at Nha Trang Airbase to refuel; it was past noon, and he bought me a sandwich because we did not have enough time, another person got on the plane, this guy was tall, handsome, dressed in a suit of black, a black watch with luminous hands, a dagger at his side, he carried a small black bag, sat in the back of the new chopper with two pilots; only this man and me, he looked at me, I looked at him, both of us were silent, the chopper is quietly flying, then dropped him right on a hillside without touching down, he jumped down and disappeared behind dense trees. It was then I found out that he was part of the special commando team on a mission...

The chopper landed at Da Nang Air Force Base after stopping at Chu Lai Airport to refuel. When I got off the chopper, I could clearly see the person giving me a lift: he was a lieutenant, a name tag reading Nguyen Hoang An…He drove me to the Squadron reception room, not that far from the chopper bunker, to wait for the flight to Hue, and then I had a chance to meet him again on January 18, 1974. At that time, I was waiting for a plane to Hue with my brother to celebrate Tet. My brother had volunteered to go out with the South Vietnamese Navy Fleet, and he picked Captain An to go with him because China was besieging the Paracel and Spratly Islands. The squadrons sent out the two best pilots for this special mission; that was the last time I met him, because I always stayed in Saigon after that, and did not have the opportunity to return to Da Nang Airport as before.

On March 28, 1975, at night, due to heavy shelling by the VC into Da Nang AFB, all kinds of jets or transports flew to Phu Cat AFB or Nha Trang Airport. Without any orders from higher Air Force officers to retreat, a number of helicopters flew over to a former nearby American airfield: Non Nuoc (Marble Mountain MMAF) to avoid shelling, and a number of choppers were still able to follow each other to the south.

That night, although it was February 16 of the lunar calendar, the moon was full and bright, but the sky was cloudy and foggy due to bad weather. These pilots, familiar with such conditions, decided to take off at night rather than waiting until sunrise, to fly further south, because the helicopters had to refuel at Chu Lai AFB in Quang Tin: there was not enough fuel to get to Phu Cat AFB or Nha Trang Airport, when leaving in a hurry, many of the choppers were not full of fuel, not enough to go to Phu Cat AFB, now Chu Lai airport has fallen to the VC, so some planes had to add more fuel, perhaps the Communists were aware of that and assigned their troops to these areas. Some helicopters were shot down, some had to make an emergency landing along the coast because they ran out of fuel and were arrested, all calling each other for help on a "*guard frequency*".

His helicopter carrying refugees had to land because it was about to run out of gas; soon afterward, it was surrounded, they were disarmed by the local VC, and among them were senior officers. They forced a pilot to use the helicopter to fly into Quang Ngai City, just as a trophy and to take them to observe the front; he volunteered to go, his co-pilot who flew with him from Da Nang, Second Lieutenant Dang Vu Dang, asked to become his co-pilot again with him but he refused, saying that he alone was enough: the co-pilot and other soldiers should stay as hostages. Mr. Dang protested, he only saw that at that time, Captain An's eyes looked at him very fiercely, bloodshot, just like he was giving an order for him to stay, just like a last look to say goodbye. He used Captain Hung's helicopter because it still had fuel, so the Viet Cong officers boarded the chopper, and guards with guns ordered him to fly south on this one.

He took off, but he never landed again, because he soared higher and higher, and then decided to dive…in fact he *"crashed"* intentionally at a really high speed…the chopper shattered on the surface of the sea, in front of everyone there…

At least 25 years later, during the South Vietnamese Helicopter Squadron Reunion in the United States, the witnesses to his last flight on March 29, 1975, including his co-pilot, vividly brought his story to life. I heard the news of his feat; I was shocked, I could not believe it, I was sad, I cried, but then I was glad that he did not die in battle, like so many of his comrades, but he decided to sacrifice his life. It would not be easy for many people to do this; not being greedy for life, afraid of dying…not surrendering to the enemy, shamelessly heroic…he may be dead, but he is still alive forever in me…He left behind a young wife and two young children, the smallest son less than a year old.

He flew high, soared high on his last flight, never to return; but in my heart, there is always a rose for him, just looking forward to a day when the country is truly peaceful, I dream of walking on Nguyen Khoa Nam Boulevard, Le Van Hung, Le Nguyen Vy, Tran Van Hai, Ho Ngoc Can, Pham Van Phu, Nguyen Hoang An...

Written on March 29, 2009

The late Captain Nguyen Hoang An-

Artist Co Khai Vu - Australia 2013

Added March 29, 2013

The 38th anniversary of the death of the late Captain Nguyen Hoang An

Before his 37th death anniversary (2012), I was able to contact his co-pilot, Second Lieutenant Dang Vu Dang in Oregon, residing in US after more than 5 years in a re-education camp (He confirmed the news I had received about Captain An 3 years before. He was a living witness when Captain An died. He sadly told the story and was informed that his wife and her children had settled in the United States. Before the 38th anniversary of his death, which his family chose on March 29 of every year, I requested artist Vu Khai Co from Australia to come up with a canvas painting, and sent it back to California to his family on March 29, 2013. Captain. An's son, Nguyen Hoang Bao, who is residing in Southern California, received the painting from me on behalf of his family.

Captain An: You know, even though you are gone, people never forget and always remember you.

REMEMBER A FRIEND–BIM BANG BUI

I don't know when the American Cultural Center, also known as the *"Vietnamese American Association"* in Hue, the office on Ly Thuong Kiet Street initially opened, but this was where I often rode my bicycle to read books because the small house contained a library inside with air conditioning. Here, my favorite was the Free World magazine, the most beautiful color printing that at that time was the 11th flight of the Apollo spacecraft, depicting many pictures of the earth on the way to the moon, and this was also a place to apply to learn free English-language courses, taught at night, but they held classes at National Academy Quoc Hoc school's classrooms because of the large number of learners. My primary foreign language was French, then up to grade 10, my school added English as a secondary language, so I applied and they gave me a placement test so that students with similar levels could easily learn together.

I met Bim here and we two were placed in the same class after the test. We studied at night at the National Academy; we often arrived early and went to class together. Bim had an older sister who also studied English; she often rode a PC scooter; QH School allowed students to enter the main gate on Le Loi Street, park their scooters or bicycles at a place only for professors and staff to enter the classroom during the day.

Our class, mostly taught by American professors working at MACV[58], had an office on Duy Tan Street. Once, a blonde American English teacher brought a classical guitar to class; he wrote some lyrics on the board and started singing folk songs; the first one was "500 Miles" [59]:

If you miss the train I'm on, you will know that I am gone

---

58. *U.S. Military Assistance Command, Vietnam (MACV) was a joint-service command of the United States Department of Defense (DoD) and US State Department.*

59. *This is an American folk song in the 1960s, also known as "500 Miles Away from Home" or "Railroaders' Lament" famous for three musicians Paul, Peter and Mary. In 1966, my brother Chau brought back a Sylvania 33-tour phonograph, who when training in the United States to join the Air Force, also about a dozen discs with folk songs, which were all good. This machine is automatic, stacks a stack of plates, it will fall down one by one, after the last one it automatically turns off. I love this machine and the discs he brought back then.*

You can hear the whistle blow a hundred miles
A hundred miles, a hundred miles, a hundred miles, a hundred miles
You can hear the whistle blow a hundred miles...

I don't know if it was the English teacher's confession, an American soldier or a civilian working with the US Department of Defense or State Department who had been sent to Vietnam for military duty, diplomacy, volunteered to teach English to natives in the evening – still, it was a good song that he sang and played very well. The song's meaning is *"a lament of a traveler far from home, running out of money and too embarrassed to return"*. I was listening at home, through Peter, Paul, and Mary (PPM) on a vinyl record, but saw Bim attentive; maybe it was his first time to listen... after class I said "When you are free, go to my house and listen to it on the record player as many times as you like.

Next time, the teacher sang **BLOWIN' IN THE WIND:** Bob Dylan

How many roads must a man walk down
Before they call him a man?
How many seas must a white dove sail
Before she sleeps in the sand?
How many times must the cannon balls fly
Before they're forever banned?

The answer, my friend, is blowin' in the wind The answer is blowin' in the wind.

The English teacher sang every song very well, accompanied by his guitar. The one that I found my friends most admiring and pondering was: DON'T EVER TAKE AWAY MY FREEDOM by Peter Yarrow, also known for his PPM recording, which has the following words:

Chorus: *Don't ever take away my freedom, don't ever take it away We must cherish and keep that one part of our lives And the rest we're gonna find one of these days... One of these days*

I always thought that I'd see it in my own lifetime An end to poverty, injustice, and war But now I've learned that that job will take a long, long time So there's one thing that must endure.

Not sure about my friend's thinking, but in my life, this was the most special and memorable English class because the young blond American teacher did not teach grammar or vocabulary as in other times, instead spending time singing folk songs to his students. When I came to America, I realized that this way of learning helped me a lot, and surely why my friends also liked it, because I noted that you were more attentive than the times when you were studying with teachers who focused more on grammar.

In 1972, after the general mobilization order, my classmates were born in the same year as I went into the military, one by one, including Bim, and the English classes also no longer had American teachers because most of them had returned back to their country. "Vietnamization" in the military; also English classes transferred to Vietnamese teachers, focusing more on vocabulary and grammar instead of dialogue. The school also became an evacuation place for people along the northern border area. I lost contact with Bim in subsequent times. After finishing military school, Bim returned to serve in the South, but from 1973 to 1975 when I was in Saigon, I didn't have the opportunity to see my high school friends in Hue who had joined the army, except Chanh (Security/Intelligent Officer) and Hai (Commando).

Through Pendleton refugee camp, I searched for old friends and Scouts, besides Chanh who went over at the same time as me to Thailand, Hai also exited at the last minute. Other friends were all stuck in Hue or around Vietnam.

When I was writing an English version of my book, about a month ago, I typed in Google Search to try and see if I could find my friend Bim or his sister Ms. T. Cuom on Google or social networks, but nothing showed up. The names were especially difficult to match with anyone. On Sunday morning, November 20, I got up early, finished my coffee, and tried Facebook to see if there was anything new. I usually don't like social networking sites because of the confusion, so just to listen more than talk, I suddenly saw the page of Mr. Le's memoirs[60] showing up with a young picture

---

60. *Mr. Phieu Le was an officer of the Republic of South Vietnam Air Force with the F-5 fighter jet stationed at Da Nang Air Force Base. In March 1975, even as a F-5 pilot, he could not evacuate on time, got stuck and went to re-educate prison of the Communists. He rewrote memoirs on Facebook and Youtube recounting the wars of the Republic of*

of my friend, only the title below stating *"The Unstoppable Hero would rather die than suffer humiliation"* chilled me: that was my friend. Listening to the voice reading, I felt like I had gone back to Long Ho, Song Muc, in Thanh Hoa Province, a place I did not know, a re-education camp in the deep forest, poisoned water told only by a living inmate. survived the reprisals and trampling on the dignity by the winning cadres. This is also the place where my friend Bim passed away forever on the 30th day, Lunar Vietnamese New Year's Eve (February 17, 1977)[61].

You have chosen to die bravely here on the last day of the lunar year of the Dragon, before you turned 24 years of age, a dear friend that I knew when I had overcome suffering as in the song you and I heard in English class, a death that my friends' family only found out about two years later because of the harsh, revengeful rule of the victorious Northerners at that time. Perhaps your outspokenness caused the victors to try to ***"Silence and kill you"*** because the Communist's method is to kill and blame the victims, ones who can no longer defend themselves. Your mother, a mother like many other Vietnamese mothers, loved her children, still going to your camp to bring food for you after the day you died *(forbidden for prisoners to tell any true stories outside the camp)*, not knowing that her child has gone to another world, and finally, 45 years after you died, your story has been told by your fellow prisoners. A belated incense stick for you, even though I have been trying to find news about you for the past 48 years. Now, for the rest of my life, every New Year's Eve, I will light an incense stick for you.

"Hero died, his spirit immortal".

Farewell Forever my friend Bim Bang Bui.

South Vietnam.

61. *The article about the details of Bim's death was told by Mr. Le on Youtube in Vietnamese:https://www.youtube.com/watch?v=4_0YNFJenE0*

STORY OF MY BROTHER'S FRIEND

233rd SKY HAWKS SQUADRON COMMANDER

(Rewritten according to the story he told me).

South Vietnamese Air Force Major Thanh Nguyen is the one who let me and my family and ride the Hue-Da Nang-Hue helicopter quite a few times, a pilot whom my Mom liked because he flew gently and when he landed, many passengers mistakenly thought he was still *"hovering"* in the air, hence the nickname *"mosquito"*. Major Thanh, squadron Commander of the 233rd Sky Hawks Helicopter Squadron, of the 51st Tactical Air Wing, First Air Force Division in Da Nang AFB, Air Force Command, ordered the establishment of more units to receive American aid aircraft and the urgent needs of the battlefield. Support for operations, the purpose was also to train pilots to learn to fly domestically in Vietnam after the *"Vietnamization"* program. The type of aircraft was the UH-1, most of which were *"slicks"* (military transport), i.e., the type with only two M-60 machine guns in the back, no miniguns or rockets, like the armed helicopters of the 213th Twin Spiked Mace Squadron.

On the evening of March 28, 1975, Da Nang Air Force Base was heavily shelled; following a lack of orders from higher authorities, the squadron commanders ordered helicopters to be sent over to Marble Mountain Air Field (MMAF) [62] to avoid

---

62. *After the US Marines withdrew, this base was used by South Vietnam Airforce, located southeast of Da Nang Air Force Base, near the sea, from here along the coast to Chu Lai military airport is less than 100km.*
Chu Lai AFB was built by the US through RMK-BRJ Raymond International and Morrison-Knudsen, later added Brown & Root, Inc. and J. A. Jones Construction Company (the engineer on this project Mr. Larry Courtney later my boss at Greenhorne & O'Mara Inc. in Maryland/Tampa), the airstrip could be used for the B-52 flying fortress. After April 1975, when VC took over, people took all the cement from the airstrip and "taxiway", cut in pieces, took it home and used it, as an unusable airport until 2005. Although it is more than 200km from MMAF to Phu Cat AFB, if you do not fly straight and the plane is heavy because it carries many people, it will consume more fuel.
Lieutenant General Victor H. Krulak (USMC) name in Chinese Characters (Chu Lai) was used to name this air base in 1965.

damage by shelling. They were attempting to take care of their squadron, partly because there was no evacuation order, just thinking about going back to the airport after the shelling ended. Because of the bad weather that night – fog and clouds - but with was a *full moon* (16 day of the month on lunar calendar), with his experience flying night missions, he told his staff to wait until morning, if possible, and remember to take two extra tanks of gas (55 gallon drums, more than 700 lbs. of kerosene/gasoline). A plane full of gasoline that could not be refueled at Chu Lai AFB fell into the hands of the VC; it was not fueled enough to reach Phu Cat AFB or Nha Trang airport. Despite being carefully instructed, some pilots, because they were in a hurry, panicked and only filled up the tank and departed at night, crashing because they ran out of fuel and were taken prisoner, some were shot, damaged choppers also had to make emergency landings and met the same fate.

About 5 o'clock, on March 29, it was almost morning, the weather was better, he sent the squadron to evacuate to Nha Trang. As for him, along with Lieutenant Duc (copilot) he brought two JP-4 drums to land, refueled around Quang Tin, and did not forget to keep two machine guns on both sides to dissuade the enemy from coming. The choppers that could go, arrived, then continued on to Tan Son Nhut; the ones which did not have enough fuel or made an emergency landing because of being shot, and crews captured alive. Hearing the call for help on the *"guard frequency"*, a few choppers landed near Tam Quan, Bong Son because they ran out of gas, but at that time he could not do anything, although it was very painful not be able to rescue others.

Fortunately, a month before, his wife was eight months pregnant, so he brought the whole family to Saigon, and he was free to continue his mission at DNAFB. Arriving in Saigon, the family temporarily stayed in an apartment and his wife gave birth to their youngest daughter, on April 28, 1975. When the Communists shelled TSN Airport on the evening of April 28, 1975, continuing on the early morning of April 29, he decided to enter the airport to check its condition. Arriving at TSN around 6 am, he walked from Phi Long gate to the dormitory, meeting my Mom, my sister and the family of Major Hieu, his 233rd Deputy Squadron Commander. Seeing the urgent situation, he asked my brother to drive him back to the gate; the purpose was to go out back with his wife and children because he knew they needed him, but because of the 24-hour curfew, the Air Force Military Police shot warning shots into the sky and would not let him out, as was told in my own story. Major Thanh went with us to U-Tapao, then Guam and to Gainesville, and shared the same sponsor with us. Luckily, we stayed with him because he was alone during the evacuation, he could not get out of the gate at the last moment and listen to my brother; nor did he return with the Vietnamese Viet Nam Thuong Tin's ship in Guam. Otherwise, he would have just tormented his family, wife and children with more than 10 years in prison, similar to Lieutenant Colonel Cao Quang Khoi (213rd Squadron Commander and his 213rd Deputy Commander Major Ta Thai (d) or his 233rd Deputy Squadron Commander Hieu – they stayed behind, were arrested and spent 13 years in a re-education camp/prison.

After we went to work at the Holiday Inn, and they were not treated well by the owner's son-in-law (the restaurant manager), he went to find a job with the James Moore accounting firm. The owner had suffered from Muscular Dystrophy since he was 14 years old; he studied very well, graduated from school, and taught at UF before opening his own CPA company. The owner and his wife treated him nicely; he just kept their car, filled up the gas, helped him get from home to work, and then they let him study in the office. He took many courses with me, studying carefully, so his grades were very good. After finishing his course of study at Santa Fe College, he planned to go to UF, to continue studying like me (or my brother later), but he was working and going to school when he heard the news from New Orleans, Louisiana that South Vietnamese helicopter pilots coming to the US as refugees were being recruited by oil/gas companies for commuting within the Gulf of Mexico. Remember, the cost to train a helicopter pilot is very steep, and even if that person has as many flight hours and experience as the South Vietnamese Air Force (RVNAF) Officers, getting ready for the job right away is even more difficult. As a result, PHI recruited many RVNAF helicopter officers and they beckoned each other to go to Louisiana back in 1975. Now they were recruiting former US Air Force officers who had been trained in the US Air Force, serving in Iraq or Afghanistan.

He moved to the Harvey area of New Orleans, after getting his pilot's license, and with his flying experience, it was not difficult to get a job. The family of his wife and children are stuck in Vietnam and the youngest child was born on April 28, so he needed to have a stable job and income immediately so that he might help his family. Every choice has its reasons: if continuing to university, it would take another 4 years (like me) and of course during that time, it would be difficult to have any financial surplus; the scholarship would be just enough to cover his education. My brother did not pursue the same career because – as I said previously – the chopper was not armed, did not feel safe, and Major Thanh took the offer because he needed income to help his family right away. From the Huey UH-1H (Bell) in the Air Force in Vietnam, he changed to the Bell 206L-3 of Southern Natural Gas (El Paso Energy Pipeline), until he retired in 2006. In fact, he was associated with the Bell Helicopter throughout his life. He and his family moved to Northwest of Houston after retirement. In good health above 80 years of age, he still plays tennis with his friends.

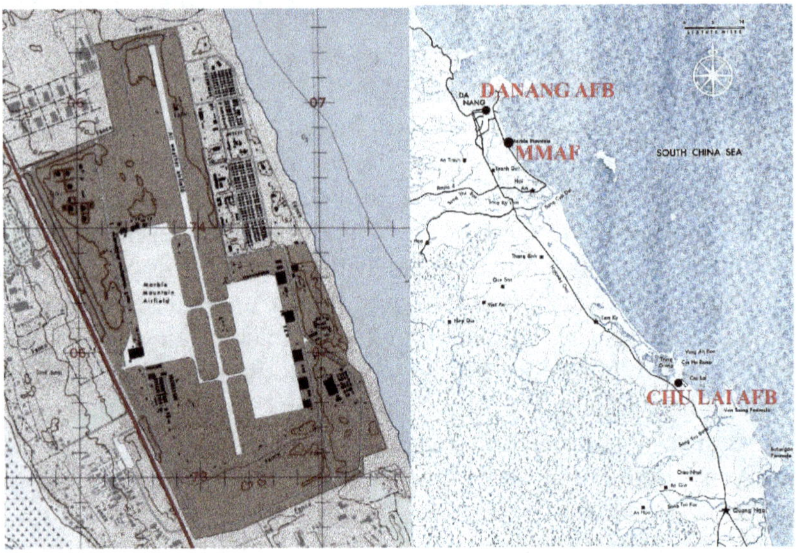

Marble Mountain Air Field (MMAF) South East of the Da Nang AFB, near the beach.

Da Nang Air Force Base (DNAFB) and Chu Lai Air Force Base (CLAFB) with MMAF location map (right).

This is a photo my brother brought with him in 1975.

Standing Rows from left to right: Lt. Colonel Khoi, Huyen, Mai, Captain Thuc(d), Major Thai(d), Tan, Captain Chau, Captain Nguyen(d), Captain Tien(d), Hai, Hau.

Front Rows from left: Long, Loc(d), Captain Duong, Major Thanh, Khanh.

The photo was taken as they finished UH-1 Helicopter training with US trainers/advisors in 1970.

A VIETNAMESE NAME IN AN AMERICAN PUBLIC PARK MONUMENT[63]

Tra Nguyen

This is an article published in the Vietnamese newspaper by Mr. Tra Nguyen when he was surprised to see the name of a Vietnamese person he knew engraved on a plaque in a park. Captain Tra Nguyen is a South Vietnamese Air Force Officer who served in the 239th King Hawks Helicopter Squadron, 51st Tactical Wing, 1st Airborne Division in Da Nang Air Force Base, whose Squadron Commander was Lieutenant Colonel Toan Anh Nguyen, who used to let me ride in his chopper as an Air Force Family Members passenger traveling many times from Hue to Da Nang. Mr. Tra has a wife and three children and is currently residing in the neighboring Town of Lake Park. He often enjoys a walk in the park amid pleasant scenery every afternoon. Captain Tra was also my matchmaker. Thank you.

In the afternoons when the sun disappears from the horizon, the sun fades away, the gentle breeze blowing from the Atlantic Ocean is gentle and soothing, my wife and I leisurely stroll through the tall condos, then to the park to exercise and enjoy the sea breeze. We used to go back and forth to this park for days, focusing only on the sights and pedestrians, but this time we stopped at the stone monuments and saw the name of the Vietnamese *Hoa Ngoc Hoang*. I am not surprised by the familiar name, Hoa is someone I have known since I was in Vietnam.

While escaping in the last day, I met Hoa at Camp Pendleton, California, then a student at the University of Saigon, young in

63. *Town of Lake Park Kelsey and Lake Shore Park located in Palm Beach County, Florida between North Palm Beach, Palm Beach Gardens in the North and Riviera Beach and City of West Palm Beach in the South.*
https://www.lakeparkflorida.gov/

appearance, in his twenties. More than fifteen years later, when I met Hoa again in South Florida, I felt different as soon as I met him. Hoa graduated to become an architect, an employee of a firm specializing in the construction of commercial and residential facilities in Boca Raton, South Florida. At this time, he looked mature and dignified, a true civil servant, at the time when Hoa was about to get married.

Hoa's brother, Captain Chau Ngoc Hoang is my senior, he attended the 65th course in the South Vietnamese Air Force Cadet, I was close to him during the days of serving in the same force, and my room was near his room, the Tran Van Tho dormitory, in Da Nang Air Force Base. He was trained to fly two types of helicopters: initially flying H-34, later transferring to UH-I, holding the position of Chief of Flying Security and then Chief of Operations of 213th Twin Spiked Mace Squadron and 257th Savior Squadron, 51 Tactical Wing, First Air Division. Before 1975, he was transferred to Bien Hoa Air Force Base. His name is prominently spread in the helicopter squadrons, everyone knows, that he was grateful and received noble medals of the South Vietnamese Air Force after the Lam Son 719 *(Operation Lam Son 719 or 9th Route – Southern Laos Campaign)* and regained the Bastogne base (on the West side of the ancient capital Hue in Nam Hoa district). He was seriously injured when his armed helicopter was shot down by anti-aircraft fire while saving his comrades at Tchepone Hill and escaped death, he brought the badly damaged helicopter back to the Base and fainted from excessive bleeding. The US Air Force had to take him to the Navy Hospital Fleet in Da Nang Bay to treat his wounds, and today he still has shrapnel in his body because they can't get it out. From the glorious feats that brought victory to the unit, he was an excellent gunship senior helicopter pilot of the First Division Air Force in particular and the RVNAF in general, he was rewarded with high medals of the Republic of South Vietnam. He is currently retired in Orlando, Florida. He was an example for Junior Officers like me to follow, courageously, passionately fighting to protect the free South, years later we replaced him and supported him on the battlefields of Tactical Zone One to retake Sa Huynh, Mo Duc, Duc Pho, Red Summer 1972, Quang Tri Ancient Citadel...

Since the day I met Hoa again, I have been in regular contact, Hoa worked at Boca Raton for a while, then returned to work for the Town of Lake Park, until today, he is currently holding a senior position in Lake Park. Once I went to Lake Park to get some permits for my local business. I was able to meet Hoa in an office upstairs, with an administration secretary to guide me, the office was spacious and organized.

The Town of Lake Park on the north side of the City of West Palm Beach bordering the Palm Beach Gardens has many beautiful, waterfront parks that make visitors notice and visit. A large park of nearly fifty acres at the end of Park Avenue called Lake Shore Park, rebuilt about ten years ago, is connected to Kelsey Park, although the two names are different, they are connected together. On both sides of the two rows of tall building condos, the park is poetic and romantic, with seawater, sandy beaches, fishing places, rows of coconut trees leaning over the water, benches to practice physical exercises, there is a barbecue place, there are tennis courts, in the afternoon the shadows of the trees shine on the water with ripples when hidden, the gentle sea breeze blowing in it feels great, we spend a lot of time to embrace and enjoy nature here. Right in the center of the park is erected a beautiful and tall stone statue with the names of sponsoring agencies and councilors who have approved the park project such as the Mayor, the Vice-mayor... about ten of them including Hoa Ngoc Hoang.

Seeing the Vietnamese name, we wholeheartedly appreciate the honor and feel proud. Thirty-seven years ago, we were refugees who came here to find a way to make a living, today we have been gratefully engraved by the indigenous people of the United States on stone monuments to commemorate, the treasures and favors that have contributed positively. Extremely constructive for the country, not only today but also handed down for generations to come, the stone stele named Hoa Ngoc Hoang remains forever. I would like to introduce to readers who have the opportunity to go on Interstate Highway I-95 exit Northlake Boulevard, go eastbound until the end of the road, meet US 1, turn right about 500 meters and you will see Lake Shore Park on the left. An American President who started the war in South and North Vietnam, President John F. Kennedy, popular with the American people said: *"Ask not what your country can do for you – ask what you can do for your country"*. Hoa was also the Scout Leader who founded the Vietnamese Lac Hong Scout Group (Cubs, Boys, and Ventures Co-op) in South Florida in the mid-1990s. At first, the activities were regular and developed rapidly, but gradually because of business, the leaders moved to different states. Due to the lack of manpower, the Lac Hong Scout Group temporarily closed its doors and heard that it would resume activities in the future.

When the Palm Beach Buddhist Association at Loc Uyen Pagoda established the Bo De Vietnamese Second Language School for our children to learn Vietnamese, I invited Hoa to guide activities, Hoa was enthusiastic and ready to help and thanks to his acquaintance, Hoa invited the Scout's Leaders came to guide the Bo De Vietnamese Language School (VNBD) at first, that was the sincere feeling of the VNBD school for Hoa Ngoc Hoang during the years when the Bo De Vietnamese Language School was still in its infancy. .

Nearly two million Vietnamese refugees are sponsored by the US government. The US government and people are benefactors of the Vietnamese refugees. To express our gratitude, we will repay the favor with great deeds. For the construction of the United States, people such as Mathematics Professor Vinh Xuan Nguyen, and Zen Buddhism Master Nhat Hanh... have been gratefully received by the US government, scattered in cities and states of the United States of America such as California, Texas, Washington a lot of Vietnamese people work for the government, contributing to the United States is both a contribution and their duty. The descendants who also volunteered to join the US Military West Point years ago have now become significant ranks such as Lieutenant Colonel, Colonel, and General and we will have a young and talented second generation of Vietnamese refugees in the history of the United States. Even our children's efforts to study and pass have also contributed to the construction of the United States of America. Because of the ideological and irrational war of Vietnam twenty years ago, today each person has responsibility and serves two countries, we rejoice and do it, because fate has been born in the midst of turmoil, in the poor little homeland of Vietnam, natural disasters, wars, separations... Oh my painful homeland of Vietnam!

MEMORIES WITH MY TWO SENIOR OFICERS TRAN LE TIEN AND PHAM VUONG THUC

Thu V. Hoang

This is an article composed by Captain Thu Van Hoang of the 213th Helicopter Gunship Twin Spiked Maces Squadron, formerly stationed at Da Nang Air Force Base about the Lam Son 719 in 1971(Operation Lam Son 719 or 9th Route – Southern Laos Campaign); my brother Captain Chau Ngoc Hoang was also assigned to this squadron before moving to the newly-formed 257th Rescue Squadron specializing in helicopters working as ambulances and resupplying besieged encampments, ones that cannot be reached by any other means. Usually, these missions happen at night, with all lights turned off and flying at treetops to avoid anti-aircraft fire. It is thus very dangerous, because there is no minigun or rockets on board, to defend – as in a Gunship.

At the time of this article, Captain Thu Van Hoang was a junior officer working under these senior officers and is currently retired with his family in Savannah, Georgia. Thank you for allowing me to print his article on my book.

The helicopter of Late Captain Tien Le Tran was shot down and he was killed at "Tran Le Tien Hill" in 1972 while supporting troops there. The late Captain Thuc Vuong Pham passed away in California in 2012, from illness.

These are the officers in my brother Captain Chau's squadron that I had the opportunity to meet and ride in their choppers along the Da Nang-Hue route. I ask for a stick of incense for those who sacrificed their lives for the homeland.

Operation Lam Son 719 on the battlefield of Southern Laos in February 71, although fierce, was also an opportunity for our helicopter pilots to just complete the UH-1 training courses (K/1-2- 3-4) at Hunter Flight School, Georgia, had the opportunity to test fire and gain more combat experience for the next battles in the Vietnam War later.

Although after more than six months of continuous military

flight, with many hours of flight and a lot of combat experience, it has been quite solid; in fact, the three of us - Tai, Hoang, and I - have not had time to train to *"check out"* to become the chief pilot, so when the Lam Son 719 came, we were only seated next to the pilots. The seniors of the 213th Twin Spiked Maces Squadron, together, threw themselves into the battlefield of Southern Laos, as both a military operation and a training mission. If we are lucky enough to survive the battle, of course, we will become Chief Pilots! Both me, Tai, and Hoang were happy to accept the exchange without repeat thinking.

Meanwhile, also because of the needs of the battlefield, junior pilots in other squadrons, although returning to the country later, were given the chief pilot first, with only a short training course by the IPs. / US of the Black Cat (USMC) squadron at the Mable Mountain Air Base. They became the core of the newly formed squadron, 233rd Squadron, and flew *"team"* together during Operation Lam Son 719. Despite the danger, it was still the pride that every pilot aspires to wait in flight; the day when you have full control of the chopper, including the right to *"swish the screw"* to your heart's content!

Nguyen Tan Tai, and Nguyen Van Hoang and I have just finished course 70-02, one of the first courses in the *Vietnamization* program. Returning home on July 13, a month later, we presented to the unit immediately (Aug. 06, 1970). Youth seems fearless, everyone is eager to join the war, regardless of fate! Hoang has a family near Da Nang AFB, so he is considered to have the luckiest number; Unexpectedly, less than a year later, Hoang was fatally wounded in a night gunship mission with Hoang Tat Dac (Hunter's group 1) outside the waters of My Khe (China Beach), Tai from Saigon, later moved to Chinook, to Bien Hoa, 237th Squadron, was also shot down and died on the battlefield of Binh Long-An Loc. All because of cruel fate that should! In the life of flying helicopters, perhaps not many people dare to rely on their talent to survive! Just better by luck.

On the day of the draw for the unit, the Major/Chief Officer/ Staff Officer at Air Force Command Center, after reading a special list of about 20 people, probably by relatives and parents, skillfully knew how to foster in the right place, those pilots were given priority to the squadrons in Bien Hoa AFB and Can Tho

AFB, considered lucky to serve both near their family and near Saigon, which would certainly be safer. The rest, then is our turn to draw for fun. Anyway, the Air Force Command Center deserves to be honored as a relatively fairer service than other combat units!

Da Nang AFB, August 1970, there were only two helicopter squadrons: 213th and 219th. All were still under the 41st / Tactical Wing with "fixed wings" squadrons such as the 516th Squadron. (A-37 Dragonfly) and 110th (L-19 Cessna). The 213th Squadron was equipped with UH-I (Huey) helicopters but the 219th Squadron was still flying the H-34 (Choctaw). The two squadrons are close, facing each other, in a strong neighborly relationship, friends also often go back and forth. Most of the 219th command levels also come from the original 213th and vice versa. Both squadrons are located behind the airport's Conference Room, near the VIP apron. Later, with the expansion of the South Vietnamese Air Force (RVNAF) and before the Operation Southern Laos / Lam Son 719, the helicopter squadrons were separated from the 41st Tactical Wing to become the 51st Tactical Wing, with additional 233rd Sky Hawks Squadron has just been established. However, during the Operation of Southern Laos, the 213th Squadron alone had a group of gunships to escort the slicks of all three squadrons 213th, 219th, and 233rd [64].

February 1971, cold winter, the entire 213th Squadron, from pilots to gunners, including flight nurses, and clerical staff ... were ordered to fly out on secondment at Ai Tu base/Dong Ha, in the old barracks of the U.S. Marines left behind. Dong Ha, the leading land near the border (DMZ), is a desert-like arid land, interspersed between mountains and sea. Inner side, west, Truong Son (Long Mountain), with mountains overlapping; towering like great walls blocking the border between Laos and Vietnam. On the outside,

---

64. *Additional notes from the book author:*
The South Vietnamese Air Force under the Republic of Vietnam (RVNAF) named the squadrons as follows: Using 3 numbers, if the first number is odd (1, 3, 5, 7, 9) then the last number will be even and vice versa (2, 4, 6, 8): The first number shows the mission of the squadrons: Liaison Squadron: 110, 120... Helicopter: 213, 215, 219, 233, 239... Task Force: 314. Loading/Transport: 423, 435, 437... Destroyer: 516, 528, 538... Observation/Aerial: 716, 720. Armament/Potential Attack: 819, 821. Training: 918, 920. The 820th Fire Dragon Squadron, the only one with the exception to use both even numbers, head and tail.
615th squadron using bombers/reconnaissance B-57B Canberra was discontinued in April 1966 because this aircraft had many problems on the battlefield in Vietnam. After that, no more squadrons used the number 6 first.

the East Sea shines like a giant mirror, the harsh sunlight burns everything, the villages are desolate, the grass is sparse, and the leaves are bare... The mountains are close to the outer edge, near the National Highway 1, only bare mountains, with military outposts such as Rockpile, Sark, Fullers ... is the gateway to Khe Sanh base. At night, the cold mist from the mountains pulls down violently, creating an immense white *"ground fog"*, no longer distinguishing where the boundary is between the Sea and the Earth. Every night, after the mission to return to the base in Dong Ha, also the forward command of 51st Tactical Wing, the crew members could only gather around cheap wine in the personal plastic canteen and boxes of C- Rations [65] as appetizers against the bitter cold winds, to find a deep sleep after a tiring day on the battlefield. Even so, being placed on the front lines of the Fire Line Region is still a common pride for every soldier, regardless of their serving units, whether it is the Army, the Ranger or the Air Force, the Airborne, the Marines...

Every morning, when the sun had not yet risen, we hurriedly took off from the Dong Ha Air Base detachment to fly to Khe Sanh on duty on the hills next to the airport or under the shade of the trees with ripe red coffee, in the old French plantation near Lang Vei, is being cleared to expand the battlefield. At night, the cold wind blows into the empty barracks, and the walls are only half covered; Sleep is restless, so it is easy for you to get up early in the morning. Helicopters, both American and Vietnamese, from nearby bases such as Ai Tu, Carroll, and Ca Lu ... flew up and down in excitement, *"beacon"* lights flashing in the sky like fireflies. Each one, then, automatically searches for a position, one after another in a vertical line, like flying train cars. They all flew along the right side of the zigzag valley leading to Khe Sanh. Below, each convoy of infantry units is also slowly and painstakingly crossing each hillside.

Just entered Khe Sanh. As it got brighter, Captain Pham Vuong Thuc and I landed at the airport; Still *"refilling"*, on frequency, the

---

65.  *C-Rations was a wartime canned food for the US military at the time called MCI-Meals Combat Individual (which was later replaced by MRE-Meals Ready to Eat). Meats, fruits, cakes are preserved in tin cans, opened with a folding lock called P-38, nicknamed "John Wayne" by the US Marine Corps, invented in 1942. The number 38 is named call because it will take about 38 turns to open the can.*

Operations Office / 51st Tactical Wing contacted for the mission to fly into the Command Center of 3rd Brigade Paratrooper on Fire Base Hill 31. Captain Thuc took the mission details: *"A gunship escorting two H-34s of 219th Squadron"*. After receiving the order, just a few minutes later, we *"rendezvous"* with two H-34s waiting on the Lao Bao Pass. Perhaps because of the lack of aircraft, the mission only had one gunship escorting two *"slicks"*. As usual, I was the co-pilot, Captain Thuc, the chief pilot of the gunship chopper.

Command Center of 3rd Airborne Brigade Hill 31, is located about 40 minutes from the Lao Bao border in the northwest direction, with Colonel Tran Dinh Tho / Brigade Commander. This route we have been in and out many times so it is very familiar, no need to look at the map. If at an altitude above 2000ft, from Lao Bao Pass, you can see Hill 30, Hill 31, and Tchepone in a triangular position which are the "checkpoints" that we always remember to easily coordinate the other Landing Zones (LZs) and fly for safety. Hill 31 is not very high, has been cleared and is very large compared to the lower hills that surround the western sides and the north or south faces are small outposts to guard the brigade headquarters on the top of Hill 31. For some reason, the East is the entry line for helicopters when it is needed to support, transport, or resupply, but it is left open without defense so it cannot be cleared, dense forests cover the whole area including the *"Ho Chi Minh trail"* system is crisscrossed like a spider's web below, not knowing which is the main road. Unlike the Cambodian battlefield, which is full of sparse old forest, in Southern Laos, the forest trees from the valley can reach nearly as high as the top of the mountain.

From this side of the border with Vietnam, West Long Mountain falls down into a vast and fertile valley. It is thanks to the dense forest that the helicopter is easy to avoid if flying at a low level. At the end of the valley is a long zigzag stream like a giant black snake, crawling across the foothills of Hill 30, the ARVN's first firebase guarded by Artillery units. Although the flight path is relatively safe, every time I fly over the valley, I always take precautions to avoid letting the chopper hover in the middle of the sky, making it a good target for air defense. The fragile ship, daring to plunge its nose into the dark stream, still clinging to the terrain, then quickly cut through. During the Southern Laos 719 period, I kept the *"low level"* position as the main flight, so lucky I never got shot. At that time, the helicopter's exhaust was not curved up like it was later, so it was very difficult to avoid surface-to-air missiles (SA or SAM), except for flying low.

Every time we got in the area, the chief pilot and I often calculated, and planned each flight position, the gunner behind was also ready in defense, and the two *"miniguns"* rose up heroically, just waiting for the opportunity to release bullets!

Although I am still a copilot, I am very trusted by my Chief pilots both in terms of map ability (navigation) as well as combat flying positions. In the sky, we trust each other, and the crew's lives are also entrusted to each other. Every time I had to change my team, Captain Tran Le Tien, Major Nguyen Van Thanh, Captain Hoang Ngoc Chau or Captain Pham Vuong Thuc, they did not want to let me go back to Da Nang AFB, considering it was both a match and a lucky together.

When I was at Thu Duc Military School, class 5/68, I was very interested in Topography and loved to learn about the brown high-altitude rings on the marching map. Unexpectedly, when I first returned to the 213th Squadron, Captain Tran Duy Ky, the new Operations Officer, assigned me and Nguyen Tan Phat, the daily task of going down to the Military Newsroom / 41st Tactical Wing Office, recording the war security news and get the map for pilots to fly. It really suits my preferences. Since then, Phat and I have also become close friends. After Phat changed to Bien Hoa AFB got shot down and became a prisoner on the battlefield of Kampuchea.

This morning, Captain Thuc and I also followed the usual schedule as before. From Lao Bao Pass fly to Hill 30, and from there take the West direction straight to Hill 31. As already communicated, three helicopters, one at a time, plummeted very low, on the dense forest surface, aiming to fly in the same direction. Two H-34s, slicks, flew ahead one after another. Our gunship, which Captain Thuc controlled, wraps around in the rear, just within sight of both, but is not required to follow a certain formation, so that each can be easily dodged for safety. The sound of the engines and propellers of the three helicopters, the slots slashing through the air, reverberated in the stillness of the early morning. The battlefield that day suddenly seemed quieter than usual! The mountains and forests were silent without the smoke of guns, the 155mm artillery guns, on the fire base of Hill 30, were still waiting quietly. Although the flight was quite long, from a distance, we could clearly see the location of Hill 31.

Previously, once, I had the opportunity to fly with Pham Van Vui, a senior from Ft. Rucker, but also just released Chief Pilot. We flew Colonel Nguyen Dinh Vinh, Deputy Chief of Staff, First Corps, into Hill 30 to Scout the battlefield after a recent attack the night before. Unlike Hill 31, it is an earthy hill, bare and low, with no trees. Hill 30 is like a vertical cliff, craggy on all sides, surrounded by dense forest, and tree tops reaching the mountain peak, helicopters are the only means of transportation to reach the top. Yet, one night, the Viet Cong commandos also climbed up to the helipad but were pushed back by our troops, the military equipment was still in disarray... I went down to pick up a green khaki green enemy hat, next to the puddles of blood that were still stained, intending to return as a battlefield memento. The hat was pierced with many holes by the Claymore mines and still had a small clump of hair stuck in it. Colonel Vinh wanted to ask for the hat back, but I refused. Later, I brought it back to AFB and hung it in my room at the Butler bachelor's residence. Every night I dream of the ghost of that VC coming back to claim his hat, so I have to burn it.

On the first day of the order to enter the interior of Laos, the marching map distributed for that day was limited to the advance of friend units. I flew with Captain Tran Le Tien, the lead gun. We accidentally flew over the map limit of a stream without getting shot. Lt. Col. Nguyen Anh Toan, Major Nguyen Van Thanh, and Captain Thuc followed suit. Four gunships with chariots, one turn, rushed into Laos on Route number 9 from the border of Lao Bao pass. The atmosphere became very exciting and fun rather than scared! Captain Tien in control, I look at the map, but my eyes and limbs are always ready to be ready so that if something goes wrong, I can still *"take over control!"* if needed. Following the convoy were the most elite soldiers of the ARVN. Armor, Paratroopers ... all together towards the ultimate goal of Tchepone. Helicopters continued to maneuver around, directly overhead, to protect the army that was groping to occupy every step of the road full of traps and dense foliage. In the face of the stormy force of our army, the NVA, no matter how strong, had to wait and we were safely back inland without a single bullet wound, rejoicing in the victory of the first day.

Later, Captain Tien was fatally wounded during a gunship mission in the mountains northwest of Hue along with copilot Second Lieutenant Ng. Trong Khanh, before the Red Fiery Summer of 1972, when he was still single. The hill was later named after him, *"Tran Le Tien Hill"*. Everyone in the crew loves him very much. With a slim, tall, handsome figure, originally from the North; cute personality, arrogant, young, he is always happy to love life ... When he is alone, he often shakes his head, clams, whistles softly a few short songs, perhaps of a song that he loves very much: *"No! No! I don't love you anymore... "*. I have seen him sing this song over and over again many times, I don't know if he has any resentment in his life for a lost love or not.

Back on the mission to Hill 31, because the UH-1 Huey was faster and more agile than the H-34 Choctaw, Captain Thuc and I had to fly around many times to wait for each other. When he and I turned around, we just saw the first H-34 fall halfway down the hill after a brief *"pop"* and a plume of white smoke in the middle of the tail. It all happened so quickly in an instant. The chopper was still intact, just a few meters from the landing area; the head was slightly tilted like a clock's hand pointing in the direction of Tchepone Command Center, the crew escaped unharmed ... Captain Thuc landed, and went to the *"bunker"* of the Airborne Command Center, to see how the crew was. I stayed and continued to keep the chopper in the *"idle"* position, waiting for about 15 minutes. The security situation around the hill is still normal, there is nothing urgent, we also never expected that the situation could change suddenly like this later; because it was the largest forward Command Center of the Airborne unit in the territory of Laos at that time. Then we took off to make room for the number 2 to land. While Captain Thuc was still planning to fly *"circle around"* a few more *"paths"* to wait for the H-34 No. 2, when the plane turned left, on the forest surface in the southeast corner, there was a powerful explosion below the belly of the plane, right next to the foothills. Perhaps, the chopper was suddenly attracted by the *"vacuum"* and jumped as if it was about to fall! At that time, the H-34 No. 2 had just landed and reported that it had been *"hit by artillery"* on the landing pad, so it could not take off! Both H-34s were downed on the landing pad, there was no room left, and the heavy gunship didn't do much either. Captain. Thuc told me to take control to fly out and let him contact the 51st Tactical Wing Command Center to ask for the *"rescue"* chopper to come in, the situation around the hill was back to normal, and there was no sign of danger sure to be safe, Hill 31 is the largest Command Center of the Airborne unit in Southern Laos, no one thinks that the Communists can take over so easily.

Unfortunately, at that time, the 51st Tactical Wing was just established, with three squadrons in the operating area without having a rescue helicopter ready in the sky like the US helicopter groups, until a rescue chopper came to rescue then it was too late. The situation at that time was not so pessimistic, we still flew out normally, and not a single bullet shot up! It wasn't until a few hours later that the North Vietnamese communists started their attack. Black smoke rose from the top of the hill like vertical antennas, visible from this side of the border. After Hill 31 came to Hill 30 and then Tchepone base, just like that, fell like dominoes! And then there are the painful and bloody pages of the ARVN's retreat to the homeland. The two crews of Mr. Giang and Mr. Chung Tu Buu, if there had been an emergency chopper in time, and surely they would not have been taken prisoner along with Colonel Tran Dinh Tho and the Airborne soldiers on Hill 31 later.

That day, everything that happened to me was like a miracle! Why was it that on the same helipad of Hill 31, all 3 aircraft landed at the same time, but 2 H-34s were shot when they landed and the gunship of Captain Thuc and I was spared? If we didn't have some sacred protection, surely if we didn't die, we would have shared the same fate with the two crew members of Mr. Giang and Mr. Buu 219th Squadron.

I have known Captain Thuc for many years, but recently before his death, I found out that he was a very virtuous Roman Catholic believer; Surely that day he also believed in some miracle and miraculous protection like me, or maybe I escaped by his blessings. The last time I had the opportunity to see him was in Houston, Texas, on the occasion of the helicopter's squadron reunion in 2010. Seeing that he was much sicker than before, I asked him, because I heard that he was ill and had no chance. He smiled gently, with his eyes still narrowed as before, whenever we had a chance to have fun. He said: *"There's nothing wrong with being sick! In the past, I hadn't died in Southern Laos yet!"*.

Reminds me of the mission of more than 40 years ago, flying with him to Hill 31, 3rd Brigade Command Center, and the memories of the day when we were still in the same squadron 213th Twin Spiked Maces Gunship Squadron ... When I was a new officer and getting married, he was also recently nominated for the position of Assistant Operations Officer 213th Squadron for Captain Tran Le Tien. One day, I was too sleepy and forgot the flight time, he had to run down to the Butler residence to wake me up. After knocking on the door and getting no answer, he went around the window and saw dimly behind the glass of my room that was full of pots and pans and dishes ... He suddenly remembered that I was newly married, so he left, not to wake me up. Later, I only listened to him retell it for fun without reproach, making me always remember and love him.

He has the ideal physique that every Vietnamese pilot dreams of: big, tall, handsome, bearded... compared to any American pilot in terms of size, so his clothes wear well of the new US pilots just right! As a copilot who has had many occasions to fly with him, I find him very gentle, his voice is also gentle, his eyes are not very big, slightly narrowed when looking at the opposite person with a smile as always easy sympathy, all contrasted with his shaggy, dark beard. On the days of the secondment, sometimes at noon, we had the opportunity to fly back to Dong Ha to go to the city for lunch. Gunners like Het, De, Mai... often wear a machete next to them, making them look cool! We are also proud to see the fear in the eyes of the other soldiers of the Airborne, Marines, or Rangers in the restaurant. Perhaps they also admired his massive size.

Later, I thought of another reason to explain why the VC did not intend to shoot the gunship of Captain Thuc and I on the 31 Hill. Unfortunately, he passed away, so we did not have the opportunity to share the old story together. I still remember very well, that day, Captain Thuc was wearing a US Marine Pilot's yellowish Nomex flight suit, with the US Navy Pilot's brown leather jacket that he used to wear, and wearing leather "boot" shoes pale red. He also wears the *"camouflage"* jungle hat of the Commando or Airborne... With his massive body, dark skin, and bushy beard; If the Viet Cong had used a telescope to observe, they would have mistaken him for an American pilot, mixed or of American origin. Perhaps that is why they gave up and did not dare to shoot, because they did not want to give the USAF (US Air Forces) a reason to intervene to ruin their plan of attack. We flew around *"low level"* over the target for half an hour, right in the range of AK guns, but they still didn't fire a single bullet but just wanted to destroy 2 H-34s of Mr. Giang and Mr. Buu. Is there really a special reason? Or was it that at that time they had tightened the siege around Hill 31 so they didn't want to be exposed to spoil the attack plan? And if the attraction of the *"vacuum"* range, due to the explosion we encountered, was also the muzzle of the artillery shell on the second H-34, then that proved that the NVA had advanced very close to the foot of the hill that the 3rd Airborne Brigade still unknown; Just like we were flying right over the target of the gun and fortunately they let us go.

After Operation Lam Son 719, I no longer had much faith in the firepower of gunships and rockets. The destructive power of rockets in the mountains and forests of Southern Laos only created a tiny cluster of smoke like a kitchen stove that had just glimmered out of the treetops that had dissolved in the wind. After becoming the Chief pilot, I went to return to flying slicks. For me, the *"Slicks"* mission is more dangerous but more interesting! Helicopters are most difficult to land, not fly, especially to land safely in the difficult conditions of the battlefield, difficult terrain, and difficult weather. The higher the challenge, the more fun it is, that's the *"Slicks"* flying beast. Each mission completed safely returned, in itself a little sense of victory!

In tactical Zone I Corps, the mountains are dense, difficult, and dangerous. All operations are located in the mountains. The UH-1 Huey helicopter is the only vehicle, besides the military operations of the Infantry units. In the experience of flying helicopters, maybe by chance but also by accident, I found a certain flying position that can be effectively evaded, so I rarely get shot; made me not believe, the battlefield of Vietnam, including Southern Laos and Cambodia, has many air defenses like other pilots often described.

In reality, I was always on guard, fearing that the airfield would be bombarded more than I was afraid of anti-aircraft shooting down. Anti-aircraft weapons are community weapons, slow to manage and require specialized gunners, more necessary for the North battlefield than in the South, so they certainly cannot be distributed indiscriminately to the enemy guerrilla; except for the large fronts with division-level troops such as the battle of Quang

Tri or Binh Long - An Loc, but it was only limited to a small extent. It is important to always have a good grasp of the situation before a mission, carefully studying friend and enemy positions around the landing pad; therefore, crews who fly regularly are less likely to be in danger than those who fly occasionally. In short, not everywhere all the time, every place has a room that is not as dense as a net of fire! Which is 12.7mm, which is SA-7, which is 37 mm, 57 mm of direct target ... All of these are probably just legends, embellished with bold colors of war and a more heroic battlefield!

Only once, I witnessed with my own eyes the orange sparks of SA-7 from a mountain in the northeast of Ba-To district shooting after Lieutenant Colonel Cao Q. Khoi's helicopter, 213th Squadron Commander. That day, Lt. Col. Khoi flew in from the direction of Mo Duc district to observe the invasion of Ba To / Quang Ngai. It was an important and dangerous landing because two squadrons 213 & 239 sent a unit from the 4th Regiment, the 2nd Army Division from Duc Pho airfield to relieve the besieged district capital Ba To for a whole week has not been recaptured. Perhaps he was worried about his juniors because a few days earlier, the 239th Squadron had to sacrifice a crew of Lt. Hoang Vu & Toan. Fortunately, that day, Mr. Khoi flew high and fast, the aircraft was also equipped with a new type of exhaust with a curved shape to dissipate the hot air from the engine, so the bullets only flew past the tail, in front of our terrified eyes. At that time, perhaps Lt. Col. Khoi himself did not know that he was being followed by SA-7!

Ba To district capital is located in the valley between 3 districts Minh Long - Ba To - Gia Vuc, surrounded by three mountains. Only the direction from Gia Vuc to fly out is the valley is quite wide, enough for 2 groups to manage in case of unforeseen circumstances. Therefore, I chose to take the direction to Gia Vu and then fly back out, even though the flight path is a few minutes longer. From Duc Pho airfield, I led 10 slicks, with 4 gunships as an escort, flying down into the jungle to the south, past Major Du's Ranger outpost, an LZ very familiar to the 213th pilots before. From there, we started low level, crossing the jungle to the West, all flying in a vertical line for easy dodging and landing one by one. Four gunships followed, escorting both sides. The two groups approached the foot of the mountain before turning right, then hugged the northern mountainside, followed the valley road, and flew back to Ba To, still at a very low altitude. Unexpectedly thanks to that change, accidentally (or fortunately), it was possible to disable the SA-7 missile batteries, if they were aimed, from the front mountain range (East), blocking Duc Pho and Ba To, which they fired on Lt. Col. Khoi's chopper, will now have no effect on us; because the SA-7 is a tail-only weapon (follow the heat) and has no effect on the *"face-to-face"* firing position. Maybe that's why the two squadrons, 10 slicks and 4 gunships, safely completed the mission, and came out, not a single shot! The mission that day I still remember had Captain Nguyen Nhu Huyen, and Captain Tran Van Hoa fly slicks number 2, and number 3 followed, Lt. Tran Tam Son's ship reported having a "chip detector" so it was put in Duc Pho airport standby!

Usually, the helicopter's *"march"* flight, during each mission, is considered dangerous, but is in fact very short! The space that you often refer to as "into the area", is only in the last 1-2 miles near the landing area, that is, in the close range. If every battlefield was full of anti-aircraft defenses, the helicopters that had just taken off would have been shot down! The level of danger to fly from one province to another is almost nonexistent, if from the province to the county level, the most dangerous area is probably not more than 1%. Similarly, flying missions from divisional to regiment level are usually communication missions with 0% danger. From the Regimental Command to the Battalion Executive Command Center is the same as from the Province to the District. Then the remaining danger is only at Company or Battalion level targets whose range is usually no more than 3 -5 miles from the Command Center / Battalion. Many landing sites have just taken off from the Command Center and have seen LZ, that distance is the true flight of each helicopter mission when *"entering the area"* of operation that each pilot can calculate according to battlefield experience. enter, land, and take off safely. Of the four ways in and out, there must be a more *"safe"* way! The most dangerous part is when the aircraft slows down to enter the *"short final"*, that is, within the last 1-mile radius around the landing area, or if the landing area is suddenly shelled by the enemy.

American pilots often pay too much attention to technical safety factors, must follow the direction of the wind, must have smoke to mark the landing area, etc. In the old days, helicopter missions also dropped pathfinders first to throw smoke and guide aircraft to land on the battlefield, so many American helicopters crashed. In the Red Fiery Summer of 1972, in the mountains west of the My Chanh defense line near Phong Dien district, Thua Thien province, American helicopters fell scattered in the valleys, beside dry streams right next to the base of the fortress, and aircraft still intact form; but perhaps American pilots always respect the principle of *"safety first!"* should flee early, less dare than Vietnamese pilots.

An armed Huey helicopter (Gunship) of the 213th Twin Spiked Maces Squadron

An H-34 Choctaw helicopter of the 213th Twin Spiked Maces squadron.

Vietnamese helicopter pilots in mountainous areas, such as 1st Corps, are no strangers to daring mountain landings depending on the demands of the battlefield, regardless of the ups and downs of the wind. Landing on the mountain is not always from the top, but if necessary, it can be scooped up from a low-level position, suddenly fooling the enemy, in case the landing area has been warned against shelling ... Want to get down quickly, respond fast and neat, must spiral down *(spiral approach)* like a funnel, with few spectacular zig-zags, to avoid *"overshooting"* the landing area. Landing on the mountain needs to be accurate, not to be *"overshoot"* but also unable to *"undershoot"* and when taking off, you must also beware of *"over-torque"* because of the high terrain, lack of lift capacity of the propeller (uplift). The higher the mountain wind, the faster it descends, the less the influence of turbulence will be. Hitting the nose down with *"cyclic"*, the plane will drop more quickly than with just *"collective down"* like the usual landing. When you come from the region while changing to the mountains, you are used to the *"normal approach"*, relax both *"flare"* and push *"collective down"*; The plane did not come down, creating conditions for the wind to rise, unable to descend the mountain. The chopper is like a kite in the wind, hovering forever in the air. Meet the landing area about 2/3 of the mountain, can only land and take off in the same direction. When entering, it's like aiming for a mountain, but when taking off, you have to *"hover"* back and quickly plug your nose into the valley and *"gain speed"* (fake) quickly lest you get *"stalled"*... are the flight tactics of the Vietnamese pilot outside the training books at the flight school. In the Iraq battlefield in 2003, after a series of helicopters were shot down, it was not until 2007 that American helicopter pilots had to change their flight tactics to avoid.

In the past, I very much admired the talent of the night ambulance pilots of the 257th Rescue Squadron. I am even more proud because they all came from the 213th Squadron, such as Nguyen Hoang An, Duong Tan Long, Vu O, Tran Long, Vu Van Hien, Do Quoc Hung, Dang Vu Dang... It's hard to land in the mountains during the day, it's even more difficult at night!

Most missions in the mountains have only one landing area, so the leader always has to sacrifice himself to find a way to get in first, if it is safe, then it's the wingman's turn. The role of the leader in each mission is very important in leading the crew to the safe landing area, especially for the *"Hot"* ones. It requires an understanding of the topography as well as the security situation around the landing area and accurate judgments of the leader. The correlation between friend and enemy positions is like a game of chess, in four certain directions will find a more *"safe"* exit. Unfortunately, in the past, the crews often flew under the guidance of Command and Control chopper ("C & C"), most of which were staff of the squadron, and only had the opportunity to go to the operating area once in a while, not understanding the situation of war changes every day.

After Operation Southern Laos, in November 1971, the 213th Squadron was seconded to Bien Hoa, reinforcing the 3rd Air Force Division which was facing the two battlefields of Binh Long / An-Loc and Kampuchea at the same time. The land was strange but there were no mountains, so most of us didn't seem too wary. Once, taking the mission alone, one slick, no gunship escort, no other aircraft flying; I landed at Loc Ninh airport in the northwest of Binh Long province to load supplies and get more security information for the mission to fly to Bu Dop to resupply the Rangers. Sure the coordinates on the map, note the necessary check points to avoid getting lost in the flight path. I took off, determined the direction of the flight, plugged my nose to get speed. Go through the dense wooden forest next to the ring of Loc Ninh airport, on the left side of the national highway, then start down the "low level" and fly along Highway 13 to the North. The road seems to have been abandoned for a long time, no cars, no people, trees covered the road like Highway 9 in Southern Laos. Bu Dop outpost is located deep in the Vietnam - Cambodia border region, in the northwest, alone in the middle of four sides of old forest, surrounded by sparse trees. The soldiers were happy to receive the supply. They *"unloaded"* very quickly, only a few minutes later. I took off and returned, looking down at the rudimentary barbed wire fence surrounding the fort and four rudimentary watchtowers, I don't know if it can stop wild animals at night. How can we resist VC attacks? Feeling sorry for the fragile condition of the Rangers who remained in the lonely outpost. Though not dead. They also deserve to be commended as the heroic suicide soldiers of the ARVN!... Still low level, the plane hovered close to the treetops to dodge, gently passing through the jagged old forest. dry without leaves, then fly back along Highway 13, land at Quang Loi airport, and continue to *"standby"* ... The terrain of the 3rd Corps is relatively flat, easy to land, but very dangerous, difficult to determine which direction is more secure. I think the most effective flight position to avoid is still *"low level"*, the lower the safer. Only at low altitudes can a helicopter, whether gunship or slicks display all of its eloquent power.

On the last mission (3/1975) Le Tan Dai and I flew into Round Mountain, before the day of Quang Ngai's loss, to resupply a unit of the 2nd Infantry Division. Thanks to the low level, the guerrillas holding AK-47s in the leafy village at the foot of the mountain, seeing the helicopters rushing in, had to panic and flee into the house. We didn't shoot so they (VC) didn't shoot back either!

After the second mission to Bien Hoa, around the end of January 1972, the 213th squadron returned to Da Nang, then plunged into the new battles of the 1972 Red Fiery Summer and the Quang Tri front. Captain Tran Le Tien died in battle, Captain Pham Vuong Thuc left the 213th squadron, transferred to the newly established 239th King Hawks Squadron, and assumed the position of Operations Officer.

Capt. Tien & Capt. Thuc are no longer alive, but their silhouettes will probably never fade in the minds of us, from whom they know especially the pilots of the 213th Twin Spiked Maces Squadron who once struggled with them across the battlefields in the Line of Fire!

Farewell, Mr. Tien, Goodbye Mr. Thuc!!!

NATIONAL ACADEMY HIGH SCHOOL 1965-1973

For my friends who studied under the same roof of Quoc Hoc (National Academy High School) in Hue from 1965 to 1973. Our memories of the old days are still there, but now each of us pursues a different life in different cities. We still remember one another and try to meet, along with our spouses and families.

HIGH SCHOOL FRIENDS 65-72 MEETING/REUNION, AFTER 45 YEARS

Front Gate of Quoc Hoc Hue High School

HIGH SCHOOL REUNION OF 2017, 2018 IN FLORIDA, 2019 IN VIRGINIA

2012: Actually, the first meeting in the US only included Liem, Chanh, and Hoa, because Liem and his wife went to the US for their daughter to get married in Virginia in November 2012. We were dragged into the girl's family side for the sake of being part of an enjoyable crowd and having fun.

2016: Then, in 2016, Phuc Hue, on the occasion of his daughter's wedding at Ponta Vedra Beach, Florida, planned to hold the event at the end of May, wanting to add to the reunion meeting of the National Academy High School. Although Hue and his wife had just settled in the United States the year before, they kindly invited all of their high school classmates to visit their home and attend the wedding, as well as taking this opportunity to meet Quoc Hoc's friends after 45 years away from school (1972-2017). May have looked easy, but hard to do.

Forty-five years from the day we left school, after the 1971-1972 school year, everyone was in a different place, with a friend who enlisted in the army, according to Huynh Xuat, *"putting pen and paper away to join military life"*. Some students stayed in Hue for college or went to Saigon to continue their education. However, we still do not forget the memories of our student life, so the event of April 30, 1975, completely affected everyone's life. The lucky ones came to America at the last minute, while the ones who stayed behind bitterly lost everything, then became boat people, then H.O., O.D.P., tourists, a reunion, finally they were able to breathe the free air that so many friends wish like our dreams across the ocean have yet to come to our homeland.

Mr. Hoe Trinh (RVNN officers), Liem, Hoa and Chanh at a wedding party on the evening of November 10, 2012 in Virginia (Liem's daughter's wedding).

The journey from the day we left Quoc Hoc has one thing in common: we share the same childhood school, and respect teachers and friends that are undoubtedly difficult for the next generation to encounter.

FIRST HUE NATIONAL ACADEMY HIGH SCHOOL REUNION, AFTER 45 YEARS

May 26, 2017: At first, really only Chanh-Linda (Raleigh, North Carolina), Hoa-Tuoi (Palm Beach, Florida), Xuat-Hang (Denver, Colorado), Chinh-Soan (Southern California) had planned to attend. Former Class President Nguyen Van Chanh was nominated as the communications and organization Director, as well as a coordinator of accommodation for everyone, because all had come from far away, except for Phuc Hue and his wife who lived locally in Jacksonville, Florida. It was not certain that there would be enough husbands and wives in this reunion, but in the end, the full attendance of 8 couples, plus De-Hong's daughter Hong Van, proved to ensure great success for the meeting. Thank you to our friends' wives for supporting and attending the meeting, because the trip was quite expensive for everyone, in terms of both time and money.

July 2018: We arranged to meet again in Florida, a little further south, so we could pick tropical fruits. This year there were 6 and a half couples, with husband and wife Liem-Phuong who recently settled in the US with their children and grandchildren. Hue-Huong, Chinh-Soan, Chanh-Linda, Quy-Hang, Hoa-Tuoi, and Xuat, only missing was his wife, Hang, because the request for a leave of absence did not get approval. Happy days swimming, going to the Turtle museum, fishing…and getting bitten by *"no-see-ums"*. Planning for next year's reunion in 2019, when we will visit Liem-Phuong's house in Virginia on the occasion of cherry blossom season in our National Capital.

March 2019: Go to D.C. and Virginia this time; also had 6 and a half couples, complete with the Xuat couple; missing was the Hue-Huong couple, but with the addition of Venerable Thich Huu Nguyen (student name Nguyen Thanh Hai), returning from Ohio. The capital region is full of interesting and strange things: we went to restaurants, saw flower displays, landscapes and especially national museums full of people. Liem-Phuong's house had probably never been so crowded. Being disturbed by all old friends. Thank you to the owner for being patient and letting the room selection by lottery win. We have also discussed contributing to the event and a scheduled to return to Hue, Vietnam in 2020 for a half-century reunion (1970-2020). Alas, the Covid-19 pandemic ruined this plan, although the airplane tickets, hotel accommodations and everything had been prepared since 2019.

February 2022: Planned to meet again in Southern California on the occasion of the Vietnamese Lunar New Year, but it also had to be canceled because of the high level of the Covid-19 pandemic. It was difficult to travel by air, as well as concerns about hotel accommodations and eating in restaurants, so only local friends got together. We promise to meet again when the Pandemic is declared over and when most of us reach the age of 70, it will probably be 2023.

2017-Florida – In front of Liên Hương-Phúc Huệ's house.

2017-Florida-Picture taken before a wedding ceremony.

5/2017-Wedding Ceremony with Quoc Hoc's friends, 65-72

Picture taken before saying "Good-bye", 2017

2018-Florida Quoc Hoc High School Reunion 65-72

2018-Florida. Picking fruits in front of longan farm in Ft. Pierce.

2019-Washington, D.C. Quoc Hoc Reunion in front of Capitol – Cherry Blossoms

3/2019 – In front of Liem-Phuong house in Gainesville, Virginia.

2022: SMALL REUNION FOR FRIENDS' 40TH WEDDING ANNIVERSARY.

The Covid-19 pandemic interrupted the annual meeting and reunion program of QH High School 65-72, several times after the meeting at the Cherry Blossom Festival in March 2019 in Virginia. It was not until 2021 that the situation brightened, once the Covid vaccine became available. However, the *but* is still wordy but evil: we bought plane tickets, booked a hotel, intending to meet on the Vietnamese Lunar New Year in Southern California, friends in California are also preparing to pick us up, would share the evenings eating and drinking with us – and probably with all Hue dishes. Near Tet, the Covid pandemic broke out again in this large and densely-populated state, restaurants were temporarily closed, seeing that going out could spread the disease, bringing the disease home to young children and grandchildren who had not been vaccinated, so the whole group stayed far away – just projecting a plan for friends in California to meet in February 2022.

Near the middle of 2022, former class president Chanh announced that everyone who wanted to meet should go *"cruising"*, just on the occasion of the 40th anniversary of Chanh-Linda's wedding and Liem's 70th birthday in September.

At the end of August, 2022 we flew to the meeting place in Seattle, Washington. There were only 4 couples because other friends would go to Vietnam or go to another group meeting, so the best we could muster included: Chanh-Linda, Quy-Hang, Liem-Phuong, Hoa-Tuoi, adding in Quy's in-laws; Tung-Hanh[66] totaled ten people in all. We met the day before boarding the cruise ship headed to Alaska; we visited Pike's Place Market, famous for fish throwing, the Space Needle that was built for the 1962 International World Fair and is kept open today for visitors. The building, located on the top floor must be reached by elevator, and rotates slowly around an axis. It is built of unbreakable glass, looking down.

The next day, we boarded a large cruise ship called *"Ovation of the Seas"* from Pier 91, containing several thousand people, eating and drinking as much as they like. The ship called at rendezvous places like Juneau, Alaska (the state capital). Skagway, Sitka and the last stop Victoria in neighboring Canada. Each place had its own beauty, a natural beauty preserved as precious, making my heart feel even more sad for our homeland.

We celebrated Chanh-Linda's anniversary with a dinner on 9/4, small but all friends. After nearly 8 days of sailing, visiting the wharves, the group returned to the pier and headed for the airport to return home. All 10 people had to be tested negative for Covid before getting on the ship as required; coming back to make sure, we tested again; this time only one person tested positive: the Doctor's wife, so it was not too bad. Will see all of you and perhaps more friends on the cruise on other occasions next time.

---

66. *By lucky chance, I first met Doctor Quy's brother-in-law (married with his wife's younger sister, in Vietnam we joked that he control the boat's front and the one married with the older sister controlled the rear of the boat) and discovered that he was Dentist Tung, who let Pharmacist Trinh and family board the evacuation commercial ship Long Ho (Dragon Lake) on the 30th day of April, 1975 at Bach Dang Pier in Saigon. The person I interviewed two weeks ago about his story. It is a fate that did not make an appointment to meet and never expected to meet him in personafter I wrote his friend's story just 2 weeks before that.*

Four high school friends (left) and their wives, not in order (right).

Stopover to visit Skagway, Alaska and Victoria, British Columbia, Canada

CHAPTER IX

ACHIEVING PROFESSIONAL CERTIFICATION

CAREER AND RETIREMENT

WORKING TOWARD PROFESSIONAL CERTIFICATION

In the United States as well as around the world, life changed when the *Internet* started. Before that, *email* [67] changed the lives of people everywhere. In 1980, when IBM released the personal computer, it not only upgraded the lifestyle of individuals but also affected their way of working, because small companies were suddenly able to compete in their way of working without any problems. Before that time, only large companies or government agencies could afford expensive computing rigs called *"mainframes"* that were able to network. In 1970, the US government gave the Republic of Vietnam an IBM computer system in Saigon that changed the paper-based tests to tests called *"IBM exams"* but the drawback was that they required highly-trained and qualified personnel to operate the system. It was not until later that they had more and more modern, compact, and easy-to-use products.

When we studied at the University of Florida and graduated before 1980, all we had to use was a *key punch* system; that is, write a program, put it in a typewriter, put a card on top of it, and type the words in. The letters on the card would be punched it according to the available boxes. The students had to struggle, holding a box of cards bought at the bookstore, waiting for a machine to become available, and then taking their turn to sit down and type. Next, wait in line, and put your card into the reading machine; the reader is fast, runs smoothly, and then returns the card, if the machine is unfortunately stuck, then the card is damaged, and you have to go back to the typing room to type to replace the card with a new one. All students understand that at the beginning of the course, the computer room is almost empty, but as soon as a teacher gives an assignment, they have to wait, sometimes an hour for their turn, but not everyone is good at computers. Coming up with a correct

---

67. *The Internet began in 1983. E-mail, or email for short, has been tried at the University of Massachusetts Institute of Technology (M.I.T.) since 1965, but it was not until 30 years later, 1995 that it became popular. Today in the world, every individual has at least one email and the internet for communication and daily use via computers or cell phones.*

answer the first time, that's called *"learning"*. With the same solution, some people only use a few cards, others a whole box. Until the final exam, oh well, why is it so crowded, long lines of students, standing in long queues waiting their turn in Weil Hall, those who know how to plan ahead, do it early, some people wait until the last minute, submit papers even they know the results are wrong; there are many opportunities to go back to the same class next quarter. Many students sleep during the day and wait until nightfall. Fewer people, sometimes a wrong estimate, day and night see the same volume of students... then there are chances to ask for a medical excuse from the doctor, drop the course without penalties. Student life is full of joys and sorrows – not necessarily because of themselves but caused by machines.

When I joined the Town in 1998, there were no computers, no email, and no internet, everyone used pen and paper, and records were required to be kept by law, some for one or three years, some for eternity. Over the long run, it was a problem, because the cartons in the office were getting bigger and bigger, have to be sent off and stored in air-conditioned places to avoid decay.

At first, when IBM introduced its compact products from *"Junior"* to *"XT"*, *"AT"*, using hard drives and floppy disks, at the same time, outside the market, Radio Shack also released their *"Tandy"* brand machines, while other unnamed companies imitated them. exactly what we called *"clones"*, cheaper and sold better. Thus, the IBM office that made personal computers in Boca Raton slowly laid off employees and ended up not being able to compete with clones made in other cheap-labor countries, or assembly in a garage to cut costs.

The computer industry in information technology, now because of the inventions of new chips and machines and software, has become common for factories and even at home, becoming indispensable, without the need for TVs, phones, televisions ... If you have a computer, you will have everything, and then Apple on June 29, 2007, released the first *iPhone*, and our world of information technology was turned upside down. Many convenient inventions on the market require a deeper understanding on the part of the user. It is easy to give an iPhone or iPad to a baby who can't walk, he or she already knows how to swipe, and swipe back, but if you need to know why in detail, there must be people like us.

The computer field began to require I.T. competence, for positions from Director or above, not only to have experience but because technology changes daily, they must have leadership to overcome challenges.

After the machines got smaller and smaller, universities had to train students in technology, to do their homework with laptops, and not to need to wait in line to use a keypunch... but leadership and higher levels are rare. Universities began to offer professional training programs and in 2005, Florida State University, through the Florida Institute of Government in Tallahassee, began piloting the CGCIO (Certified Government Chief Information Technology) program and CPTM (Certified Public Technology Manager), lower level, at first with 1 year of training, then 2 years and then down to 16 months. Supporting the program is the Florida Local Government nformation Systems Association (FLGISA).

Acceptance for admission to study, in addition to the requirements of the degree, also involves having worked 10 years in government, holding a position of Director or higher, most of them are members of the association. I had to wait until the 5th class before I packed up to take the courses after the city paid the tuition and my boss allowed it. After studying for two years, they must write a thesis called a *"Capstone Project"*, which is approved by the teaching board and a mentor, about their field. It must be presented to a panel of judges, consisting of instructors and members who have graduated from classes before receiving a PASS (P) or FAIL (F). This is a thesis that the candidate relates to their field and will be working on in a specific industry. My case was quite special: my project was about: *"Leadership beyond technology: Playing multiple roles in a small municipality"*. My topic had not been attempted by anyone, because those who had been in class and graduated before never held the power of City Manager, able to work directly with the Mayor and Council members, and taking the opportunity to hold that power for the time being, I had strengthened my Information Technology Department. In politics, it is not unusual for the President of the United States to come from a state and in return to help his own state. It is only natural: anyone who has the opportunity would do it so that when I returned to my old position, people liked or respected me more.

After the class, I was certified in 2011 and recertified every three years after completing 120 hours of CEU.

The Florida Institute of Government
at
Florida State University

recognizes

Hoa Ngoc Hoang

Certified Government Chief Information Officer
Successfully Completed
120 Continued Professional Development Hours

Certified Through
2020 - 2023

CGCIOFlorida
CERTIFIED GOVERNMENT CHIEF INFORMATION OFFICER

WORKING AND RETIREMENT

Arriving in the United States of America as a refugee with empty hands, like many other, previous ethnic groups, required a long time to integrate and succeed. I still think that this is my *"second homeland"*, just staying temporarily because of the war. When I was younger, I tried to study hard, so that in the future, I would possess the ambition to return to build my country, Vietnam, like America, never imagining that I would stay here for the rest of my life.

With that desire, also the prediction from my father when I was born. I studied Architecture instead of engineering, like many of my friends. In the College of Architecture, because of limited space, every year, only fifty students are accepted; I was the only Vietnamese: all the rest were white Americans. After finishing school, with a degree in hand, I was going to go around the US but stopped in Kansas City, now either wavering, as I could go West (California) or East (Washington, D.C.), I choose the East. After being introduced by friends, I stayed at the house of Mr. K., an Air Force officer, 223 Lightning Bird Helicopter Squadron, the biological brother of my classmate, who also knew my brother in Arlington, Virginia.

LEE GARDENS, ARLINGTON, VIRGINIA

Lee Gardens apartments consist of many buildings for rent; this is a residential apartment with 2 bedrooms and one bathroom. I don't know how long they had been there, but when I moved in, the house was crowded but very happy, with people all cooking together. From time to time, a few ladies appeared to visit, because of the handsome host. Mr. Son was working for NASA. Alas, his wife and children were still stuck in Vietnam. Mr. Hung [68], outside

68. *Mr. Hung, from An Bang village, Hue, served on the South Vietnam Navy (RVNN) at Da Nang, using the US-aided ship Patrol Craft Fast (PCF), also named Swift Boats with a speed up to 32 knots, 15 meters long, range from 600 to 800 km. On March 28, 1975 they evacuated from Da Nang to Cam Ranh, then Vung Tau, on board were General Truong, commander of the 1st Corps. On April 29, they went out to sea and transferred to the Yangtze ship Nha Trang HQ-505 to Subic Bay and Guam. Admitted to the refugee camp Ft. Chaffee, Arkansas he settled in Kansas City and then Northern Virginia.*

of work and school hours, volunteered to take care of Vietnamese refugee boat people coming to DC and surrounding areas through the resettlement program of *"Giac Hoang Pagoda"*, a volunteer agency. Having just come to the US for about 5 years, although the means of transportation were limited, everyone lived together happily. When I had a job in Maryland, I moved to Jim Bo's house to be able to work more closely.

1980: HELPED MOVING CROSS-INTERSTATE, ENOUGH TO GET AN ELECTRIC RICE COOKER

One day, Mr. Hung invited me to move/relocate a family he helped settle in Manassas but who wanted to stay with a brother's family in Salem, north of Boston, Massachusetts.

The family had 7 members: 2 of them followed me on a large U-Haul carrying all their belongings, Mr. Hung's Ford car carried food and the rest followed behind. When I entered New York, it was just getting dark; the road was *"detour"* due to construction, and the traffic was quite crowded, so we could not follow each other, there was no cell phone at that time, so after stopping and check a map to be sure I was traveling in the right direction, I decided to stop and buy hamburgers and drinks for the three people in the car because all the food was left in the small car with the rest of the family. We then drove straight to the new location, with no waiting involved.

There was no GPS locator at that time, so we were only guided by a paper map. Arriving late, too tired after a long drive at night, I asked the owner to lend me a bed to sleep in until morning. Waking up, listening to the noise outside, Mr. Hung's car and his family had arrived and were unloading things from the moving truck. We had lunch and said goodbye to Salem. On the way back, we decided to stop by New York's Chinatown for dinner, then bought a rice cooker to take home. Calculating the cost of gasoline, the small amount of money left over between the two of us was just enough to buy the rice cooker. The moving trip that the apartment now has a new rice cooker; no need to cook rice in a regular pot and cooked rice is always available.

THE FIRST JOB

THE AMERICAN ROAD NAMED "FREEDOM" IN VIETNAMESE

1980: Sending *"résumés"* to multiple firms around the Washington, D.C. *"metro area"* (Virginia, DC and Maryland). I was called for an interview by JMT [69] in Silver Springs, north of Beltway 495. This was the first time I had had to go in for an interview; of course, I was inexperienced in terms of salary, no experience – I needed to learn how much I should get paid, because when they asked me how much money I made after graduating, I could give them no number, so I let them decided how much they would pay. Mr. Ben (Benjamin) agreed to hire me; the main job was to take care of the drawings (drafting), large *"size D"* (30in x 42in) on *"vellum"* or *"Mylar"* (drafting film paper), both in mechanical pencil and a Koh-I-Noor Rapidograph *"Pelican"* pen. This is a hard clear 3 or 4-mil thick polymer that you can see through and should be ready to on draw both sides. The back of it is meant to draw existing topography in 2-foot intervals, incorporating existing data; it does not change unless field survey verification is superseded, which means that you have to draw backward, sometimes you have to line both things on a drawing table with a light bulb underneath large enough for the drawings. I call it a *"light table"* to draw on the bottom/ mirror side (backward), usually the topography and buildings of the land are developed for roads, houses ... and existing drainage systems. The main (top) side of it is the part that will design the future of the project, so if you need to delete it to change it, you won't have to touch the unaltered terrain on the back. They devised a way to embed blueprints on both sides, including the design and existing together; this was what was needed for the construction of roads, sewers, earthwork, and new houses to pass along to the construction department. This part about planning and land development belongs to both civil and architectural engineers: each house has its own structure, and outside, the landscape architect takes care of it. Note here that there are four different majors in the School of Architecture in the US: Architecture (Architect),

69. *This is a firm of Planning and Civil Engineering: houses, roads, bridges. Johnson, McCordic (Mirmiran) & Thompson, P.A., in Silver Spring, MD, was founded in 1971 and is still operating today, more than 50 years late.*

Landscape Architect, Interior Design, and Construction. All fields must work together as well with Civil Engineers and Surveyors as a team, to get the best possible projects.

Most people did not know this but when necessary, I could draw with either hand, so within 3 months, the projects that needed to be prepared on the back were continued by me, then I went to find my boss to get more work. Mr. Ben joked: *Slow down*…After three months of work, one day he invited me to lunch with Jim, my trainer, while waiting for the restaurant to bring out the food, he said: *"I didn't get a chance to apologize to you until today..."*. I looked at Jim and he said: *"A confession, maybe..."* I asked him, *"Why did you apologize to me like that? You treated me right from the beginning"*, he said: *"Not really..."* and explained when he hired me, he also hired another person, one with the same degree but from a different University and because I was a foreigner, with English as a second language, he paid me less because he thought that the other guy was an American, he probably wouldn't have any problems with communication – even though my résumé was better, and both Jim and he saw what was wrong after 3 months of work: with my talent and technical abilities, language wasn't an issue, so *he would correct his mistake and give me a raise over the other guy!*. I thought that was the end, they acknowledged their error and corrected it right away, proving that they were good people to work with. Three months later he resigned; I asked him where he was going and he said he intended to start a new firm with an old boss; he also took my friend Jim Bo with him. I stayed and continued working with a new department head. He was taciturn, quiet, and unfriendly, so I avoided as much contact as I could, just doing my work.

About a month later, I received a phone call from Ben, inviting me to lunch. When I got there, I joked: *"Maybe this time you will give me a raise, even though you are working for another company."* He replied: *"You are only 50% right ..., I want to hire you to work for our new company"*. I asked *"You already know my salary; now how much do you intend to pay me if I take the new job?"* He replied with a sentence that I still remember forever: *"I pay you double if you accept"*. Easy to understand English, and without any necessity for further negotiations, I answered: *"Ditto"*. I returned to the office, gave them my resignation letter, and worked the last two weeks as per my notice; the boss asked me where I was going, and I told him the truth: I planned to work for Ben. He said: *"If you stay here. I will match his offer"*. I knew his character (Tinsbloom) because he was jealous of Ben, so he would do that, but I honestly did not have enough trust to work with him any longer; without disclosing the salary Ben promised to pay I just said: *"I will learn a lot from Ben and have more opportunities and responsibility with his firm"*, so *"Thank you anyway, but I am leaving"*. I thought he would say OK but the most surprising thing was that he retorted *"So you don't need to work the last two weeks; you can leave now"*. It is true that some people know and respect the skills and talents of others; some people do not the important thing is to be able to trust each other when working.

So I didn't have to stick around the last two weeks I gave notice for. I went to work for the new company earlier, happy because the new salary is twice as high as what I had made before. When I arrived at the new company, called *"KML"*, I was surprised to find that the office was mostly empty, so I had to cut some plywood to make a temporary drawing table, because the Heritage Harbor project was in Annapolis, a suburb of D.C. There is a famous US Navy officer training center there. More than 825 acres of land and nearly 2,000 US homes in Anne Arundel County for people over 55 years of age: a retirement community. Ben let me name the new roads because he was so busy. He told me to use names related to the Marines or based on Italian/Latin as the source, as long as they were not duplicated from the list the county had for existing roads. The small road I named *"Freedom"* in Vietnamese is also here; at first, they thought I meant TUDOR Ct., so the county added an *"R"* on the end, but I had to tell them to take the R off to get it right *"TUDO"* and surprisingly or maybe just luckily, they did. I am not sure whether the people living on this road ever got the real meaning.

To name street and get approval, computers were not yet available; the names must not be identical and not too special, so the names I proposed on the list were not approved, even though I took out the marks, such as CamRanh Bay, Saigon, Dalat, MyKhe (American GI's favorite beach), and only two names that are a bit off the list are TuDo Court and Lanna Way were accepted (*"Lanna"* is Lan Anh's nickname for my niece that the family used to call when she was young in VN). For me, Tu Do Street in Saigon lost its name after changing hands, but the small and short Tu Do Street I named is a spiritual symbol of why I and other Vietnamese people came here to find it, and also with the hope that one day a road bearing the same name will be present in Vietnam again, to bring a new source of vitality for the people to enjoy [70].

Google Map: *Tự Do (Freedom) Court, Annapolis, Anne Arundel County, Maryland 21401*

1982: TRIP TO THE WORLD'S FAIR

(Rewritten and edited according to the Diary, after taking out the personal thoughts)

This year's World Fair was held in Knoxville, Tennessee, and was opened by President Ronald Reagan on May 1, 1982, the first time it had been held in the southern part of the United States, with 22 countries participating. It was considered a success. However, after 25 years, in 2007 the city paid off $46 million in advance loans it had taken out to organize the event. The fair ended on October 31, 1982.

During this time, since I had just bought a house, I was still driving an old VW Bug. I was really not sure I could take it out of state and complete my trip, to be more confident I rented a car, a red Dodge. The journey started from my home in Maryland, stopped

70. *The new government renamed the old streets in Saigon after April 1975, in which two famous one-way streets, people have placed two verses, both literal and figurative:*
"Nam Ky Khoi Nghia destroys Justice,
Dong Khoi rose up and lost Freedom".
Two other roads name are also lost, namely Thong Nhat (Unified) and Cong Hoa (Republic), these four basic things no longer available after Saigon changed hands.

in Virginia to pick up Mr. K., and drove straight to Charlotte, North Carolina to pick up KM (also my girlfriend [71]) at UF.

On the way, we visited a small mountain known as "Chimney Rock". The site is located near the city of Ashville, N.C. To get to the top of the mountain, you have to go along a small path. The flagpole is the highest peak, after 499 steps. We climbed to the top and here it is, 2,280 feet above sea level, though the mountain itself is only 315 feet high.

THE 1982 WORLD'S FAIR 40TH ANNIVERSARY CELEBRATION
KNOXVILLE, TENNESSEE, U.S.A.

2022 – Sun Sphere after 40 years – Photo courtesy of City of Knoxville.

71. *Note explain here about the different cultures between the East and the West. In our Vietnamese tradition and culture, the names calling boyfriend(bạn trai) and girlfriend (bạn gái) and dating does not means to have the physical or sexual activities like the West. Further relationship as romantic partners or lovers are different than boy or girlfriends. Friends of both sexes in mental until get married by respect each other, sometimes, even holding hands or kissing are prohibited in old tradition and family members also involved in decisions of select future husband and wife, wrong or right.*

Chimney Rock Mountain-Photo Courtesy of Chimney Rock State Park Media Room

Leaving the small mountain, we went to Knoxville – another two and a half hours by car, where a couple, Buddhist family friends of Mr. K., met us at a rendezvous location. Mr. and Mrs. Tam/My were very enthusiastic. As soon as they picked us up, they took us out and around the city. The next day, there was an unfortunate reoccurrence of Mr. K.'s old illness; we had to take him to the airport to return to Northern Virginia immediately, leaving only me and my girlfriend to drive back to North Carolina.

From Knoxville to Charlotte, the road is about 250 miles long and is hilly with curves, difficult to navigate quickly, especially at night. It was pretty late; we stopped at a gas station. After filling up the tank, I had a strange premonition and when I went to the restroom, saw a group of men gathered nearby, although they did not see me. My sixth sense alerted me that many people were paying attention and looking at me. I returned to the car, carefully told my girlfriend in the car to let me in first, whether it was safe or not, and then go to the toilet later. I gave the car keys to her and told her to lock the car and wait inside the car; not to open the door for anyone. When I walked across the corridor, I saw many people standing in a circle as if waiting for me to enter. The decision was very quick: I changed my mind, went moving quickly in the opposite direction got out of the car, started the engine, and drove straight to Charlotte, not daring to stop anywhere. I didn't tell anyone this story (except for my diary) because really driving at night, going to the strangest places, in remote areas, it is easy to be robbed or assaulted, especially with women following along and being an Asian. I am not afraid of what that crowd might do to me, but I know for sure that I could not protect my friend who was waiting outside the car; at that time, I did not have a cell phone as I do now to call someone for help; nor did I have a gun permit.

World's Fair First Day of Issue Stamps 1982.

The next day, driving back to Maryland alone, feeling numb after the happy days, no one to accompany and talk to on the long highway as at a departure, only alone to think a lot about life myself. Looking back at my postage stamp collection, at that time each letter cost only 20 cents and there were 7 people visiting that day who signed autographs to enrich my stamp collection. An unforgettable memory, even after more than 40 years.

1985: A large Engineering firm in the Greenbelt, Maryland area where some of my friends work, where I started using an Intergraph mainframe computer for Civil and Architecture drawings. The company has many branches in the US and will open offices in Atlanta and Florida in the future, so they asked me to come and work for them. Brandon Smith, the new boss, is a real gentleman, so I went to work for him until the Company opened a branch in Tampa, when I volunteered there to help with the new office in 1986, coordinating with the new boss in Tampa, Don D. Kreider (died 2014).

1988 TRIP TO VIETNAM – BACK TO THE HOMELAND

In October 1988, I decided to go to Vietnam, the reason being that we had made surety papers for Mom and my sister's family, but my Mom at that time was afraid that if she moved to the US to settle down, she would have to stay forever, so she said she had to have one of her children come back, then continue to complete the immigration paperwork. My oldest brother is working for the US Department of Defense, but at that time under President Reagan Vietnam was still under embargo, so he was afraid of losing his *"Security Clearance"*, since he had served in the Republic of Vietnam Air Force. In fact, his friends are still in prison, condemned with the epithet *"air pirates"*. He was afraid of being detained, so he didn't dare to go. My next brother's children were still too young, so as the only single one I was on the spot, and eligible to go to Vietnam.

The year before, Mr. Hieu, my vice-patrol in the Scouts, had returned to Vietnam and went to Hue to visit his family. He said that he had had no difficulty but had to arrange his trip through a tourist group in Canada. I contacted them, bought a ticket, and departed with a Philippine Airlines flight to Manila and then connected to Saigon. The flight departed from Los Angeles airport, which is mostly Vietnamese, and I have never seen a worse airline than this one, from the receptionist to the staff at the counter to the stewards. At that time, because the US did not have any trade with Vietnam, everyone had to make a copy of their passport so that they could stamp it when they arrived in Vietnam, avoiding the original for fear of problems later when returning to the US. When the plane arrived in Vietnamese airspace, for some reason my heart ached, there was no calmness as usual. Before I left, I made all the copies and gave them to my boss, explaining to him if for any reason I was detained in Vietnam, please contact and provide the information to the local newspaper and publish it, so maybe I could come back to America. At that time, I was concerned that when I came to a communist country like Vietnam, they could use any excuse to detain me there, and without diplomatic relations, I couldn't report it to the Consulate or the Embassy like I might be able to in another country.

The airplane landed at the familiar airport I had left 13 years previously, on the last military flight. Looking at the airstrip, there was no difference, even though it had been 13 years, somewhat older and worse than before because the new government probably didn't care about the South at all. Passengers getting off were greeted by two rows of uniformed policemen; will they greet us or intimidate us? When I went inside, I saw the place to check luggage and papers was built on a high platform, surrounded by glass, and a uniformed border customs officer sitting inside. I stood below and looked up like a defendant looking at a judge after hearing a guilty verdict.

Handed the passport to him but did not see or know what he did (even though on the airplane before, many people returning to Vietnam but not on their first trip told us to put twenty dollar bills in our passport to avoid being asked many questions that would delay you and cause them to inspect your luggage item by item). A week before my return had been the closing ceremony of the 1988 Olympic Games in Seoul, Korea; many people looked at me and thought I was a Vietnamese athlete returning from the Olympics. All money brought in is counted because they will review what you have when you go out, see what you do, and declare everything, everything must have a sales receipt to add up the amount you brought in.

Leaving the luggage station and passing inspection, noting a crowd of people waiting for relatives, I dragged my luggage along with me and temporarily returned to an acquaintance's house in Nguyen Huynh Duc. From there, I rented a minivan with an extra fuel drum and two boards behind in case of bad roads; the driver was a secret policeman in plain clothes, who would follow me the whole trip to make a report later. Very challenging trip, where I had agreed to carry along money from my friends to distribute to their families. When I went to spread around the money and asked Shou, my friend's brother, to take me on a motorbike, I realized that my work was not in vain, as everyone was happy, because they were so desperately poor; everything was precious and appreciated. Seeing my hometown, after 13 years of changing hands, even poorer than it was before I left, made me very sad. I come from the richest country in the world, wasting so much and throwing usable things away while my country, poor and going backward after 13 years, I witnessed right in front of my eyes.

Searching for an address of a house to give money from my friends to their families, Ms. Hieu, Mr. Hong, Mr. Trinh's family, Ms. Thanh...but finding a house in Saigon is not the easiest task for a visitor; people move around because the new government lists them as *"enemies"*. Shou took me to find a *public well* near her house, as suggested by my friend in the US. Ms. Hanh was a teacher, there is a well in the alley at every intersection; who knows where to find it? Which one is correct? However, we did manage to find it; the people in the alley saw that I had the appearance of not being a local man, as I had pale skin and wore neat clothes, perhaps looking for lost friends or families, so they enthusiastically guided me; people at that time were so nice and polite.

The minivan that I had rented carried more than 14 people from Saigon to Nha Trang. It was late and dark, the roads were bad and there were many potholes, no street lights, and people were drying grain next to the road, so the car did attempt to run quickly; its speed was about 30mph on average. Stayed overnight at the Hai Yen Hotel (about US$3.00 per room per night) and the next day we drove all day, arriving in Hue in the evening. I could not recognize any places or anywhere from before, after being away from my hometown for only 13 years. Everything had changed and I could only see the gaunt faces of the people to guess how poor and demoralized they were, compared to life before I left.

Arriving in Hue during the flooding season in October, the rains delayed our return trip to Saigon and the flight to Manila by a week because of the storm. Mom and my sister were clearly happy and she had no problem supplementing her documents to her to settle in the US. Mr. Quy, my brother-in-law, also understood when I explained to him the matter of a future for his children and grandchildren; elderly folk will be sadder and find it tougher to live in another country, learning another language from that spoken in their homeland. But the words of freedom and a future for the children are hard to find unless you come to America.

Returning to the US but now *"Seeing it is believing it"*, and I am clearly helpless to do anything for my country; my lack of power echoes even more sadness.

A SAD LOVE STORY… Broken because of religious differences

GOING BACK TO FLORIDA FROM MARYLAND

While in Maryland, during a weekend gathering of friends of Mr. K.'s social group in Virginia, I happened to run into my former girlfriend, whom I had known in Hue when she was at her house at 16 Ly Thuong Kiet. She is *"running away from her fake husband"*, she said: he is an uneducated, violent man who threatens that *if she had any boyfriends except him, "...he would go and kill you both"*. Another difficulty is that both of them made a fake marriage, to bring her from Canada to the US to settle down, after escaping by boat (one of the boat people) she was accepted by the Canadian government to settle there. Although she had gone to court, and the lawyer filled out a divorce application at the Fairfax County, Virginia court to wait for FDD (Final Divorce Decree) after coming to the US, he refused, determined to make it difficult, so the situation persisted, the Vietnamese lawyer was not good, so it was not solved until 1986. Somehow he found my address, perhaps through the University of Maryland (U of M), sending many threatening letters, almost daily mail from Marina del Rey, California. I reported it to the local Montgomery County police and they sent a detective officer assigned to the case. I had to translate some of his letters from English into Vietnamese for her to understand; he used dirty, low-class words. I had worked on a rig, so I was familiar with plenty of these words. The police just told us to be careful, however. They said they could do nothing about it until he managed to find her when she was studying at the U of M for assault; she suffered an injury; the police had to make a PFA (Restraining/Protective Order) report. Seeing that the situation was not good for either of us – there was no shame in avoiding crazy people – I persuaded her to move to Florida with me to have an opportunity to go back to school when the company opened a branch there.

One day we were both driving down the road, and a bird hit the front windshield of the car, not breaking the glass although I am not superstitious, I had a feeling that something bad would happen to us. Before that, when she sent her belongings from Canada to my house, she left the white mourning headband in her luggage, for her grandmother who had died earlier; she forgot to take it out:

that was another bad luck sign.

As a *"valedictorian"* of the girl's high school in Hue, and completing her Bachelor of Economics in Saigon before coming to Canada, it was not difficult for her to go back to school, just a few years of study to complete BS/MSEE of USF. However, our love affair became increasingly complicated because of our conflicting religious convictions. Seeing that this disagreement could not be reconciled and that the two of us were still young and had no children, *"Everyone went their separate way"*. Prolonging the separation would only make both lives miserable. I believe that husband and wife, in addition to love, must have a predestined relationship to be together. This is probably the time when my love life was at its lowest point, but thinking that I had done a good deed, and I would be lucky later.

At that time, my best friend in Maryland, *"Jim Bo"* (as I called him), was my roommate, before buying my own house. Jim and I worked with Planner-Engineer-Surveyor agencies like JMT, KML, and G&O in the suburbs of Maryland. Jim had graduated from the College of Architecture at Catholic University in Washington, D.C.; although he was a year younger than me because his education had not been interrupted by war, he graduated before I did. At my first job, Jim was the one who trained me in drawing, especially roads, drawings called *"street grades"*, where you must draw plans and profiles to calculate the slope of the roads; these must be calculated by hand according to the Pythagorean/Right Triangle method, which requires mathematical knowledge. As a member of Math B in Vietnam and one who has taken Calculus classes at University, I like to do these things the most. It was easy to calculate by hand, although it took time. Without knowledge of math, people were scared, but it was fun with the slopes and bends of the roads, we had to follow the safety and speed rules. Roads in the state of Maryland have elevations and slopes of up to 10%, but in Florida later, residential area roads are sometimes less than 1%. A few years later, everything was calculated neatly by computer. He bought a townhome with two floors and a basement, so when I moved here, I rented a room and considered it the whole house because the place was large. Sometimes we traveled together by car to work; he had a habit of needing to eat breakfast, so we stopped at McDonald's on the way to buy McMuffins. I don't eat in the morning, even until noon. In the office, he spent time talking to someone on the phone; on the table was the Wall Street Journal. Later, I learned that he was dealing with his broker about buying and selling stocks that his grandfather had bequeathed to him.

Jim called to confide that he and his girlfriend had decided to get married. The two of them had lived together for 8 years without any problems. Jim's family was close to me, so when I received a card from the bride's family (according to American custom, the bride's family took care of the cost of the wedding), they thought the bride's family had forgotten to put a stamp on the return letter (a small R.S.V.P. card to indicate whether the invitee would attend or not), but when they knew that I have received no return stamp either, both sides realized that *"small thing becomes big"*. Having had religious conflicts before, and both families being pious (Jim's family is Catholic and his wife a Protestant), the two families decided to break up this couple. If they had been two orphans, it probably would not have happened. Later, Jim moved to Connecticut, got married again, and had two daughters; the family was very happy. The first daughter eventually got married in Charlotte, North Carolina; the youngest, a PA major, worked in Boston. Jim and his wife run the Dairy Queen store left to them by their parents, both working and retired.

AMERICAN CAR OR JAPANESE MODEL – WHICH ONE IS BETTER?

Before I bought a small townhouse in Maryland, I had a new Chevrolet Monza. Even with less than 18,000 miles on it, the car was shaking like an old woman; I brought it to the dealer, and they said they found nothing wrong with it. Jack, the boss, checked out my beautiful silver-blue car and decided he wanted to buy it for his daughter for her 18th birthday. I told him it had a vibration …he said it was okay, and let him show it to his mechanic. They discovered problems: two engine mounts had loosened, so the entire engine was shaking. He bought it from me so I had to go and buy a used Volkswagen Bug. The car runs fine but when winter comes, I already know the sun's direction, so I chose a southern-facing building to avoid snow. The VW Bug does not have a *"radiator"*, but it is cooled by air; the engine is in the back, not in front. When it got cold through a freezing night, I poured boiling water on the windshield first, thinking of melting the thin layer of ice, but the hot water froze up into a thicker layer of ice and the car had to run for a long time for the engine to heat up. I only cleaned a circle in front of me, carefully driving slowly until the engine warmed up, like driving a tank with a small window.

Financially stable at last, I decided to change my car again. After graduating from school, and after years of studying in the US, I didn't know what my friends would think, but I just wanted to buy an American car to support the domestic economy (later, American cars were assembled abroad and sent back from Canada, Mexico, etc.). Going to the Pontiac-GM dealer near my house, I bought a Pontiac 2000, although the GrandAm was good –the price was higher. The car ran fine, but when I moved back to Tampa, near the city, the car stopped running. I carried it to the local dealer, only to find out that the *"timing belt"* was broken, even though it only had 40,000 miles on it. Repairing it cost quite a lot of money because it was out of its warranty period; now it is still running but no longer dependable – it makes me wonder about the workmanship of American cars. I went to buy a Camry LE; at that time, Japanese cars were not so very popular; the Camry had just been released, but the one I bought had been assembled in Japan and exported. It is running hundreds of thousands of miles and is still good. Later, when I bought another car, I gave the Camry to my sister, and she used it for a long time. The car was so good and reliable; it never broke down, so as a customer, I am not considering buying an American car again.

Sometime later, I applied to work for an architecture firm (Lee & Sakahara) in Boca Raton. This is a company with a headquarter in Costa Mesa, California, a top ten firm in Orange County; most of its employees are Architects of Asian origin, who were students at the famous University of Cal-Poly, Pomona) so the architects here are all top-class [72].

---

72. *In 1970, Italian architect Paolo Solari (1919-2013), founded the village of " Arcosanti" or Cosanti as a non-profit company in Yavapai County, north of Phoenix, Arizona. The Italian words "cosa" and "anti" combined mean "against things", Here, Architecture students come to visit, learn and volunteer to help make bronze or crockery bells, making different sounds, no two are alike. They poured it out in clay molds. The village rarely has a population of more than 100 people, everyone comes to volunteer and everything is "homemade".*

Lee & Sakahara Architects I work with, with its main office in Southern California, has

Then about 1989, the economic situation went downhill again (in the architecture and construction industry, it periodically sinks once every 10 years – at that time there were only layoffs, then you applied for unemployment benefits). The Florida branch only had 5 people, and I was the only one given an option by my boss in California to keep my job if I agreed to move and work in the main office in Costa Mesa. Knowing that they decided to keep me thanks to my multi-purpose talents, and being sad because of my broken love story earlier, I packed up all my things in the Camry, headed west, and went all the way down Interstate I-10, from East to West.

Arcosanti crockery and bronze bells are given annually by Lee&Sakahara.

---

a tradition of giving employees a Cosanti bell at the end of the year. After each year of work, the gift bell gets bigger and bigger. More bells mean longer stays with the company, and the louder and louder the bells, the more valuable they are. This is a "top ten" firm in Orange County, which people often say is hard to get a second bell if you're not good. This company also has a tradition that every Friday afternoon, employees stop working at 4 pm, employees are divided into groups, taking turns to take care of snacks and appetizers weekly, the company takes care of drinks for social hours. That hour is called the time to discuss things outside of daily work. If something is satisfactory or not, it is time to discuss it.

EASILY GOING TO CALIFORNIA... GOT CHEATED WHEN RENTING A HOUSE

Arrived in California after more than two and a half days of driving continuously, only resting and sleeping in hotels during the night. I rented a temporary room, in a house with my own entrance, for $300 a month, until one day, I met an old friend from National Academy in Hue and his wife; their children of two girls and a boy had come to settle in the US, temporarily staying at his brother's house, and the house of five people was cramped, so he proposed that we rent a house together. Finding a two-story house in Westminster, with a swimming pool, and five bedrooms for only $1,200 a month, with the only condition that we let the landlord temporarily stay downstairs for a month before moving out, we were eager to "sign a lease" for one year. At first, seeing the big house, spacious enough for everyone, everyone was happy, when entering the house, there was a small altar on the floor in front of the house with an Earth God statue, lonely and gathering dust, dirty. I guess no one took care of it; my friend's wife took him to the bath, cleaned him up, and bought flowers and fruits to worship.

For a few days, my friends were enthusiastically cleaning the flower garden in front of the house, as we were going to buy flowers and plant them to be beautiful, when someone suddenly stopped their car in front and asked: *Do you live in this house?* Answer: *Yes*, they continued: *So did you know this house is being "foreclosed on" by the bank?* After asking more questions, they revealed that they were from the bank and had come by to check on the condition of the building before bringing it to *"auction"*. We endeavored to find the owner of the house, purportedly staying in a room downstairs, but he was nowhere to be found. His furniture was also gone. My friends were shocked and crying because they had paid a deposit and rent for the first month and last month, totaling $3,600.00. I lost only a few hundred; for them, having just come to the US, several thousand dollars was quite a big amount. I immediately called the Westminster police department to report having been cheated, but they told me that we had to go to *"small claim court"*, maybe to reclaim nothing or at most part of it back if we were lucky; they sent a lady detective to work on setting up a case. Only a few days later, this detective somehow found the purported owner of the house, hiding in an acquaintance's bakery. She told us that we should find him to resolve this problem privately, as the police department could not do anything – it was a *civil* case, not a *criminal* matter for the police to get involved in.

I took my friend and his wife to find Mr. Sinh. By chance, he was standing in front of the bakery, unable to hide from us. Speaking seriously but politely, I told him that I had reported him to the police; they found out where you were, but our purpose was just to get our money back, not to cause trouble or punish anyone, because my friends did not have much money: they had just come to the US. *"If you cheat them like that, it's so pitiful."* He replied: *"I know it's wrong, but I don't have money to pay you. I've lost it all at the Casino!"* He continued, stating *"Before, I was rich, had a restaurant with several hundred seats; I had helped this bakery's owner, that's why he let me stay here temporarily. But because of my addiction to the Bicycle Club, I lost everything through bankruptcy, including my house, and had to deceive people. Now I am ashamed."*

In a difficult situation like that, we knew we couldn't do anything, so we gave him two weeks. I said if you hide, we may not find you but the police will eventually catch you and the crime will be more serious. If we go to small claims court, you will have trouble building up your business in the future; we warned him about this even though we were not sure he could break his gambling habit. Two weeks later, by appointment, we met him again at Dong Ba Restaurant. He brought a lady friend, introducing this woman who had previously done business together with him, had advanced money to pay for him to get the house back… What a good friend; she also confirmed that it was only because of his passion for gambling that he had to cheat others, even though he had previously had a successful and prosperous business. This just confirmed the proverb that warns *"Gambling is a poor uncle"*.

Get the full amount back; my friend's family was overjoyed, and ran back to the old house, moving everything out, and my friend's wife did not forget to bring the altar and the statue with them. She said that when she moved in, thanks to bathing and fruit for this Earth's God, she believed she got back all the money, as the previous owner probably hadn't taken care of the altar for a while. I don't know if it is accurate, but being tricked into renting a house with gamblers without losing money and then getting it all back without going to court is a rare thing in this world.

Only 6 months later, California's economic situation fell behind that of Florida, so the company did not have enough work coming in: from more than 40 employees, only 12 people remained. Seeing how I would pack up to apply for unemployment benefits, I called my old office in Florida, and the situation was clarified once more. I went to the computer store, and bought a computer powerful enough to draw CAD; at that time the software and the hardware were both still rudimentary *and* expensive: I had to pay 10 thousand dollars for the machine and the big 14" screen.

GOING BACK TO FLORIDA FROM CALIFORNIA

1990: Most Vietnamese had a slogan: *"Easy to go to California, but not easy to get away"*. The main reasons are weather, ethnic foods, many services, and many choices of entertainment. Back in Florida, my two former bosses arranged for me to split the profits; I was the only one who had a CAD drawing-enabled computer at that time. Then one of my bosses also let me stay in a room upstairs for free, instead of renting an apartment. He cooked very well – especially Cajun dishes from Louisiana and French cuisine, so every evening after returning from work, he cooked for the whole family, even preparing extra food to bring to the office for lunch the next day. I only took care of washing dishes. The house and the office were both in Boca Raton. His wife's son (early marriage) was about 11 years old at the time. They treated me like a younger brother in the family, so the job and accommodation were considered stable – even though this time, architecture firms were having difficulties. Everyone knew that it would pass like the previous times. I was so fortunate to have a support person(s) like my boss and his family.

The group in the company numbered up to 5 men; I was the only Vietnamese. When attending the annual AIA (American Institute of Architects) conference in Atlanta, everyone was poor, so Mr. Dale (principal of API) rented a two-bed Hilton hotel room; he checked in first; then, we all went up after learning the room number; three of us had to sleep on the floor, leaving the bed to the person who had paid for it. The love was so wide that, despite a lack of means, everyone was happy because of these memories, and even invited each other to visit the Underground in Atlanta. Now that Dale Meaux is in heaven (died in 2021), all of us continue to remember and honor him as a teacher, a master, a mentor or a good American brother.

PREDETERMINED PIECE OF LAND – A NEW FAMILY AND A NEW HOUSE.

March 25, 1992: When the economy revived, in 1993, I bought 5 acres of land in Rustic Ranches, moved to Palm Beach – north of Boca Raton, planted exotic tropical fruit trees, grapefruit, mango, star fruit... intending to build a house after getting married or when I retired. I observed architecture firms going up and sliding down every 10 years; it was fun to work, but I guessed I would have to move to a more stable job.

January 16, 1995: I was hired by Sunland, a firm specializing in the construction of small offices and private houses. This was a compact company that had models of houses for customers to choose from, which could be modified or built according to their preference (Custom Build and Design). I was the person in charge of the job of making customers happy, including difficult customers or those who abided by the principles of Feng Shui.

Some people just wanted a larger bedroom or an extra garage to store things. Many American customers tell stories about their homes that they truly believe, so they are looking for a way to build a new home. Most American home architecture shares similar features, such as a kitchen, if there are multiple floors, there are bedrooms or showers above because of plumbing, on the garage there are bedrooms above, plumbing and drainage, because of the simplicity of construction, it violates two factors: water and fire, most Americans do not going into details because they don't know, just heard or read books, difficult to understand, when I know and understand these principles I try to avoid what they believe without having to change a lot to avoid cost overruns when building. Only once, a Vietnamese couple, when they first met me to build a house, thought they were foreigners, so we spoke English. When the wife handed over the sketch paper of the house, there was a note in Vietnamese, I just blurted out: *Are you Vietnamese?* and with a drawing unlike any existing American house, I knew immediately that it was according to the *bagua*, the five elements. When they moved to a new house, not only did they encounter bad luck like in the old house - this made them believe it even more. Later we became close friends.

I met my wife through an acquaintance when I asked where a dry cleaning store was. I was in DC, and Cali which are cold states, so when I moved back to Florida, my clothes were full of wool/ felt that couldn't be machine washed. She was the youngest child, often helping her mother at the alterations and dry-cleaning store. By bringing in clothes to clean, I met a new lover and remarried in 1995.

My wife had traveled to the US during the last days of April, through her adopted father's sponsorship; the papers were returned to the US Embassy in Saigon, but fortunately, a friend hand-delivered them to their house, so she and her sister were able to complete the procedures to get an early evacuation through the Defense Attaché Office. One of the early arrivals at Camp Pendleton was allowed to enter Camp One, which was the first camp open in the USMC barracks with air conditioning instead of tents (like the latecomers) also because of an existing sponsor, they did not have to wait, so they got out of the camp next day and flew directly to Florida. From the time she arrived in the US, she had only lived in one place until one day, because of predestined reasons, she went to a shop to help her Mom and met me.

Around 1996, the Company had a small piece of land divided up to sell and build houses for customers, according to their wishes. I asked the owner, Frank Y. if he could sell us one lot to build a house, although I already had 5 acres of land. I'm a Scout, I like nature but my wife is a city girl, so she was even afraid of a cockroach. Thus, I did not plan to build on 5 acres. My mother-in-law wanted to live together with us, so we had to build a special and affordable house. We asked him which lot we could choose; he said that except for the ones near the lakeside and without a house in front of a conservation area were the lots that had to pay an extra *"premium"*. We decided to choose the small lot in the back, which had only a limited view of the lake – and only had to pay a three thousand dollar premium.

Three days later, I went to the office to meet Ms. Cheryl, the owner's sister. She was the one who handled closing documents for the Company, along with transfer papers, as well as being ready to do a survey and design the house. When I pointed to the map of the land, she said: *Sold!* I asked again: *Sold to me?* She said: *"No, there are customers who have signed papers to pick the house they will build, put down a deposit and we are applying for permits."* I said: "*Ma'am, the boss agreed to sell that piece of land to me the other day.*" She said: *"I didn't know anything about this..."*

But that was true; perhaps no one informed her, and her office only counted deposits or full payment to reserve a lot, unless there was a verbal order from the boss. Hearing a loud voice, Frank walked over from the next room and asked: *"What's wrong, Cheryl? What is going on here?"* I explained that Cheryl had already sold Lot 67 to someone else – the one he promised to sell to my wife and me the other day! He then said: *"There's still another lot available!"* I asked him again: *"But that piece is suitable for our budget there is a little lake view."* He continued: *"Hoa, then choose the piece with the lake view..."* Not sure of my ears, I thought he was joking, I asked him back: *"The waterfront lot? No premium?"* He looked at Cheryl and said firmly: *"No premium!"* Very quickly, before the boss had a chance to change his decision, I looked at Ms. Cheryl, who was staring at her brother with wide eyes: *"Do you have any left for me?"* She said she had two pieces left: Lots 41 and 47. I told her: *"I will give you an answer tomorrow and a deposit so I can go home tonight and ask my wife what she would like."* Walking back to the office, I joked with Cheryl: *"Don't sell those to anyone without going over my dead body! I will move to live with you or Frank."* She replied with a smile: *"Sure, my dear!"* [73].

It is true that Americans when they promise something, like a nail in the wood, they mean it. Mr. Frank let me choose the land for the sake of his employees, at a loss of a premium. As I said, I liked Lot number 47 because there is only 1 neighbor on one side; on the other side is the conservation area. But my wife chose Number 41. If there had not been a customer, then choose Lot 67 we had selected; or had Miss Cheryl not sold it or the owner hadn't been generous, maybe we wouldn't have got the piece of land with the

73. *The construction company Sunland of my two bosses was established quite interestingly. When they were still poor, two friends Frank and Chris, working in construction for other firms, found that every day, in the dumpsters for the construction works, there were a lot of construction materials wasted, like plywood, only partially used, screws half used. Seeing the waste, they gathered to build a house, sold it cheaply, after having enough income, they decided to open their own firm.*

lake view behind the house. It is true that when choosing land, vehicles, houses, or husband and wife, each has its own charm. What belongs to anyone is predetermined.

At the beginning of 1997, I completed the design of the house on the computer, consulted with my architect (boss/friend Mr. Dale Meaux), and started to apply for a permit to build our house. I asked the sub-contractors to come up with a proposal and cost estimate for the walls, roofs, doors windows, etc., and indicated I was willing to pay more money to make the house stand up to hurricane-force winds of up to 140mph=225kph, by adding cement in fill cells, and reinforced steel for strength.

The state of Florida is located on an annual hurricane axis, from May to November. After August 1992, when Hurricane Andrew blew in and devastated South Florida, new building codes were passed for Miami and Dade counties, stipulating structures to be modified and upgraded to withstand high winds, from the foundations to the roofs. They discovered that before, solid steel reinforcement went up from the foundation to the bottom of the exterior walls to retain them, but strong winds blew off the roofs. Now, roofs had to be supported by steel extending from the foundation, known as "Simpson hurricane straps" or "ties". Some houses would find it difficult to resist wind forces when they blow in, from the bottom to the roof. Wind and rain also damage windows and garage doors, and rushing into the house through these cracks, causing heavy damage to the inside of the house, so there must be protective barriers outside when applying for a building permit. We find it difficult each time before storm warnings, so you had to attach protective aluminum shields called Hurricane Shutters outside windows; I built an automatic electric-powered partition to go up and down. Now, modern technology has developed glass panels called Impact Windows, that can withstand high wind forces and are cheaper now, without having to have an outside panel like before, but when I built a house, their price was still quite high. Structural Engineers work together with architects and manufacturers to get better materials and construction methods, more resistant to the natural disasters that hit us every year.

At this time, my wife was pregnant with a baby. When visiting the house under construction, both my Mom and her Mom carefully advised me that we must *"not move into a new house when pregnant"*, but to wait for the birth; then, after a few months, we may enter the new house. The elders are superstitious or experienced because something happened to them; they became widows so they advised their children not to make this mistake. She was born in late June and we moved into a new house after Thanksgiving in 1997.

1998: LEAVING THE PRIVATE SECTOR; AND WORKING FOR THE GOVERNMENT

Now, after nearly 10 years, the economic situation again assumed downward momentum. I concluded that working for the government, I would not be subject to the 10-year cycle; seeing that there was an advertising job for renovation projects at the Town of Lake Park, I submitted my résumé and was called in for an interview.

On Friday afternoon, when I arrived, the City Hall conference room was being cleaned to prepare for renovation. The Town Manager directed me to temporarily go to the dining room for an interview, instead of the meeting room. There were a total of 6 people on the interview panel: Ms. Terry Leary, Town Manager

[74], Director of Public Works and Assistant TM, Brian Sullivan, a consultant architect and Mr. Lee Collum (PE) a Professional Engineer in charge of projects, the Human Resources Director and TM's secretary. They rumbled me until 6 pm with questions, after studying my portfolio.

The interview team said that the renovation/new project works would include redoing the main road, known as Park Avenue, passing through the city's *"downtown"* as the first project. Then, they would build a new fire station, city park, City Hall (Historical Building) outside and inside, a Marina parking space... A lot of work – but all scheduled for only 3 years and a budget of only 10 million to be borrowed, before taxes of the people (the Town, after a vote from citizens, adopted a Bond Project Money program, borrowing money first for restoration and then paying it back every year from real estate taxes paid in by the public; in about 10 years, the debt would be cleared up). This was a special program, perhaps only relevant when the projects were not funded or people had to approve a loan by ballot. If there was to be no debt taken on, the areas needing renovation would have become more and more seriously run down.

The Manager knew that for me to accept a job offer, the salary would have to be higher than I was earning at a private company, and must contain a long-term job guarantee. So, the following week she called to reassure me, she promised, *(She is of Italian descent and has kept her word)*, but to increase wages she would have to go before the Commission, including the Mayor, Vice-mayor, and three other members: in the government, the Manager herself cannot raise salary offers for prospective employees, as in private firms. The second thing is that she would transfer me to another position after the end of the contract, and the end of the Bond Project money, meaning that my salary must be transferred to the state budget (General Budget) and had to be approved every year, to become a permanent employee of the Town.

---

74. *Town Manager Therese (Terry) C. Leary is the one who hired me for the city to work on renovation projects that are expected to take three years, then move on to a full-time employee upon completion to establish about the future computing system for the city that had not yet begun. What she planned for my job came true later, although I only worked for her for less than two years. She died on November 4, 2018 in Hilton Head Island, South Carolina after retiring.*

February 2, 1998: I brought my entire CADD computer [75] to the office because at that time the Town did not have a computer: only two ATs were available, creating documents with Word Perfect, and still using an IBM typewriter that could change typefaces by replacing a spherical ball in the middle. Three days later, she came to the office *(at that time, because Town Hall was ready for renovation, I had to work temporarily in the old office of a dentist sold to the city at 849 Park Avenue)*, saying that she had a budget for me to get a computer system, consisting of CADD-capable software, able to print large format C and D (30x42in) drawings. The reason for this move was that the city has a policy of avoiding the use of employee belongings, which could cause a lot of trouble later. And that was also the reason she found a way for me to keep the whole city's computer network system in the future, because at that time the technology was slow and expensive, and very few people knew how to use it. They used an IBM or Data General mainframe, not like later.

Buying a Gateway 2000 computer system, I did everything

75. *CADD - Short for Computer Aided Design and Drafting: Drawing and designing graphics by computer. Around the mid-1960s there was the IBM Design System. By the 1970s, Intergraph, IBM and McDonell Douglas had to use mainframe systems and applied more to technology in Engineering than Architecture. After the personal computer invented, without the need for an entire network, by the 1990s, MicroStation and AutoCAD began to become popular for graphic design in many industries. Universities also added this branch to adapt to the market, but when I went to school, drawing and writing, all by hand.*

Before computer drawings were popular, drawing by hand took a lot of time, requiring the artist to have a talent for writing beautiful letters. When you make a mistake or change something, it is easier to erase, redraw, and erase the pencil than ink because the black "pelican" ink sticks to the drawing, you must use a machine-powered eraser, moreover, if you draw a project with many floors high , like a hotel, for example, many floors are almost the same, stairs, elevators ... to fix one sheet, you have to fix it all, sometimes forgetting is normal. CADD is convenient for modification because it can see through many floors and if related, it can only be edited once. Now, the details on the job site can be put directly into the machine to line the bottom to show in the drawing the heights, what needs to be kept so as not to make a mistake, if there is a change, just replace the liner. In the past, they had to wait for the survey team to go to the construction site, bring it back to the office, make a map (tie-sheet) and then draw according to what was already there. Today all because of technology, shortened and thanks to the location machine (GPS), the accuracy is more complete. The aerials are also used for the bottom liner to draw on top. Companies also submit machine drawings to the government for documentation.

from Drafting to Design, including preparing a budget for the city's future network system, a Live Media broadcasting system for twice-monthly meetings on channel 19 of cable TV, later moved to 18 (Adelphia); they went door to door, Adelphia ran the cable and pitched in an extra 40k dollars to set up the system. The law stipulated that city meetings must be held at night after 6 p.m. when residents have returned home from work so that they can attend the meeting. Minutes of meetings must be available for all to see or view, for any public meetings. Democracy is just like that.

The first project was Park Avenue, with four lanes running in an east-west direction; there were frequent accidents because of speeding traffic. In order to reduce vehicle speeds, the project cut traffic to two lanes and designed a clock tower, right at the intersection – and that's the reason for the *"Clock Tower"*, inspired by the clock tower of Ben Thanh Market in Saigon, my motherland. The bell tower has 4 clocks facing 4 directions: East, West, South, and North and every 15 minutes, the time and clock are displayed with chimes. Clocks are made by Verdin and also have the ability to play music according to each spring, summer, autumn, and winter season (see attached picture in the appendix). Due to time constraints, the project, once approved by the Town Commission, was delivered straight to the site. Necessary changes would be decided so that the paperwork would not delay progress. The Park Avenue renovation and the clock tower were completed from the drawing after obtaining aerial photos and maps through a navigation system, from approvals until inauguration took a record time of just six months. Starting to draw and commencing construction in June and to be completed by December 1998, sometimes a construction engineer of Burkhardt Construction company was waiting for my drawings to be printed at my office, the stamp of Mr. Lee Collum, responsible professional engineer (PE), then the project is to be brought to the construction site right in front of the office, so that the project could be completed very quickly, without going through complicated paperwork, but required coordination for close teamwork: before entering the project all members went through a quick two-day training course so everyone understood each other's duties.

1998 - CADD APPLICATION FOR MY BROTHER AND SISTER-IN-LAW'S HOUSE AT PERSIMMON ORCHARD

My brother and sister-in-law bought more than 50 acres of land outside Tallahassee, the state capital of Florida, to grow crispy persimmons, soft persimmons and egg-persimmons, just because they love to eat these types. The garden is named after their children, starting with the youngest one first, named HaViNam. They asked me to draw a detailed design, after receiving a draft from Wayne Berenbaum, an Architect and personal friend who graduated from Virginia Tech University in 1973. He specializes in drawing custom-built, detached private houses known as *"dream homes"* by the owners. The house and farm were drawn and printed entirely by computer. They built it about the time I finished building my own house, and moved in in early 1998, after the brittle persimmon trees had started to produce fruit. During harvest season, the garden is open to visitors from near and far, who may pick fruit like some gardens in California. The fruit is picked, weighed, and bought at wholesale prices, so it may take only a week or two to run out of harvested fruit.

Logo of the Havinam Orchard

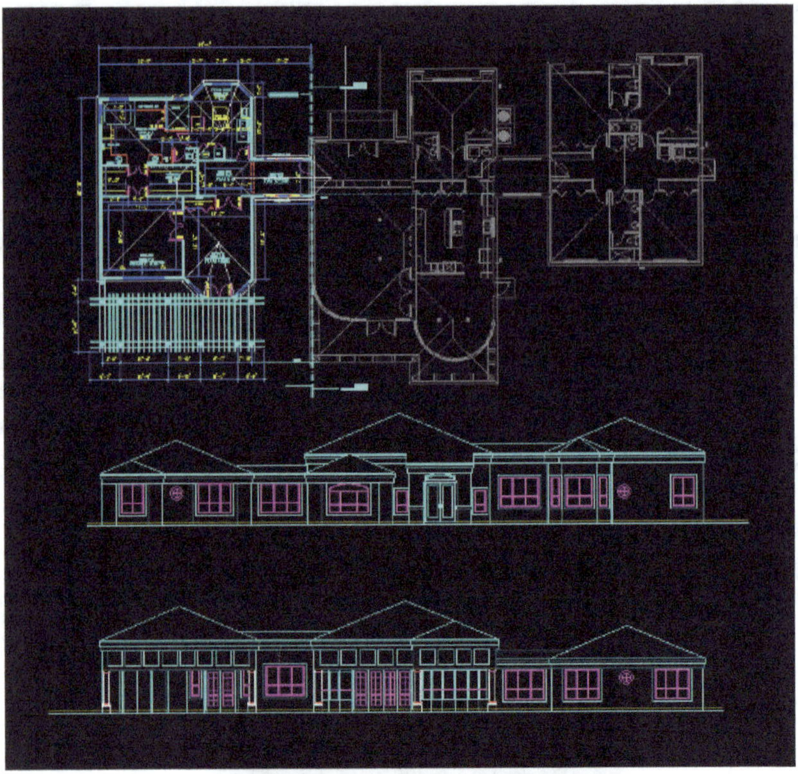

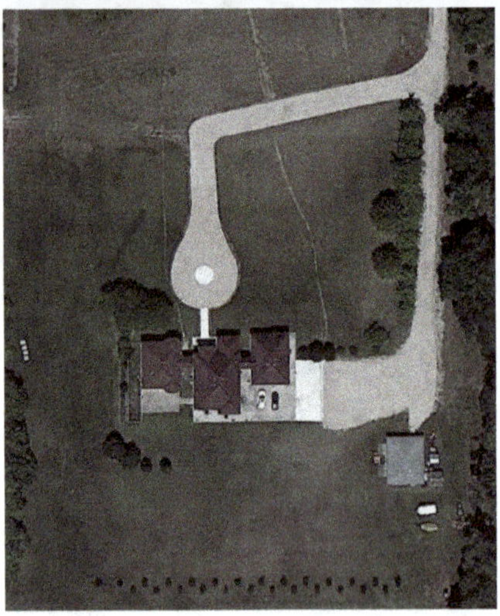

CADD drawings, Phase 2 construction, HaViNam Persimmon Orchard of my brother and sister-in-law Google Map – Monticello, Florida

HAUNTED HOUSE AT COMPASS LAKE IN THE HILLS

This is a small village in Jackson County, Florida, little known to many people including those living in the state, even though it is only a short distance from the famous Gulf of Mexico seaside resort city of Panama City. The coastal city known as *"Sugar Sands"* is located about 37 miles to the north, the city of Mariana 20 miles to the south and only 2 hours' drive from the state capital Tallahassee, but the area is still far away and strange if you're not a local or haven't been on vacation here, bringing Recreational Vehicles called RVs. The lake is 582 square acres (1 US square acre = 43,560 square feet) or 2 square kilometers. It is circular like a compass; the road around the lake goes up and down steep hills with red clay, so the official name bestowed is *"Compass Lake in the Hills"*.

Compass Lake in the Hills on Google Map and Jackson County logo, Florida

With a population of only about 1,000 (2019), this place is mostly known by locals and vacationers from faraway cities in Florida or neighboring states like Alabama, Tennessee, or Mississippi. Anticipating the future, fearing that one day when discovered, many people will pile in and risk destroying the natural environment, Jackson County has rules and regulations to build/develop single-family or mobile homes, and trailers specific to this subdivision.

It should also be mentioned that in the southeastern regions of the United States, formerly the land was wide and sparsely populated or farmed, so at the end of the 19th century, in the states of Texas, Florida, and Georgia, white American farmers after days and hours, working in the sun in the fields, their necks were tanned and burned, so they were called *"rednecks"*, after which this word became the term to describe the indigenous people here. When Jim took my wife and I to see where the land in the area would be sold, although he had advised them before, when I entered I saw a lot of local people of this type. They were not accustomed to seeing foreign faces; only my wife and I were Asian, they rushed to ask how I came to know this place. I answered that I had an introduction from Jim and Mona.

Hills in the background and Cypress trees growing on the lakeside.

Sometime in the early 1900s, a gristmill was put in using the waters of the lake, which is spring-fed, to power the mill. This mill dammed up the lake and created its northern part.

I had the opportunity to meet Jim and his wife Mona around 1996. Working in the Architecture Department for Sunland Construction, I was visited by him in my office; he introduced himself as a Building Inspector for Palm Beach County, he added, mostly on construction sites and to check the immigration legality of foreign workers, especially roofers. I asked him: *"Are you here to ask about my immigration status in the US?"* He smiled and said, *"No, I came here for personal reasons, not related to immigration or the government at all, but purely because the house I am going to build, I will ask you to design it."*. He invited me to lunch the next day to make it easier to talk in private, because he only asked me for a design of the construction plans for a permit, not through the company I was working with to build it, as he would do the construction himself.

He said he is working for the government but will retire soon. When he was younger he and his wife bought a sizable piece of land at Lake Compass in the Hills, one connected to the lake with an existing house and the other higher up than planned, to be built with a future helipad and a hangar for a helicopter that he will buy when he retires: he was a helicopter pilot in the United States Air Force (USAF), serving at a station in South Korea, and he was injured several times (He showed me the long scar on his right arm that was caused by a helicopter crash, when he had to do an "*auto-rotation*" maneuver: *Theoretically, the helicopter suddenly shut down in mid-air but still had propeller rotation; if the pilot knows how, will turn the copter in a spiral spin while the propeller provides lift from wind resistance, allowing it to land safely – although the copter will fall more heavily than usual)*. After being discharged from the Air Force and returning to the US, he worked as a *"test pilot"* for Boeing *(who built the AH-64 Cobra [from Hughes and McDonnell Douglas], an armed attack helicopter for the US military, the type that was not provided to the South Vietnamese Air Force, only operated by American pilots in the Vietnam War – the early Bell AH-1G Cobra nicknamed "snake")* and famous helicopter maker Sikorsky has branches in many parts of the US, including Palm Beach County *(those pilots selected to be test pilots are usually talented people who have no fear of death, as piloting experiment aircraft means that sometimes the plane does not obey your input; it is only luck and it was up to the pilot's ability to "improvise" because the planes tested were not yet perfected and the designer needs "feedback" from experienced pilots so that the aircraft's operating functions can be redesigned/ modified to improve efficiency afterward).*

He said that although Mona, his wife did not like him *"playing"* with airplanes when he retired, knowing that her husband had lived his life on these *"expensive toys"*, she came to accept it. She is the principal of an elementary school in the area, so when she retires, with no children, both have quite a lot of *"retirement pension"* a comfortable financial life and nothing to give up to *"charity"* at death. He and I discussed this *"hangar"* quite a lot because I also told him that, living and growing up with the Vietnam War, having a father in the Army and a helicopter pilot as a brother, I had many opportunities to *"fly free"* of many military aircraft, familiar with military airports, I would feel confident and capable of *"designing"* a landing area called a *helipad* in front of the hangar, the helicopter then will be placed on a system by a *"platform"* controlled by a hydraulic system with wheels below following the railroad track to bring it inside the hangar, storage must also be high enough for the helicopter to be brought in, the service ladder with wheels underneath must also be high enough to get above the main rotor blades. At this time the internet was not yet popular; for everything I needed to research I had to go to the library or use the *"Architectural Graphic Standards Handbook"* to get data on dimensions. In terms of construction methods, too, the standard for cement to make the landing area would also have to be higher and thicker than usual, because of the pressure and weight above, not like a regular garage.

Regarding the location of the new house as well as the *"octagonal gazebo"* built on the lake, he invited me to visit the site, to get an opinion and plan a drawing program and construction plans; just looking at the pictures, there was only an overall concept. He invited me to his recently-acquired house in Tequesta: this was just an ordinary *"single-family"* 3-bedroom house typical in the US. He said that this house was nothing special. However, the couple had been living in it for quite some time, so they were familiar with what was in it. He told me that he would rent a plane over the weekend to fly us there, but after both wives objected to flying, we went by car instead.

Driving to the location took more than 7 hours. when I was about to leave my suitcase in the *"trunk"* of the car, he said it was full, he showed me the empty gallon water bottles there. I asked: *"What are these for?"* he said to get drinking water on Lake Compass, these are deep wells and the water here is true to his word I confirmed that the water is as good and as sweet as the expensive bottled water from the island of Fiji, imported into

America. Every time he and his wife visit the site, they take some water back to drink because where they live, the filtered city water is not as good and clean as in Compass Lake. On the way, he said we would stay at the hotel in Mariana for the night because it was too late to get to his site.

I asked him why we didn't stay in the old little house on the plot for convenience, and he said that you would find out when we got there tomorrow. Early in the morning both he and I had breakfast at the hotel and departed for the destination. The road was short, but when turning on the way to the house, the dirt road twists along the lake, along the left side is the lake with rows of tall cypress trees growing under the water; this is a slow-growing tree that can live to five or six hundred years, water-resistant, so its trunk is less susceptible to decay. It is used in construction, but in the State of Florida, these trees are protected because it is good for the natural environment; trees near the river or located in the country are under the jurisdiction of the state government and are not harvested for timber. You only can cut down the ones on private property.

The piece of land he and his wife bought is divided by the road; the small piece with the lake and the house *(the plots of land with water behind, such as the shore of a lake, river or sea are valued by the length of the border with the water, the longer the waterfront, the higher the price).* The larger piece at the top is where the 'copter will land and the hangar and the higher side of the hill is flat for helicopters to land on grass. The lakeside has an old three-bedroom, two-bathroom house built solidly for a long time, but not using the foundation system around the house like later architecture. Instead, it uses a system lying on a wooden platform; the walls and roof are built of solid plaster, so although it has been around for a long time, it is still very good compared to later architectural materials. In the house, the hardwood furniture is intact, from each room to the kitchen, and dining room; everything is very neat and in order. Seeing me looking at the antique salon in the living room, he started to tell me the story: *"Once upon a time, a long time ago, when we bought this piece of land with a good house on it, the former owner was a widow who agreed on the condition that she would only sell it if we let her rent it back and stay until she died. At that time, we were young and just wanted to retire later, so we agreed, the old lady lived alone without relatives, children, or friends; every weekend she hired a local person to take her to the market to buy the things necessary for the week and every day she read books, went to the lakeside to enjoy the scenery, didn't go far until she died, then we got the house back and almost retired, so we didn't rent it to anyone else, we came here for a weekend getaway. We always stayed in the house and for all the nights we were here, in our dreams the house suddenly lit up in the night, classical music started playing and couples were dancing in the living room. At first, we were a bit surprised and scared, but then we got used to it, because we realized that these ghosts were fun and happy, not intending to scare you, but they were very happy in the dream. We didn't want you, as a stranger, to witness these things at night in the house if you stayed; so he would have rented a hotel room for me to stay the night. That is also the reason why we did not demolish the old house; but gave it to a construction worker in the neighborhood, who would put it on a crane and move it to another piece of land nearby. He joked: let the happy ghosts go with it so there is a place for them to enjoy, but if we destroy it, they would lose their place to stay. We also did not tell the new owner of the house this story like I am telling it to you now".*

Believe it or not: it depends on people and their religious beliefs about eternal life just that way: "*Eternal*". It means "*forever*". It means when life ends here, it continues somewhere else and I would know the former owner of the old house with a beautiful secluded site had a good happy life and even after death. I did not ask Jim later: *"Do the happy ghosts follow the old house to a new place?"*. But I know for sure: the new house did not have any ghosts, because when it was finished, we were invited to stay there and none of us saw happy ghosts appearing and dancing.

After spending more than enough time on the helicopter, hangar, and fuel supply pump, now is the time to design the new house, the position on the hill, with the slope of the land above higher than the bottom, I proposed to make a "*split-level*", which means two floors: the upper floor will be the main floor, the lower floor will go to the lakeside built of glass for the view. The concept drawing came out, everyone liked it, but after considering the valuation of materials and labor beyond the set amount of the budget, when finally revised, the new drawing became almost like the house the two of them were living in, only one floor and a large side garage to store things. The lakeside has a house to hold a pontoon with a roof, the crane will lift the boat when on shore, winching it out of the water. The *octagonal gazebo (correctly Feng Shui designed)* will be built nearby, with a walkway from the shore made of *trex* wood, not rotting, the metal roof for Key West style instead of ceramic tiles like most in South Florida

Cruising on the lake by pontoon boat, with a newly-trained captain.

Sophia playing with sand on the shore.

I finished construction drawings around 2000, including a helipad, hangar, and storage room, JP-4 underground fuel tank for the 'copter. Overlooking the lake is a house with 4 bedrooms, 3 bathrooms, and 3 car garages. Down at the lakeside is a house for a pontoon, a solid wooded Gazebo to relax, sit, read, even take a nap or enjoy the view. He applied for a permit with the local government himself, and hired licensed contractor to take care of the construction, because he was familiar with the work through his past supervisory position. Construction took more than a year; he bought a Gulfstream RV parked on the site temporarily after the *"happy ghosted"* old house was moved to another place. The new house was built in line with modern construction methods. After Hurricane Andrews in 1992, the new building code had changed, specifying structures that can withstand the winds of a storm, although it was not required like most of South Florida, because it was close to the coast and the Gulf of Mexico, he made it as strong as other areas, to withstand wind speeds of 110mph.

Gazebo on the lakeside, I designed it and Jim built it with a Trex walkway.

In 2002, the project was completed. They moved into the new house, they invited my wife and I and our baby Sophia to their new house to stay and relax for a weekend, ride the pontoon boat on the lake, cruise the lake in a 4-seater jet ski, sit and enjoy like summer vacation days. This place is ideal for those who love nature, surrounded by high hillsides, always breezy and quiet because there are not many people around. This is also an ideal place to retire or take a weekend getaway after a long day at work in the surrounding big cities. Many people come here, building vacation homes by the lake just for family or friends to come over for the weekend, or stay forever after they retire. I am sure the landlady had an interesting life when she was alive and especially enjoyed the happy and comfortable days at the end of her life in her own rented house, an ideal place to become a *"happy ghost likes to party"* in her eternal life. In the old days in Saigon before 1975, many families had second vacation homes in Dalat or Vung Tau, coming to relax on weekends away from the heat and hustle of the capital. It is depicted in two verses of the famous Vietnamese educator/poet/philosopher *Trang Trinh* Khiem Binh Nguyen (1491-1585):

"Foolish, I find a secluded place,
Smart people come to the crowded place."

COVID-19 PANDEMIC 2019

Note: March 11, 2020: *(After more than 118,000 cases in 114 countries and 4,291 deaths, the World Health Organization declared COVID-19 a pandemic). CDC info.*

In March 2019, our group of National Academy Quoc Hoc High School 65-72 met at the house of Liem-Phuong (Virginia) after meeting in Florida in 2017, 2018. The cherry blossom season is a special feature of the capital; it is cold at the end of March. We had good days together because most of our friends are retired, except for two, Dr. Quy Tran and me. We promise to return to Vietnam together for the reunion of 50 years away from the school, which is planned to be held in March 2020 in Hue. After preparations, buying airline tickets, and securing visas, it is already the end of the year and we are ready to go. Total participants are 10 persons (5 couples).

At the beginning of 2020, we called each other to prepare our luggage; at the same time the bad news for all travel spread, because of the COVID-19 pandemic raging in the Chinese city of Wuhan and because of the concealment of the Chinese government. The virus had spread all over the world. The death toll was mostly elderly people, making people worried and anxious to avoid spreading. Countries closed their borders, especially airports because there is no medication to prevent or treat this disease. The news spread that the pandemic was getting worse and worse, so we were confused, not knowing whether to go or postpone the trip, afraid that once we went out, the US government might close the border, we would be homeless, nowhere to go, the whole world, not a country affected, and without vaccines or medications for the new disease. So in the end, we had to cancel the reunion to be safe, which is summed up in the proverb: *"A plan belongs to man; success belongs to God"*.

The Covid pandemic brought everyone from one surprise to another, public and private offices had to close if their employees were sick, because the pandemic spread very quickly through respiratory droplets and long-lived germs on shared objects such as furniture. door latches, toilets... *no one knows where the virus is or is not.*

I don't know why but because of Covid, I'm busier than before. The main concern is how to meet demand: employees can't come to the office but still have to work. If the office is closed, how can it serve the people in the area? If anyone has read or watched *"Journey to the West"*, they know that the Sun Wukong has magical powers, heavenly eyes, and heavenly ears, sitting in one place and being able to see everything and control it from afar. Now, because of advanced technology, communications are anywhere thanks to the internet connection can also see and control other places easily. In my office before the pandemic, there were only 3 people, including me, who were able to work remotely, i.e., anywhere. We could use laptops to connect to the main server system. This required a laptop computer, internet access, and firewalls that allowed entry after considering *"friend or foe"* because lately, hackers from other countries have been boring into public systems, especially the US Government, to hold some organization hostage for ransom called *"Cyberware"*. This dangerous situation has led many large companies or government agencies to create a new position in the IT industry called Chief Security Officer (CSO) to just take care of the security of their systems.

Doing *"remote"*, and not coming to work, will create a hole for these hackers to attack. Both anti-pandemic and anti-hackers. Call the laptop manufacturers: Dell, HP, Lenovo... the next surprise because their offices around the world are closed; they only have a limited amount for sale because everyone is in need of gear to work remotely. I saved 10 laptops for government programs (Public Sector), even though I don't know where to get the money to pay for them.

Only two days later, when we learned that we needed 10 more and that we would have a separate budget for this to let more employees work from home, they told us to wait 2 more weeks because they were all sold out. From 1% of employees working remotely, within just half a month, I had to increase this number to 90% remote, especially the Finance staff, unable to stop taking in revenue or paying, including salaries and wages.

Alone, I think about when I was a maid, (I played the chain system called *Taylorism, a System of scientific management advocated by Fred W. Taylor. In Taylor's view, the task of factory management was to determine the best way for the worker to do the job, to provide the proper tools and training, and to provide incentives for good performance),* so when my laptops came back, I borrowed the big office of Ms. Town Clerk Vivian to make two long tables, leaving 10 laptops at a time, networking thru Ethernet cables, which was more reliable than Wi-Fi, so I could log into the server and go through the firewalls, put in the software, wait for the number 1, then I jump to the keyboard number 2, and so on until the last one... I don't need to stay right there and continue the remote setup work, one update after another, then firmware updates, and then install all new software. Well done, whatever is done I would assign it to Staff after they get their information for the second authentication with Duo software. In the remote log file, this is easy because the remote machine will have to ask for details via cell phone. If not, access will be denied, to prevent an outsider attack. This is safe because no one can exchange laptops with someone else, and if they use any internet connection other than that in their home, they won't be able to access it. A Staff Member in the Special Event Department called me and said there was no way to get into the department's system today, but a few days ago it was OK, I saw the firewalls flashing continuously and asked if she was at home. She said that she went to a relative's house today, so I brought my laptop to work from there… A few minutes later she could do it and I told her when she got back home to work, she had to let me know in advance; otherwise, the laptop would be a brick.

My family and I discussed whether to retire at this time, finding it too troublesome to work, because the disease was spreading, especially for the elderly, they have no vaccine yet but the Town needed me; I decided to inform my Town Manager I intended to retire after the Covid pandemic stabilizes, so he should start to search for my replacement now.

It took a year for the search, then interviews through Zoom or Microsoft Teams, not face-to-face meetings as before, although the vaccine started to be available and a third dose had been given. The first dose had to wait after making an appointment and was only for people over 65 years old, the second dose 4 to six weeks later saw a decrease in the number of people waiting, and the third and fourth injections when they arrived; the nurses waiting are happy to see patients. Running out of space on the little vaccine cards: if you need to inject again, use a second one, who would think about the fourth and fifth shot? Hopefully one day the Covid pandemic will end so that everyone can have fun like in the old days.

September 2021, after my replacement arrived, I gave him a bunch of secret keys. I officially retired on October 29, 2022. The boss and staff held a party to invite my whole family. I officially put the *keyboard* and *mouse* in the drawer. From now on, I don't have to be afraid of *mice* that don't run every morning anymore.

MY DAUGHTER

2015: Sophia entered Oxbridge Academy in 2011 and is estimated to have completed the 12th Grade by the summer of 2015. Since she was a child, Sophia has been interested in knitting, so when she was 8 years old, my sister taught her the basics and Sophia took extra self-study on the Internet. Sophia went up to stay for a week in the summer with her aunt in Orlando to learn to knit. When she entered Oxbridge, the art teacher saw that Sophia had a talent for sculpture, so she encouraged and taught her how to make pottery, displaying it at school. They found it beautiful, and the teachers sent her to compete for regional art prizes, including photography, painting, projects, and sculpture.

After winning regional and Florida sculpture awards, they applied for permission to send them to the national competition, all shipping costs covered by major carriers like FedEx or UPS, free of charge. If selected, all winners must go to New York to receive the award. In June 2015, after the announcement of the award list, Sophia was named a recipient of a gold medal. Two art teachers from the school and their families went to New York to receive the award with Sophia and two other students. This was an honor, not only for the individual student but also for the school the students who were attending; so most of the parents and teachers tried their best to attend, even though they had to pay trip costs out of their own pockets. In order for the contest to be fair, the judges in New York were only allowed to see the artworks, but could not possibly know the names of contestants.

The gold medal-winning sculpture is displayed in the exhibition hall.

Koala Bear couple- Knitting (left) and pottery (right).

The Rabbit family, Sophia's knitting art.

In Carnegie Hall, New York, before the award ceremony opening.

The teachers and winners receive an award in front of Carnegie Hall, New York.

After seeing the schools and applying to Universities, all schools accepted her but she decided to attend Florida State University in Tallahassee, to major in Accounting. This is a state school, famous for this field, mostly female students. During 4 years of study, although she lived in a dormitory, thanks to her Uncle (my brother) living in the same city, each semester we had a place to stay when we came up and kept her belongings locally, instead of having to bring them home. By 2019, Sophia finished her Bachelor's Degree (BS); the school accepted a small number of students (about 86) to continue studying for a Master's degree (MS) in the same field, especially within one year, instead of two years as usual.

Fortunately, the COVID pandemic only affected a small part of the final semester, so Sophia finished her Master of Accounting in May 2020. The COVID pandemic was at its peak, so the school awarded the diploma by mail, and the graduation ceremony had to be postponed. Sophia was accepted to work for a large accounting firm in Tampa; also, because of COVID-19, she did not come to the office, only working remotely from home.

2022: Sophia spent time studying for a professional degree, and by June 2022, she completed her professional degree and state practice. My daughter was better than her father because she got a Certified Public Accounting (CPA) before her 25th birthday.

In addition to her studies and profession, Sophia's hobbies are knitting, crocheting, and making pottery and crockery. Although she has been highly trained in classical piano, it seems that she does not like to play music like her father.

The ceramic art of Sophia.

My job after retirement is to gather manuscripts, diaries, facts, and photographs to complete my book, both in Vietnamese and English, before the last days of April become half a century in 2025.

CONCLUSION

Perhaps because of the last days of April, my life, along with that of other Vietnamese people, has changed. I was fortunate enough to see a new horizon, a new life, and enjoy what my second homeland has brought me. A typical refugee like me came here and thanks to the merits of their predecessors, just over two hundred years from the founding of this country, they have built what a person like me could never have dreamed of, not even in my homeland, despite a foundation of more than 4,000 years of civilization. They fought bravely with foreigners and created *independence, freedom*, and *democracy* for the country.

The Constitution and its Amendments underpinned the growth of democracy in the United States, beginning with three words: *We, the People*... which I had previously known only through the limitations of books and lectures, as taught at school. Hearing is not equal to seeing and seeing is not equal to practicing yourself, all for the people and for the people.

Thanks to the Scouting movement and activities since childhood, I have been imbued with more confidence and courage to overcome many challenges in life, but the ambition of an individual like me is to grow up, in addition to education. family, school, and then the journey to serve the nation and society, contributing what is in their power to have a comfortable material and spiritual life. Or not equal to luck: the luck we encounter more than others also yields advantages on the thorny and challenging path of life, enabling us to contribute to society more than those who are less fortunate. Had I been stuck in Saigon after the last days of April, if I had not gone to prison because of my father's past, I would have been like my friends, getting married and then worrying about making a living, having to giveup everything – the scandals that you see every day – in order to survive.

Nearly half a century later, looking back at friends, relatives, or people around, some have passed away forever, the rest have a new life in their second homeland after fortunately leaving Saigon during its final hours. They settled and continued living with the profession they had in Vietnam before 1975; others started a new life with empty hands, creating a place for themselves in society after finishing their education at American universities, a second generation, having more opportunities, enjoying success in a country where their fathers settled with a rather special case.

Personally, like some other lucky people, I have been granted a second homeland to take refuge in stormy days, to wait for the opportunity to return and contribute my experience to my poor homeland. It seemed like a problem with an immediate and easy answer, but the harsh reality is that my small wishes and ambitions were difficult to fulfill, for many reasons. What I learned and what I contributed to the United States and others I should have also contributed to Vietnam, my country, where more practical and necessary contributions are needed, but unfortunately, that place lacked many necessary and sufficient conditions for me to be able to do it: Freedom, justice, independence, and democracy.

The small dreams of the writer are also common dreams of many Vietnamese living abroad or even right at home. Hopefully, one day soon, those dreams will come to pass, even though knowing that with Vietnam's important position and position in Asia, it is difficult to get independence; they just want democracy and freedom. Other things will come naturally, as we have seen in the United States.

As an individual born and raised during the war in the South, one more or less feeling a responsibility to lose his free homeland to a dictatorship and party rule, only the truth in this book may serve as a part of expressing the desire for real peace in the homeland, so that the events of the country's history from 1954, 1968, 1972 and 1975 are commemorated, instead of celebrating victory as is seen today.

When this book was published, in only less than a year, the ruling Communist Party in Vietnam would celebrate their victory and liberation of the South for 50 years, 1975-2025, unifying the two regions. Half a century has passed. As a Vietnamese, why am I not as happy as when I saw the history of the United States at the conclusion of the Civil War, ending on April 9, 1865, or East and

West Germany united at the Fall of the Berlin Wall *(Mauerfall)* on November 9, 1989, without any bloodshed? Hastening the collapse of dictatorships in Eastern European countries, such as Poland, Romania, Bulgaria, Czechoslovakia, and Hungary in 1990, and the Soviet Union disintegrating in 1991. The sad thing in Vietnam and the difference is the hatred of the victorious faction, corruption, selfishness, discrimination, dictatorship of the party, and the ambition to take power by a minority leads to the risk of losing roots and even loss of the fatherland.

Special thanks to my family, friends, and colleagues for their encouragement and spiritual support, so that the book can be completed successfully, just a typical true story of one or a few lucky individuals who escaped the dictatorship, the party rule, at the last minute, without losing his life in the Far East Ocean as one of the nameless *"boat people"* by sea or in the jungle when trying to escape by land, to enjoy a life of freedom, justice and independence and happiness in its own right.

APPENDIX
PICTURES
PROJECTS AND COMPLETED WORKS

"The Last Flight" Watercolor Painting 11x14 – Hoa Ngoc Hoang

"The Boat People", watercolor painting 11 x 14,
Hoa Ngoc Hoang, 2023

There are no statistics on the number of Vietnamese people crossing the sea or land across the border who died or went missing, because many families or boat people who departed never reached a far shore, due to weather conditions, were captured or killed by Thai pirates, the road on which before departed, they knew the probability of death more than life. The price to pay for seeking Freedom outside of their motherland.

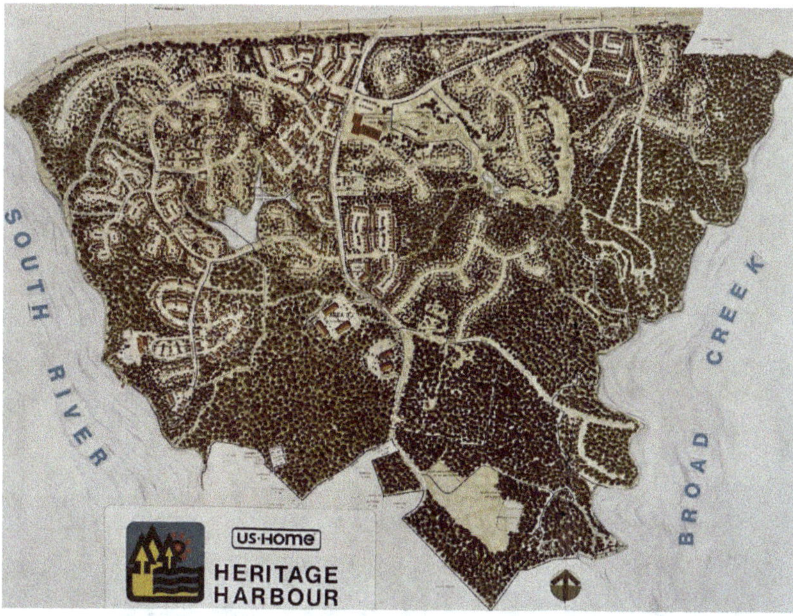

Heritage Harbor Rendering with KML-US-Home,
Annapolis, Maryland 1981-1982

Commercial/Shopping Center Elevations – Lee&Sakahara 1989

Poster for APACAF-Event 2002. Calligraphy by Artist Vũ Hối.

Organizing Committee with Khánh Hà's family APACAF November 17, 2002 in Northern Virginia for Lu Lien's event.

Fundraising Event for the Asian Pacific American Cultural Arts Foundation (APACAF).

2010- 10-year Anniversary Writing on America – Viet Bao California.

Writer Nhã Ca and Sophia - 2010

2010 - Viet Bao 10-year anniversary after Writing in America

ASSORTED DOCUMENTS

TOWN RENOVATION AND REDEVELOPMENT PROJECTS

COMMUNITY REDEVELOPMENT AGENCY

TOWN OF LAKE PARK, FLORIDA

1998-2022

FUNDING THROUGH THE TOWN OF LAKE PARK'S BOND PROGRAM COUNTY GRANTS, STATE OF FLORIDA, AND FEDERAL GRANTS

the John Scott Dailey
FLORIDA
INSTITUTE OF
GOVERNMENT
at Florida State University

July 21, 2011

Maria Davis
Town Manager
535 Park Ave
Lake Park, FL 33403

Dear Mrs. Davis:

During the Florida Local Government Information Systems Association Summer Conference an exciting event occurred that we were sure you want to share in celebrating. Hoa Ngoc Hoang was honored with the designation of Certified Chief Information Officer (CCIO) in local government from the Florida Institute of Government at Florida State University. Each CCIO received a plaque and a personalized letter of congratulations from Florida State University President Eric J. Barron for their commitment to grow and serve the people of their communities and the state.

Mr. Hoang was part of the Fifth class of Florida's Certified Public Technology Leadership program for Certified Chief Information Officers, a program designed to raise the professional standards for government technology leaders and help prepare individuals to serve effectively within their organizations' leadership teams. Mr. Hoang worked for more than a year to obtain the certification of CCIO. Each participant attended 80 hours of classroom activity, accomplished 80 hours of out-of-class work designed to engage new knowledge, and completed a significant capstone project to concretely apply key and important leadership, planning, management and progressive service principles in a manner directly relevant to your jurisdiction.

Thank you for your support of Mr. Hoang by allowing participation in this program. We know that the knowledge gained from this experience will significantly benefit the Town of Lake Park. To remain timely, this certification requires continuing education to allow Mr. Hoang to continually grow the critical skills needed to provide outstanding technology services in your organization. We ask that the enclosed Certificate be used in recognizing Mr. Hoang within your organization, at an appropriate time, so that everyone can share in the dedication Mr. Hoang has to quality service. Also enclosed is a picture from the ceremony at the FLGISA Conference.

Again, we thank you for your personal support and the endorsement of the Certified Public Technology Leadership program.

Sincerely,

Jeff Hendry
Executive Director

FSU Research Complex ▪ 3200 Commonwealth Blvd ▪ Tallahassee FL 32303
Telephone: (850-487-1870 ▪ FAX: (850)487-0041 ▪ http://iog.fsu.edu ▪ e-mail: info@iog.fsu.edu

Award of CGCIO Certificate after graduation

Plaque in front of Town Hall June 2003

Town Hall Façade after renovation-1998

PROCLAMATION

OF THE COMMISSION OF THE TOWN OF LAKE PARK, FLORIDA

WHEREAS, the Town of Lake Park desired to complete the Park Avenue Streetscape Project, within a very limited time frame with a high quality end product while holding the line on costs, the Town of Lake Park joined with Burkhardt Construction, Inc. to form a "partnering" team to perform the work. In this agreement both parties agreed to set the goal of working together toward successful completion of the project, and to join forces to solve any and all problems which might arise,

WHEREAS, Burkhardt Construction, Inc. along with their Subcontractors in addition to fulfilling this "Spirit of Partnering" met and exceeded all conditions of the agreement thus producing an extremely high quality product for the long term enhancement of the Town of Lake Park, and

WHEREAS, certain employees of the Town added to their existing workload or performed with exemplary service, and

WHEREAS, Burkhardt Construction, Inc.'s Project Superintendent, Mr. Scott Murray, excelled in his duties with relentless pursuit of meeting an extraordinary deadline, and maintained highest standards of quality,

NOW THEREFORE, Be it resolved that the Town of Lake Park express appreciation to these parties by issuance of a **CERTIFICATE OF APPRECIATION** to the following:

BURKHARDT CONSTRUCTION, INC.
SCOTT MURRAY
D. S. EAKINS CONSTRUCTION CORPORATION
ROBERT J. WALKER, P. E.
ROY-FISHER ASSOCIATES INC.
HOA NGOC HOANG
MERRY ANN CATASUS
CAROLYNN MIGUEL

IN WITNESS THEREOF, I HAVE SET MY HAND AND CAUSED THE SEAL OF THE TOWN OF LAKE PARK TO BE AFFIXED THIS Sixth day of January, 1999.

William H. Wagner

William H. Wagner, Mayor

Proclamation - January 1999.

PROCLAMATION
TOWN OF LAKE PARK, FLORIDA
COMMENDING HOA NGOC HOANG

WHEREAS; Hoa Ngoc Hoang commenced employment with the Town of Lake Park on February 2, 1998 as a Computer Aided Design Drafting System Specialist; and

WHEREAS; in recognition of his performance in that capacity, Hoa Ngoc Hoang was appointed as the Assistant to the Town Manager on March 29, 2001, a position which he continues to hold; and

WHEREAS; Hoa Ngoc Hoang has prepared construction documents and provided field management for successful capital projects of the Town of Lake Park, including the design and redevelopment of Park Avenue and construction of the clock tower; construction of the Lake Park Pavilion and tennis facility; renovation of the Lake Park Post Office Building; and renovation of the historic Lake Park Town Hall; and

WHEREAS; in recognition of his leadership and management capability, Hoa Ngoc Hoang was appointed as Interim Community Development Director on March 29, 2003; and

WHEREAS; in view of his expertise in the area of computer information systems, Hoa Ngoc Hoang, was appointed as Information Technology Manager on April 29, 2003; and

WHEREAS; Hoa Ngoc Hoang was appointed as Interim Town Manager by the Commission of the Town of Lake Park on May 15, 2003 and served in that capacity until July 1, 2003; and

WHEREAS; despite his many responsibilities, Hoa Ngoc Hoang has established an employment record of the highest caliber while at the same time earning the respect of all who have come to know him; and

WHEREAS; the Commission of the Town of Lake Park wishes to publicly recognize and honor Hoa Ngoc Hoang for his contributions to the Town and for his accomplishments;

NOW, THEREFORE, on behalf of the Commission of the Town of Lake Park, I, Paul W. Castro, Mayor of the Town of Lake Park, do hereby publicly commend Hoa Ngoc Hoang and express our gratitude for the services which he has rendered to this community.

***IN WITNESS WHEREOF, I** have hereto set my hand and caused the official Seal of the Town of Lake Park, Florida to be affixed this 23rd day of July, 2003.*

BY: Paul Castro
Mayor Paul Castro

ATTEST:

Carol Simpkins
Carol Simpkins, Town Clerk

Proclamation – July 23, 2003 after promotion to Interim Town Manager.

PROCLAMATION
TOWN OF LAKE PARK, FLORIDA
IN HONOR OF HOA NGOC HOANG

WHEREAS; Hoa Ngoc Hoang commenced employment with the Town of Lake Park on February 2, 1998 as a Computer Aided Design Drafting System Specialist; and

WHEREAS; in recognition of his performance, ***Hoa Ngoc Hoang*** was appointed as the Assistant to the Town Manager on March 29, 2001; and

WHEREAS; throughout his career with the Town of Lake Park, ***Hoa Ngoc Hoang*** has prepared construction documents and provided field management for successful capital projects of the Town of Lake Park, including the design and redevelopment of Park Avenue and construction of the Clock Tower; construction of the Lake Park Pavilion and tennis facility; renovation of the Lake Park Post Office Building; and, the renovation of the historic Lake Park Town Hall; and

WHEREAS; in addition to lending his vast architectural skill and expertise to the development of important Town projects and facilities, in view of his knowledge in the area of computer information systems ***Hoa Ngoc Hoang*** was appointed as Information Technology Manager on April 24, 2003 and as such he was solely responsible for the establishment and implementation of the Town's internet and email systems, where none previously existed, and for working to ensure the ongoing security of the Town's cyber systems pursuant to best practices; and

WHEREAS; Hoa Ngoc Hoang has served in important Town leadership and management positions consisting of Interim Community Development Director to which he was appointed on March 29, 2003, and as Interim Town Manager to which he was appointed by the Town Commission on May 15, 2003; and

WHEREAS; Hoa Ngoc Hoang was appointed as Chief Information Technology Officer on February 21, 2007, a position in which he has continued to serve with distinction; and

WHEREAS; on June 30, 2011, ***Hoa Ngoc Hoang*** graduated from the 2010-2011 class of the Certified Chief Information Officer Program through Florida State University, a program that required special dedication and perseverance in order to successfully complete such a challenging course of study; and

WHEREAS; on December 21, 2020, ***Hoa Ngoc Hoang*** was elevated to the position of Information Technology Director; and

WHEREAS; throughout his employment with the Town, ***Hoa Ngoc Hoang*** has continuously devoted his time and energy on behalf of the Town of Lake Park and has earned the friendship and respect of all who have come to know him; and

WHEREAS; the Commission of the Town of Lake Park wishes to publicly recognize and honor ***Hoa Ngoc Hoang*** for his contributions to the Town and for his accomplishments.

NOW, THEREFORE, on behalf of the Commission of the Town of Lake Park, I, Michael O'Rourke, Mayor of the Town of Lake Park, do hereby publicly recognize and commend ***Hoa Ngoc Hoang*** and express to him our sincere and enduring gratitude for the service that he has rendered to this community.

IN WITNESS WHEREOF, *I have hereto set my hand and caused the official Seal of the Town of Lake Park, Florida to be affixed this 20th day of October, 2021.*

By: Mayor Michael O'Rourke

ATTEST: Vivian Mendez, Town Clerk

SEAL — TOWN OF LAKE PARK — FLORIDA

Proclamation in October 2021

Hoa Hoang

Final Evaluation to a 25-year career with

The Town of Lake Park

Evaluator's Comments:

Hoa, the Town of Lake Park as your employer, has the distinction and honor to have you as a twenty-five-year employee. I am honored to serve with you. Your accomplishments over the past twenty-five years are significant. You have upgraded our hardware and software systems at least two times in the past six years in our time together. We plan to upgrade our audio/visual communications in the Mirror Ballroom and the Commission Chamber. We are now live with closed caption, and under your leadership, our municipality has grown in the use of technology. We have streamlined our integration of technology in every aspect of the delivery of services. You have upgraded our servers and protected our municipality from cyberattacks while other communities paid ransom to receive their stolen information back. Your achievements outlined above are only a few of the many accomplishments as a loyal servant of the public trust and interest. The implementation of Fiber Optic infrastructure will permit our town to move forward with Wi-Fi for all public places, provide faster, more reliable transmission of information from departments, buildings, and the general public.

Your vision of a separate IT and Records Retention building will keep our information safe from natural and human hazards. In addition, the building will be state of the art in terms of protecting our data and records. The difference you make is measured in generations rather than years. The improvements you advocate are changes that last a long, long time. Your contributions are numerous and will precede you by generations to come.

When you came to the Town of Lake Park, you inherited the accomplishments and failures of previous boards, commissions, and employees. However, your vision resulted in upgrades to the town's internet capabilities from zero to cutting edge internet capabilities, including Voice over IP phone systems integrated with employee desktop computers. As a result, you had left our town far better off than when you inherited it. You are a faithful public servant who has carried forth the desire to make not only your life better here in America, but you have made our lives better through your work, dedication, and commitment to serving the public.

Thank you, Hoa Hoang, you will be a tough act to follow, but you will always remain in our hearts as a model of public service for others to emulate.

Congratulations on your much-deserved retirement. Your Lake Park Family will miss you.

Education and Training Programs:

Write your book and go fishing!

Goals and Objectives:

Live a long and healthy life (keep breathing).

Hoa,

As we wish you well today, we do so with great sadness. There are very few of us who have known the Town of Lake Park without you in it. You will be missed both personally and professionally by everyone here (or at least most of us, but those are still pretty good odds).

We will also send you off with a tremendous amount of envy and jealousy in our hearts. As we all wake up to the early alarm tomorrow, we will think of you, at home and probably still sleeping, and say @#s%&!!

You may notice at your retirement party that none of us are using our cell phones to take photos of the event. That's because they are all being charged, since there's a good chance the Town's phones and computers are going to crash about a minute and a half after you pull out of the parking lot for the last time. You know this. We know this. It's inevitable.

And we probably won't even be able to use those phones for very long, because you won't be here to remind us to update them.

But while we may joke to hide our sadness, the fact is that Lake Park would not be what it is today without you. You have been directly involved in the renovation of Town Hall and the construction of the Clock Tower, two of the most recognizable parts of the town; you have served as Interim Community Development Director and Interim Town Manager (simultaneously, and while holding down your actual job as Information Technology Manager); and you have literally been the person who single-handedly kept Lake Park functioning first as IT Manager and finally as IT Director. You have engaged and educated us with your stories about the Town's history and, more importantly, your own. You have done all of this while you kept us laughing with your dry sense of humor. We have been privileged to know you and work with you, and although we won't see you every day, you will always be a part of this town.

Unfortunately, now it is time for us to say goodbye. We need to go start installing the docking stations.

With Admiration And Respect,
Your Lake Park Family

Clock Tower- Architectural works modeled on Ben Thanh Market, in the US.

Original Ben Thanh Market in Saigon, the Capital of South Vietnam before 1975.

Renovation Project of Lake Shore Park – Design by Hoa Ngoc Hoang – 2007

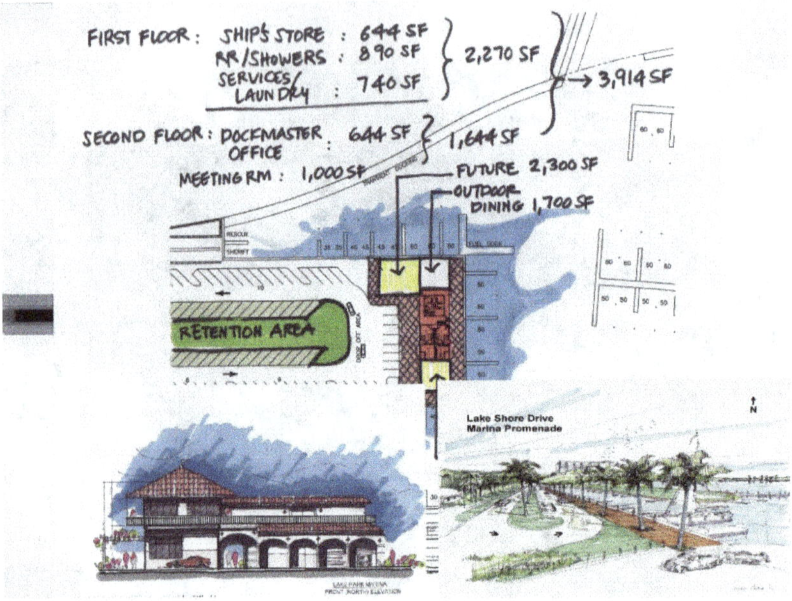

Marina Renovation Project – Conceptual Design.

Lake Park Marina – Design by Hoa Ngoc Hoang

Conceptual plan by Hoa with Restaurant above – East side Elevation.

Opening Ceremony when completed- April 29, 2006.

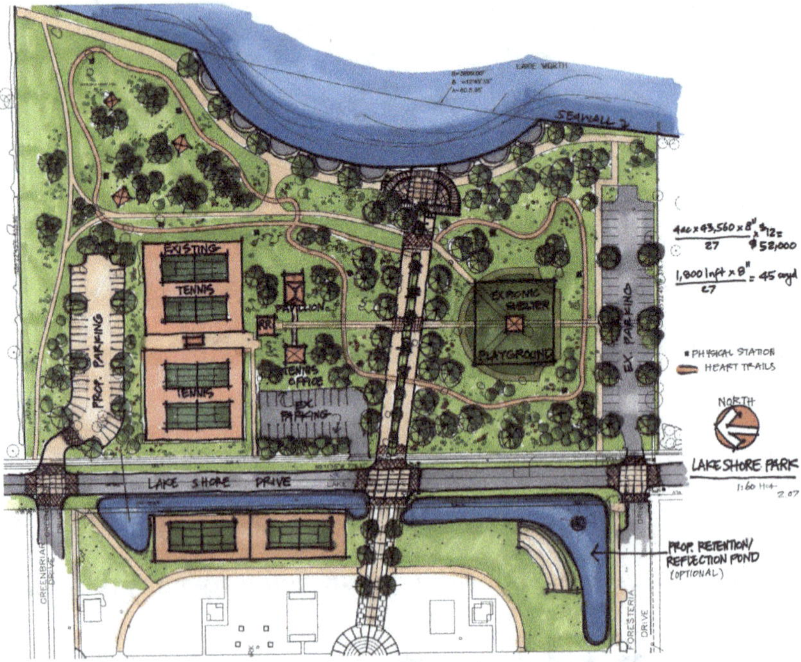

City Park Renovation - Drawings and aerial photos when the project is complete

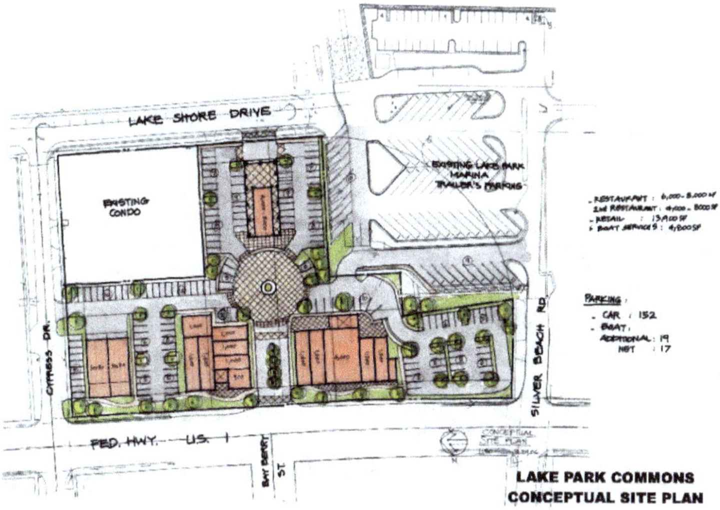

City-supported private investor concept – 3/29/2006.

Project drawings supporting private investors 2006. Later became Nautilus 220.

(The project on the plot of land that I initially drew (March 29, 2006) is only three floors including condos, restaurants and serviced offices. For private investment to be continued so the project will be completed, 14 years later, the city has changed the law to go up to 24 floors of high-rise buildings (1,150,017 sf) to provide a number of residences as well as investment costs, with sufficient profit for the project).

With approval to modify from 3 floors to 24 floors in 2020: The Nautilus 220 project has been drawn up and planned to be completed in 2024. Renderings and design photo courtesy of Nautilus 220/Forest Development LLC and Town of Lake Park.

Completing the renovation project of Mirror Ballroom in the City Hall – 2005

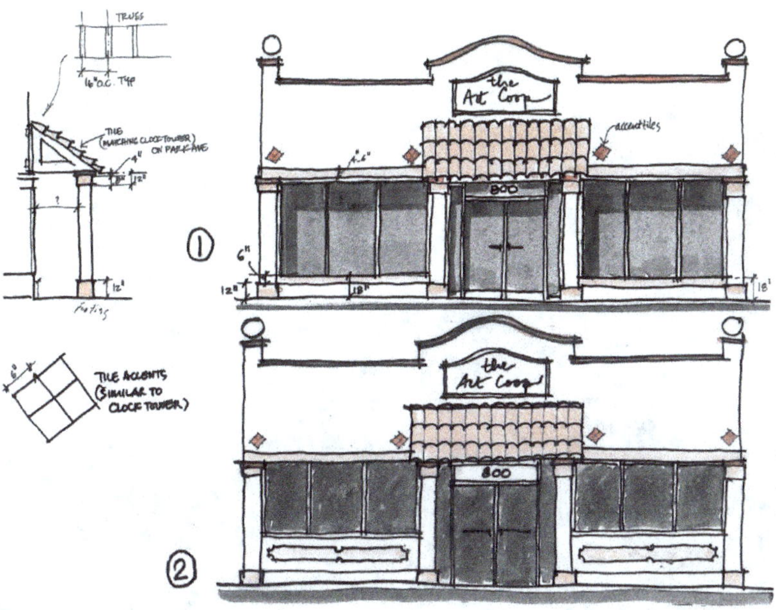

Project and construction drawings before and after completion.

Before and After – 800 Park Avenue

Ilex Park Renovation, completed with funding through Community Development Block Grant Programs (CDBG)

200kmh Hurricane house
Designed and Built: Hoa Ngoc Hoang – 1997

Bamboo bushes, after summer, and Poinciana flowers bloom on the lake.

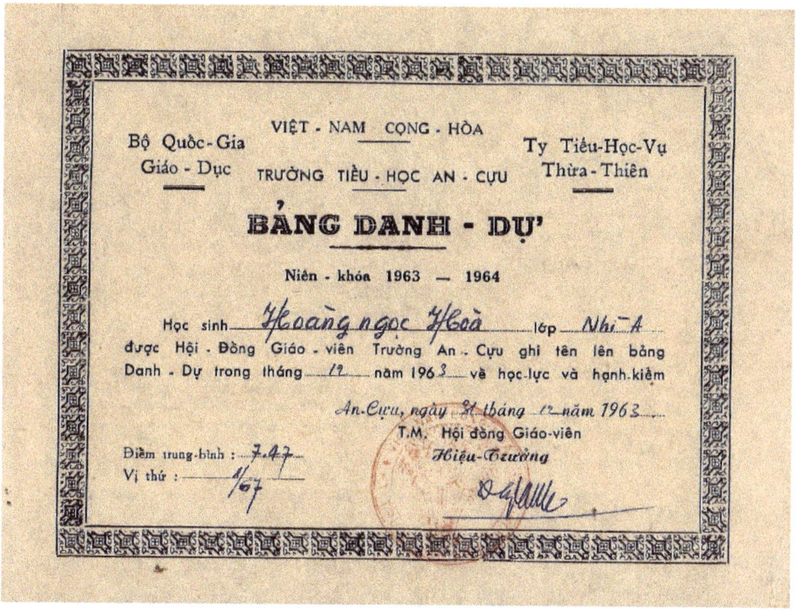

VIỆT - NAM CỘNG - HÒA

Bộ Quốc-Gia Giáo - Dục | TRƯỜNG TIỂU - HỌC AN - CỰU | Ty Tiểu-Học-Vụ Thừa-Thiên

BẢNG DANH - DỰ

Niên - khóa 1963 — 1964

Học sinh Hoàng ngọc Hòa lớp Nhì A

được Hội - Đồng Giáo - viên Trường An - Cựu ghi tên lên bảng Danh - Dự trong tháng 12 năm 1963 về học-lực và hạnh-kiểm

An-Cựu, ngày 31 tháng 12 năm 1963

T.M. Hội đồng Giáo-viên

Hiệu-Trưởng

Điểm trung-bình : 7.47

Vị thứ : 1/67

Student of grade 4 with teacher My Ky, in 1963

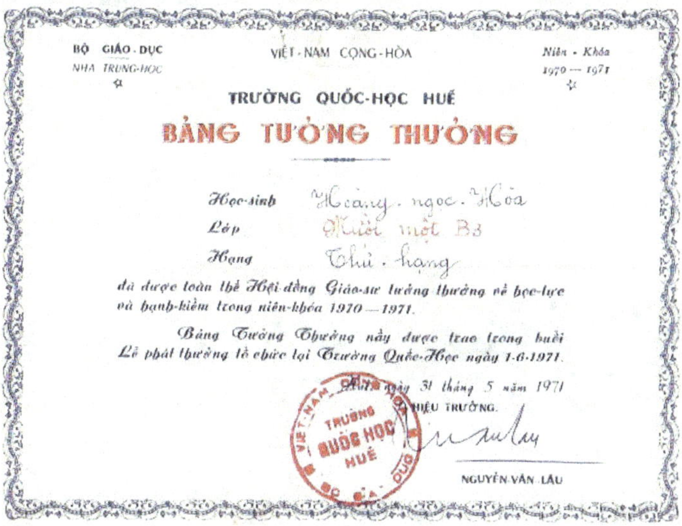

BỘ GIÁO - DỤC
NHA TRUNG-HỌC

VIỆT - NAM CỘNG - HÒA

Niên - Khóa
1970 — 1971

TRƯỜNG QUỐC-HỌC HUẾ

BẢNG TƯỞNG THƯỞNG

Học-sinh Hoàng - ngọc - Hòa

Lớp Mười một B3

Hạng Thủ - hạng

đã được toàn thể Hội-đồng Giáo-sư tưởng thưởng về học-lực và hạnh-kiểm trong niên-khóa 1970 — 1971.

Bảng Tưởng Thưởng này được trao trong buổi Lễ phát thưởng tổ chức tại Trường Quốc-Học ngày 1-6-1971.

Huế, ngày 31 tháng 5 năm 1971

HIỆU TRƯỞNG.

NGUYỄN VĂN LÂU

QUỐC-GIA VIỆT-NAM

QUÂN LỰC VIỆT NAM
ĐỆ NHỊ QUÂN KHU
TIỂU ĐOÀN 255

Số : K /TĐ255/NTB

TỜ TRÌNH

về sự rủi ro trong vụ chết của Đại-úy HOÀNG NGỌC TÚY Tiểu-đoàn-trưởng Tiểu-đoàn 255

Kính gởi,
Đại-tá Tư-lệnh Đệ-nhị quân-khu
(Phòng Hộ-tịch)

KBC. 4.217

Tiểu-đoàn chúng tôi kính tường trình quý Bộ thẩm tường:

Ngày 24.2.1954 lúc 2 giờ 30 chiều đoàn xe của Tiểu-đoàn chúng tôi gồm có 5 chiếc : I JEEP 2 4x4 2 G.M.C. chở rất nhiều vũ-khí, quân-trang và đồ phụ tùng Truyền-tin của Tiểu-đoàn chúng tôi. Đoàn xe khởi hành từ HUẾ ra QUẢNG-TRỊ đến đồn AN-LỖ 5 chiếc xe này còn dừng lại đợi nhập với các xe khác của Tiểu-đoàn 24 và của Bộ-đội pháp theo hộ tống kết thành một đoàn gồm có II chiếc rời khỏi AN-LỖ lúc 3 giờ 30 chiều.

5 chiếc của Tiểu-đoàn chúng tôi chạy theo 4 chiếc Hồng-thập-tự và thiết-giáp còn 2 chiếc 6/6 của Tiểu-đoàn 24 chạy sau.

Dọc đường vì chiếc xe 4/4 trục trặc và Tài-xế bị cảm sốt nên phải chạy chậm, Đại-úy HOÀNG NGỌC TÚY thấy tình cảnh như thế sợ e xảy ra tai nạn dọc đường đành dừng xe lại để cho đoàn xe lướt qua và tiếp đuổi nhau đến PHÒ-TRẠCH.

Trong thời gian dừng lại thì đoàn xe đã cách nhau chừng một cây số, Đại-úy HOÀNG NGỌC TÚY liền rời khỏi xe jeep và để tay lái lại cho Binh TRƯƠNG TIẾU số 2II.I57 tài xế lái còn Đại-úy lên cầm lái chiếc xe 4/4 lúc xe gần đến Phò-trạch độ chừng 700 thước thì bị Việt-minh đã phục sẵn, bắn vào chiếc xe Jeep một loạt đồng thời hô xung phong bảo dừng lại, trong lúc ấy Hạ-sĩ-nhứt NGUYỄN VANG số 204.8IO theo hộ tống Đại-úy và Binh TRƯƠNG TIẾU số 2II.I57 tài xế đã bị thương và chiếc xe jeep bị chúng bắn nằm ngang giữa đường còn chiếc xe 4/4 của Đại-úy lái, định dấn hết ga cho băng qua, nhưng rủi vấp phải gò đất cao xe trược lên hai bánh trước và tự nhiên tắc máy.

Trong xe gồm có Đại-úy HOÀNG NGỌC TÚY Tiểu-đoàn-trưởng Tiểu-đoàn 255 bị trọng thương và chạy lui được một đoạn thì ngã xuống chết ngay tại đó cách đường độ chừng 15 thước còn Hạ-sĩ TRẦN QUYẾN số 203.535, Binh TRƯƠNG NHƯ HỒNG số 238.376 nhân viên phụ-trách Truyền-tin và Binh HỒ LỢN số 237.? tài xế đã bị chúng bắt dẫn đi (hướng Tây Nam) còn đồ đạc trên xe jeep cũng bị chúng lấy hết (tư trang)

Đại-úy HOÀNG NGỌC TÚY là một vị Sĩ-quan gương-mẫu, đầy kinh nghiệm và là một cấp Tiểu-đoàn-trưởng đáng tin cậy, xứng đáng là một cấp chỉ huy trong quân-đội.

Hồ-sơ hộ-tịch Tiểu-đoàn chúng tôi sẽ đệ trình sau./.

KBC. 4.070, ngày 2 tháng 3 năm 1954
Trung-úy TRẦN VĂN TUẤN Sĩ-quan Thứ-ba Hộ-tịch
Tiểu-đoàn 255
(ký tên và đóng dấu)

NGUYÊN-VĂN Số : 0057 /TVI /T4T/CNVK

VIỆT NAM CỘNG HÒA
QUÂN LỰC VIỆT NAM CỘNG HÒA
BỘ CHỈ HUY [illegible]
PHÒNG TỔNG [illegible]
CHI NHÁNH I VĂN-KHỐ

KBC. 7.83, ngày 21 Th.BA 1966
Thiếu-úy ĐOÀN LĂNG KHOA
Trưởng Chi-nhánh I Văn-khố.
(ký tên và đóng dấu)

Official Report of my father's death – 1954

Nation of Vietnam

REPORT

Vietnam Army Ministry

Second Military Region

255th Battalion

About the risk in the death of 255th Battalion Commander

Dear Colonel, of the Second Military Region Commander of the Civil Registry

KBC 4217

Our battalion respectfully reports for your consideration:

On February 24, 1954 at 2:30pm our convoy consisted of 5 vehicles, one Jeep, two 4x4s and two GMCs carrying many of our battalion's weapons, equipment, and communications equipment. The convoy departed from Hue to Quang Tri Province and arrived at An Lo station. These 5 cars also stopped to wait for other vehicles of the 24th Battalion and the French Army to follow the escort, to form a convoy of 11 vehicles to leave An Lo at 3:30pm.

5 vehicles of our battalion followed 4 Ambulances and Armored vehicles, and two 6x6s from the 24th Battalion followed.

Along the way, because the 4x4 had problems and the driver had come down with a fever, they had to slow down. Seeing such a situation, Captain Hoang Ngoc Tuy was afraid of an accident along the way, so he stopped his car to let the other vehicles pass, and follow each other to Pho Trach.

During the stop, the convoy was spread about 1km apart, Captain Hoang Ngoc Tuy immediately got out of the jeep and left the steering wheel with Private Truong Tieu to drive, and the Captain took the wheel of the 4x4, when it was 700m from Pho Trach.

The enemy was already waiting to ambush; they shot at the jeep with a series of bullets and shouted "Attack" at the same time to order vehicles to stop, while Deputy Corporal Nguyen Vang accompanied Captain and Private 1st class Truong Tieu. The driver was injured and the vehicle disabled. The jeep was shot and disabled in front, blocking the road, while the Captain's 4x4 car forged through, intending to jam on full throttle to cross, but was accidentally caught over a high hill; the car skidded on its two front wheels and suddenly shut down.

In the car, there was a Captain Hoang Ngoc Tuy, 255th Battalion Commander, who was seriously injured and ran back a distance, then fell dead right there about 15m away from the road, while Corporal Tran Quyen and Private 1st class Truong Nhu Hong were in charge of communications and Private 1st class Ho Lon, the driver was taken by the enemy (to the South West) and the jeep's belongings were also taken by them (personal belongings).

Captain Hoang Ngoc Tuy is an exemplary officer, full of experience and a reliable Battalion Commander, worthy of being a commander in the army.

Civil status records of our battalion will be submitted later.

KBC 4070 March 2, 1954

Lieutenant Tran Van Tuan, Officer of the Civil Registry

255th Battalion

THE WHITE HOUSE

April 24, 1984

Hoang Ngoc Hoa
8626 Welbek Way
Gaithersburg, MD 20879

Dear Hoang Ngoc Hoa:

Allow me to take this opportunity to convey my heartfelt gratitude for your recent donation to the Reagan-Bush '84 Committee. Our success in this campaign is greatly enhanced by the enthusiasm and generosity demonstrated by you and other loyal Americans.

As you and I both know, the future of America is approaching a critical juncture. Working together, we can ensure that our nation continues in the right direction. With your assistance we can guarantee a future with peace and happiness.

Again, please accept my personal thanks for your continued support and I pray your commitment will remain strong during this crucial period.

God bless you.

Sincerely,

Ronald Reagan

Ronald Reagan

Paid for by Reagan-Bush '84, Paul Laxalt, Chairman, Angela M. Buchanan Jackson, Treasurer.
Not prepared or mailed at Government expense.

FRONT COVER, HISTORY AND MEANING

The front cover art was created by digital artist Khai Co Vu, an illustrator who specializes in space painting; note that he is also the author of the following drawings in this book: the A-1 Skyraider, A-37B Dragonfly, Huey UH-1, Choctaw H-34, the late Captain Nguyen Hoang An, 257th Squadron, as well as the late Major Tu Duc Trinh, 516th Squadron. Several of his artworks supplement the heroic stories of the men of the Republic of Vietnam Air Force (RVNAF).

His father was Mr. Dung Dang Vu, a lawyer/attorney and former Counselor and Head of the Central Supreme Court of Hue Bar Association. Born in Da Nang, studied with the son of Colonel Vuong Van Nguyen, former Air Force Commander of the 41st Tactical Wing, 1st Air Force Division - Da Nang AFB and also a lover of the Air Force; he thus had many concepts and learned the lore of the RVNAF from childhood.

He currently resides in Melbourne, Australia.

The meaning of the front cover painting: The last C-130 Hercules, a transport aircraft of the Republic of Vietnam Air Force, belonging to squadrons 435/437, 53rd Tactical Wing, 5th Air Division, took off from the taxiway at Tan Son Nhut Airport, on the morning of April 29, 1975 ferrying the author and other Vietnamese to the US military airport at U-Tapao, Kingdom of Thailand, to take refuge, before Saigon fell into the hands of the North Vietnamese Communists, thus ending the government of the Republic of Vietnam (symbolized by the flag of the Republic of Vietnam) and leaving the country. his homeland (the city of Saigon with the river below). He then emigrated to the United States, through a channel of political asylum, because of the war (represented by the American flag), under a blue sky, symbolizing democracy, freedom, independence, and a challenging and hopeful new life in a second homeland.

The author had the opportunity to meet the artist, not in person, but first on the website canhthep.com, because of the drawings of military aircraft of the Republic of Vietnam Air Force, often signed under the name Co Huong. In 2012, by chance, the story of the great sacrifice of Captain An Hoang Nguyen, the 257th Salvation Squadron, emerged, of them evacuating from Da Nang on the morning of March 29, 1975. It needed a drawing for the article and a picture of his family. On the yearly anniversary of the event, Khai Co Vu (VKC) did not hesitate to help, and later it became known that VKC was familiar with the family of Captain Thuc Vuong Pham, a brave pilot of the 213th Double Mace armed squadron. In the same unit as his brother, and at the same time, Thuc's older brother, the late Lieutenant Colonel Fulro Thang Van Pham, 530th Squadron, 72nd Pleiku Tactical Wing, was killed in a Skyraider mission in Kontum in the summer of 1972. When asked to design the front cover, Vu Khai Co even accepted the task, despite being busy with his daily work. Sincere thanks to the talented artist.

ABOUT THE EDITOR

Proofreader of the English-language Edition

Byron Allen Black

FROM THE AUTHOR

Appreciation to my Nhan Anh Publisher Mr. Han Le who introduced Byron Allen Black as the English Editor of my book: *The Last Days of April, 1975*. He was his English teacher and Program Coordinator, appointed an Assistant Professor of Linguistics at Fresno State College. I feel incredibly fortunate to have had the opportunity to work with him, and I was excited to see the final product of our combined efforts. His dedication to my book is evident, and I am confident that the book is better for it.

I wanted to take a moment to express my deepest appreciation for all the incredible work he has put into editing my book. His dedication and expertise have been invaluable throughout this entire process, and I cannot thank him enough for his contributions.

Thank you for his hard work, expertise, and unwavering commitment to the book. He has truly made a difference, and I'm excited to share this final book's English version with the world, knowing that it is the best version of itself, thanks to Mr. Byron Allen Black.

Nhân Ảnh
2024

Contact the Author:
Hoa Hoang

xuanphuongh@gmail.com

Contact Nhan Anh Publisher:
han. le3359@gmail.com
(408) 722-5626

www.ingramcontent.com/pod-product-compliance
Lightning Source LLC
LaVergne TN
LVHW052223200926
848481LV00001B/200